Global SAP Systems — Design and Architecture

 PRESS

SAP PRESS is a joint initiative of SAP and Galileo Press. The know-how offered by SAP specialists combined with the expertise of the publishing house Galileo Press offers the reader expert books in the field. SAP PRESS features first-hand information and expert advice, and provides useful skills for professional decision-making.

SAP PRESS offers a variety of books on technical and business related topics for the SAP user. For further information, please visit our website: *www.sap-press.com*.

Martin Murray
SAP Warehouse Management: Functionality and Technical Configuration
2007, 504 pp.
978-1-59229-133-5

D. Rajen Iyer
Effective SAP SD
2006, 365 pp.
978-1-59229-101-4

Marc Hoppe
Sales and Inventory Planning with SAP APO
2007, 441 pp.
978-1-59229-123-6

Alexander Davidenkoff, Detlef Werner

Global SAP Systems —
Design and Architecture

Galileo Press

Bonn • Boston

ISBN 978-1-59229-183-0

© 2008 by Galileo Press Inc., Boston (MA)
1st Edition 2008

German Edition first published 2007 by Galileo Press, Bonn, Germany.

Galileo Press is named after the Italian physicist, mathematician and philosopher Galileo Galilei (1564–1642). He is known as one of the founders of modern science and an advocate of our contemporary, heliocentric worldview. His words *Eppur si muove* (And yet it moves) have become legendary. The Galileo Press logo depicts Jupiter orbited by the four Galilean moons, which were discovered by Galileo in 1610.

Editor   Eva Tripp
English Edition Editor   Jon Franke
Translation   Lemoine International, Inc., Salt Lake City UT
Copy Editor   Barbara Florant
Cover Design   Tyler Creative
Layout Design   Vera Brauner
Production   Iris Warkus
Typesetting   Publishers' Design and Production Services, Inc.
Printed and bound in Canada

Contents at a Glance

Contents

Preface

In the past few years, information technology and computer hardware have continued to develop rapidly. Consequently, today's use of IT is a matter of course for supporting all of an enterprise's business processes, and can even be the *conditio sine qua non* for the company's survival in the global market. In this context, Enterprise Resource Planning (ERP) software is an essential prerequisite for the long-term and outstanding positioning of a company. Enterprise Resource Planning supports entrepreneurial efforts to use existing resources as efficiently as possible — for example, capital, operating resources, or human resources.

When planning or operating a global ERP installation, one of the main issues is how to implement the software solution. Does it make sense to position one system in each country, or should all functions be integrated into one installation that all international users can access? Or should a few regional systems be used to support business processes? These questions cannot be answered quickly, because the decision as to the used topology depends on several factors. This book describes the advantages and disadvantages of the different implementation options of global SAP® systems (such as SAP ERP) and shares the practical experiences of SAP customers.

Chapter 1 (Introduction) provides basic information on global SAP and explains the importance of information technology within the scope of globalization, as well as its historical and future development. **Chapter 2** (Business Requirements for Global Systems) describes the software's requirements — the underlying hardware that the international business world must meet.

Structure of this Book

Chapter 3 (Overview of Architectures) shows you which options generally exist for the system architecture, and discusses different aspects and properties, which are explained in more detail in **Chapter 4** (Factors Influencing System Architectures). These are important for the description of factors that influence the decision-making process for a suited topology. **Chapter 5** (IT Implementation of Architectures) describes the planning and implementation of the IT, and introduces the utilities that are available for implementing, maintaining, and operating it.

Decision Guidelines

In **Chapter 6** (Customer Scenarios and Decision-Making Processes), you learn more about the experiences of SAP customers with different architectures. It also provides information on the benefits of the individual solutions. Specific guidelines round off the suggestions and remarks presented in this book. Enterprises can use these guidelines to select the appropriate system topology, based on their own business processes as well as other aspects.

Some readers might prefer to read separate, selected chapters or sections of the book; for example, Chapter 6 is suited to SAP customers with many years of experience who want to quickly prepare for a decision regarding a change to their system topology.

All explanations lean heavily on the value of direct references to practical examples. For many years now, the employees of SAP Globalization Services have actively supported SAP customers worldwide — from planning global systems to optimizing their daily businesses. We have also learned, from numerous workshops, which topics and aspects are most important to customers.

Acknowledgements

We would like to take this opportunity to thank all the SAP customers, partners, and colleagues who helped with the creation of *Global SAP Systems — Design and Architecture,* particularly for the valuable discussions. Our particular thanks go to SAP Globalization Services for the opportunity to write this book.

Dr. Alexander Davidenkoff, Dr. Detlef Werner

If an enterprise wants to be successful, it must be able to imple-
ment global business processes flexibly. IT plays a central role in
this task. Because innovations must be quickly implemented, IT
solutions tailored to specific business models ensure a competitive
edge over omnipresent, international competitors.

1   Introduction

This chapter explains the importance of IT in today's business world
and identifies which requirements a global system architecture must
meet. An appropriate enterprise model is critical to fulfilling business
requirements via optimal and coordinated use of business models and
processes, software solution portfolios, suitable technologies, and useful
component architectures. Basic technology principles are provided, and
we describe how SAP software and hardware technologies have developed in the context of global systems.

1.1   The Role of IT in Globalization

Which enterprises will claim the global market leadership in the coming years? This is not an easy question to answer. Rapid changes in
international markets, accompanied by the need to reduce costs while
improving quality, make it necessary to run core business processes on a
global level while keeping those processes as simple as possible for local
employees. Moreover, reorganizations, company mergers, and spin-offs
are continually changing enterprise structures around the world; and
they require speedy action. Previously separate, large, and considerably
diverse IT systems must be transferred to new, shared IT infrastructures
in to fully exploit the modern synergy.

However, there are certain trends in the global market that are quite independent of the market and industry sectors:

▸ Business models that can be changed quickly, and rapid innovations as well as related strategies, are increasingly considered critical business factors.

▸ A consolidation wave will hit many markets, and only a few global players will come out as winners.

In light of these trends, superior IT is increasingly considered an essential factor for success. Today's enterprises depend on the performance and reliability of IT systems more than ever before. Previously, computer system failure had limited consequences that could be planned for; now, enterprises can expect enormous financial consequences, even from temporary errors. Estimates indicate that, for example, a two-day failure of the network or core applications can lead to the collapse of a bank, financial service provider, insurance service provider, or just-in-time manufacturer.

> **Example**
>
> Let's take a look at a widely used example: The competitor of a well-known computer manufacturer had instructed its suppliers to send lists of the components that the computer manufacturer had *not* purchased. Then, the competitor built design patterns for computers made up of these components. These computers were then sold in Internet auctions at low prices and only manufactured upon receipt of order. For this IT solution, all processes (from ordering the parts to delivery) were automated. This new and innovative business process led to considerable cost reductions and consequently to a clear competitive advantage.

To meet today's requirements for a global IT solution, software must handle global and local processes at the same time, and still be flexible enough to accept changes. For instance, English might be the general companywide language, while local languages are used in the countries in which marketing or production occur. Therefore, the concept of globalization means developing software that handles all of the business requirements of companies operating globally. An appropriate ERP solution must consist of a *neutral* core (internationalization), but which can be easily adapted to the requirements of individual countries (localization).

Some functional elements, like time zones, fall into the area of internationalization, while others belong to localization, country-specific reporting requirements, for example, and some belong to both areas, such as currencies or languages. The support of global processes represents another example: An international procurement chain can be implemented via many systems and software components, as well as by connecting third-party systems of retailers. Different languages must be processed through different interfaces during data exchange.

Globalization, localization, and internationalization

Figure 1.1 illustrates the interaction of global and local software functions.

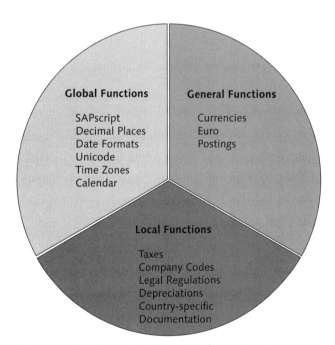

Global Functions

SAPscript
Decimal Places
Date Formats
Unicode
Time Zones
Calendar

General Functions

Currencies
Euro
Postings

Local Functions

Taxes
Company Codes
Legal Regulations
Depreciations
Country-specific
Documentation

Figure 1.1 Global, Local, and General Software Functions

When an enterprise commences activity in a new country, the locally applicable legal requirements must be complied with, date or decimal formats taken into consideration, and local specifications of business

SAP Country Versions

processes noted. For this purpose, SAP offers country versions that have been developed to reflect the specific requirements of individual countries. These versions are continually updated by SAP Globalization Services in order to keep them up to date on the latest changes. All standard SAP country versions can be combined as needed into a single installation. Some examples of the local functionality covered by SAP country versions contain the following:

▶ Charts of accounts

▶ Depreciation rules

▶ Tax calculations

▶ Payment processes

▶ Reporting

▶ Sales processes

▶ Payroll

SAP software is also complemented by functions that supplement industry-specific requirements, such as the unique business processes of the automotive and chemical industries.

Currencies   In addition to the comprehensive functions that enable companies to operate in diverse countries according to local industry specifications, ERP software can also map other specific requirements. Certainly, every global company must work with more than one currency in the course of business processes, so the software used must support different means of payment. For this reason, there is no *primary* currency in the SAP system; rather, all possible currencies are handled at the same time, and a company can add new currencies whenever needed.

Therefore, a U.S. company would invoice its clients in dollars, while its subsidiary in France would use Euros, and the production facility in Thailand could work with Baht. At the same time, company groups can be consolidated into different, freely selectable currencies. Another option is the simultaneous tracking of payment transactions in more than one currency, and it is also easy to use the different currency conversion rates for conversion and display.

Typically, users think and act in their local times and expect business   Time zones
processes modeled by software to be used similarly. A global company,
however, has processes that involve different time zones, or systems and
users who work on very different schedules. This can lead to problems
when postings are delayed or batch jobs don't start on time. Therefore,
it is important for applications to store times and dates correctly, and
convert them if necessary. Note that the manner of technical implementation can differ, depending on the specific requirements. The system
primarily differentiates between system time, user time, and object time,
and can, for example, correctly display a stored production time in the
local time zone of the production plant.

Every globally active company is faced with the challenge of having to   Languages
handle different languages. The software used must therefore have the
following functionality:

▶ Support for different languages in the user interface

▶ Translation into different languages

▶ Display and printing of characters of different languages

▶ Simultaneous operation of all the requirements listed above

These requirements are illustrated in Figure 1.2. Depending on the logon
language selected, the SAP system displays a menu that is respectively
translated, and users can enter and save characters in their native language (or any other language, if required – the system should be based
on Unicode).

There are several different reasons for these language support requirements: First, users who log into the system want to see the user interface
in their own language, or enter text and data in that language. Business
partners expect invoices and business letters in their native language. In
this context, it is especially important that every country imposes legal
requirements for the availability of individual documents in the national
language. In SAP ERP 6.0, for instance, there is support for nearly 40
languages. The software also includes different options for performing
translations.

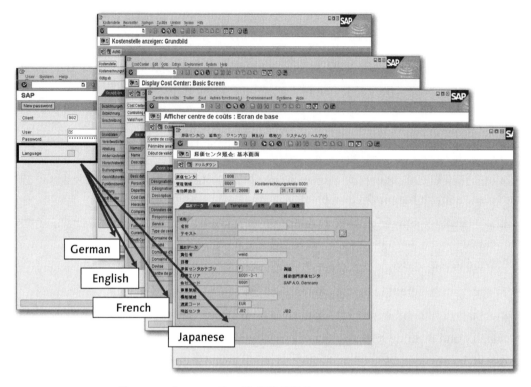

Figure 1.2   Language-Specific SAP ERP Menus

Although ERP software covers these functionalities completely, and enterprises have recognized the importance of an ERP solution, IT budgets have continuously been reduced for some years now. Therefore, budgets are barely sufficient for maintaining existing solutions and leave little leeway for investments. For this reason, temporary solutions are often developed in response to pending innovations. Over the long term, these solutions have negative effects on system complexity or maintenance costs.

SAP's strategy: Enterprise SOA

SAP therefore integrated a Service-Oriented Architecture (SOA) into ERP that enables individual application functions to be used as Web services based on the existing system architecture. This allows quick and cost-efficient development of innovative functionality. In addition, the complete logic for mapping business processes is also integrated. This concept is referred to as *Enterprise SOA* (Enterprise Service-Oriented Architecture).

Enterprise SOA enables companies to efficiently combine individual business process components with new functions at very low cost.

Considering all of the previously mentioned requirements for an up-to-date IT solution, an essential question arises, which will be answered in the following chapters of this book:

> *Which system topology is best suited to support this complex, multifunctional software solution?*

1.2 The Importance of an Appropriate Enterprise Model

Before you learn more about the appropriate system topology in the following chapters, one aspect must be taken into account: The areas of conflict between IT, enterprise strategy, and business processes, which are illustrated in Figure 1.3.

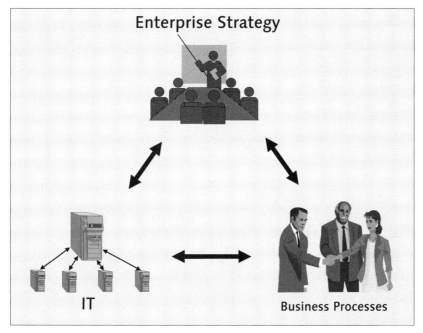

Figure 1.3 Areas of Conflict between IT, Enterprise Strategy, and Business Processes

Areas of conflict Nearly every enterprise has three *parties* that each have their own, specific interests and options:

▶ Management (or upper management) is responsible for the strategy.

▶ Employees implement the business processes defined and perform different tasks — for example, the production or sales department.

▶ The IT department serves as a service provider for both parties.

Due to this organizational structure, numerous dependencies, potential conflicts, and disputes may arise, for example:

Examples of dependencies ▶ Faced with an ever-tighter budget (defined by the management), the IT department must provide enterprise-relevant data for upper management in an increasingly shorter amount of time. For this reason, IT requires up-to-date software. The new software updates and changed user interfaces constitute a major challenge for employees. The IT department, however, must use these latest ERP system developments to support the current innovations of upper management.

▶ Management must be able to alter its enterprise strategy to quickly react to changing market conditions. This can irritate employees, due to the changes in their work environment (processes, instructions, etc.).

▶ To reduce costs, management wants to combine the local ERP installations into one central system. Because of this system downsizing, IT teams in the affected countries feel unappreciated and therefore refuse the strategy.

▶ The IT department must occasionally shut down systems for maintenance purposes; however, sales employees in countries with ever-changing legal regulations depend on continuous software updates and need these legal changes to manage their daily work.

▶ Employees want their software to operate in their native language. However, translations for all countries in a large, global installation is impossible, because management cannot afford this — not only the software, itself, but the time it would take IT to implement it.

▶ Upper management must quickly communicate new processes to employees, and therefore instructs the IT department to install a portal as a communication platform; but employees don't immediately recognize the advantages of the portal and consider it as additional work.

In order to avoid these potential areas of conflict and to ensure smooth operating procedures, it is advantageous to implement models that include all parties and enterprise units, and reflect the processes defined for the company. Figure 1.4 illustrates this model. Each enterprise will have its own version, which will harmonize the previously mentioned areas of conflict by the use of clear descriptions and specifications.

Better communication due to models

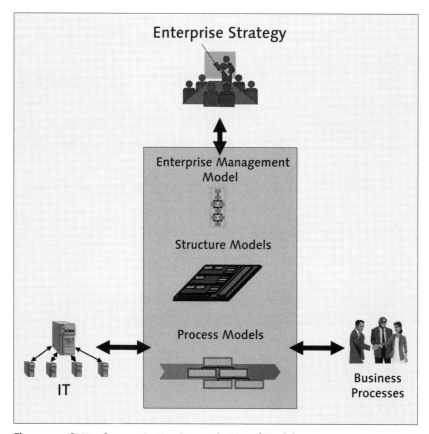

Figure 1.4 Better Communication Due to the Use of Models

Enterprise models   *Enterprise models* clearly reflect the relationships and responsibilities of the business units and locations, and at the same time indicate the implemented business processes. Moreover, this modeling shows how processes are mapped with IT. You can roughly distinguish between three possible approaches:

- A process can be implemented via the standard functions of the system — ERP, for example. Only one system is required.

- A process requires a customer's specific add-on (development) that runs on the system as a supplement (e.g., to the ERP system). Only one system is required.

- The process requires splitting the systems into several subsystems.

System topology   Modeling must therefore also *split* the systems (*system topology*) optimally and include the configuration of all interfaces required. The following tasks have to be performed at the beginning of each modeling process or successful solution strategy:

- Define the general business strategy; for example, purchasing has to be performed on a global basis, and we want to implement shared service centers for some business areas.

- Define clear company objectives; for example, accelerate the processing of complaints by 20%.

- Clearly define the regional and organizational scope of the solution.

- Define the organizational (target) structure.

- Define business (target) processes.

- Clearly delimitate the processes — global, regional/divisional, and local.

- Replace/integrate legacy systems and their related strategies.

- Conduct a performance analysis — number of users, number of transactions, technical restrictions, and so on.

Analysis and solution strategy   In this analysis, mutual dependencies must always be closely considered. This may involve some iterations to identify the best model, as shown in the overview in Figure 1.5.

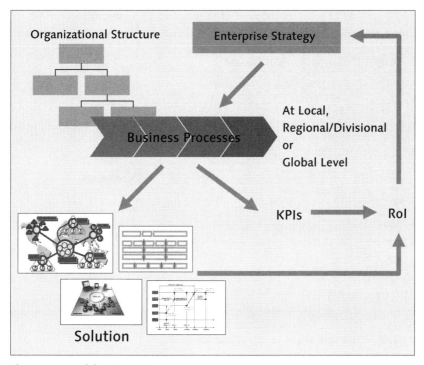

Figure 1.5 Modeling Strategy

Figure 1.5 also illustrates that financial aspects are directly integrated into the modeling strategy. For example, business processes are directly linked with *key performance indicators* (KPIs). KPIs are figures that enable an organization to measure the progress or achievement of important objectives or critical success factors. The *return on investment* (ROI) also serves as a way to periodically measure the success of the capital that is controlled within the company. In addition to KPI results, experiences with the solutions used and other parameters are also included in ROI calculation.

KPI and RoI

1.3   Six Steps to Your Enterprise Model

Company experiences from various projects show that you can roughly divide the path to a complete enterprise model into six steps. This applies to the planning of a new implementation, company mergers, and expansions, as well as internal structural changes (*re-engineering*):

▶ **Step 1: Analyze the enterprise**

    ▶ Analyze strategy and objectives.

    ▶ Consider proven procedures (best practices).

    ▶ Include the latest technologies as well as future possible trends.

▶ **Step 2: Classify the process**

    ▶ Define global, regional/divisional, and local processes.

    ▶ Define the organizational units involved.

Clustering processes

▶ **Step 3: Consolidate processes**

    ▶ Cluster the processes to logical units, considering the process classification.

    ▶ Assign the software functionality to process clusters.

    ▶ Consider legacy systems.

▶ **Step 4: Define the structure model**

    ▶ Assign the organization's structure to the model of the software functionality.

▶ **Step 5: Model object flows**

    ▶ Define essential object flows between individual components (business-critical processes).

    ▶ Determine any process gaps or weak points.

▶ **Step 6: Define the target architecture**

    ▶ Perform a high-level definition of a suited target architecture/system topology (the subject of this book).

    ▶ Specify a migration path.

A project management point of view

From the point of view of project management, when the project team performs these six steps, clear tasks and expected results are defined. Table 1.1 lists the tasks and results.

Task	Objective/Result
Enterprise Analysis and Check	
Create an overview of the company's businesses. Analyze strategies and objectives. Analyze the organizational structures. Analyze business processes. Analyze the IT infrastructure.	Enterprise model
Solution Definition	
Classify the processes. Assign components. Create a structure model. Create possible architecture scenarios. Validate technology. Decide the preferred solution alternative. Analyze for errors/weak points.	Target architecture model
Definition of the Migration Path	
Define the rollout strategy. Specify an implementation strategy.	Rollout/Migration strategy

Table 1.1 Tasks and Objectives for Project Management During Enterprise Modeling

Finally, the defined enterprise model must be analyzed in detail. This can be done using the following two approaches:

Analyzing the enterprise model

▸ In the first approach, the project team explains the model to the users by performing the daily steps according to the typical sequence of the work processes (*day-in-the-life approach*). This procedure is respectively carried out for the different areas of the enterprise (controlling department, production department, sales department, etc.).

▸ The second approach (reporting approach) is based on issues regarding current business transactions and processes, and in this way checks whether the model can provide the appropriate and required results. Possible questions include:

  ▸ Which data do I require?

  ▸ In what format should the data be provided?

> ▸ From whom and from which systems must the data originate?

> ▸ When and how often is the data supposed to be provided?

> ▸ For which purpose is the data required?

Best solution strategy for the enterprise model

After all the steps for enterprise modeling have been completed, including the final analysis, a uniform basis will be established in which the solution strategy meets the business requirements by providing the optimal and coordinated use of business models and processes, software solution portfolio, appropriate technology, component architecture, and migration path (see Figure 1.6).

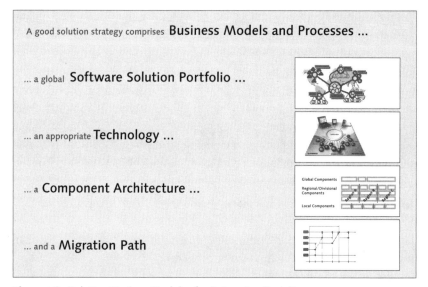

Figure 1.6 Solution Strategy Modules for Enterprise Modeling

1.4 From Mainframes to Distributed Systems

This section describes how the development of computer technology has been continuously booming over the past years, and how this growth has influenced SAP software products for global systems. We'll only discuss the topics and technologies that are relevant to this book; a complete historical overview will not be provided. However, some information on SAP-specific origins will be included, because this is important for understanding our discussion on the topology of the client/server architecture and components of SAP NetWeaver.

IBM introduced the first personal computer in 1981. In the following years, mainframes were replaced by networks of medium-size servers, workplace computers, and PCs. This gave rise to the client/server architecture — an architecture also used by SAP. The *client/server concept* is a model that describes how computers communicate with each other and exchange data. Figure 1.7 illustrates this approach. It is based on a very simple idea:

The client/server concept

▶ The client requests something.

▶ The service provider or server provides it.

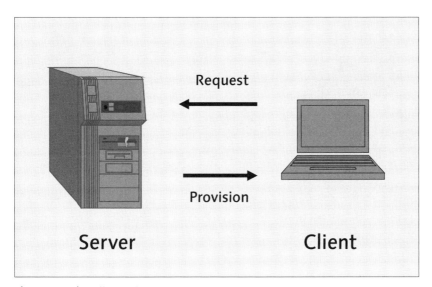

Figure 1.7   Client/Server Concept

Clients request services and, at the same time, provide services, thereby becoming servers. The same concept applies to servers — just the other way around. Moreover, it is important to understand that the terms "client" and "server" do not refer to the size or capacity of the respective computers, and that the medium used to request and provide the service can be freely selected. This means that the computers must be able to communicate, for example, via the Internet or Remote Function Call (RFC), as well as synchronously or asynchronously.

SAP recognized the importance of the client/server approach at a very early stage and subsequently developed SAP R/3, a portable system with an inherent client/server concept and a standardized graphical user interface layout that enables the use of relational databases — even on the hardware of other manufacturers.

Three-level configuration

The client/server concept is used for a three-level configuration of a common ERP system, and is most frequently used for SAP R/3. Separate computers are used for presentation, application, and database services, as can be seen in Figure 1.8.

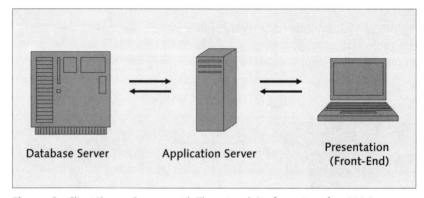

Database Server   Application Server   Presentation (Front-End)

Figure 1.8   Client/Server Concept with Three-Level Configuration of an ERP System

Client/server concept and system topology

In contrast to the installation of software on a mainframe where software is installed on only one computer system, the client/server concept offers many new options, because the previously fixed one-to-one links between software and computer are removed.

▶ You can physically separate the database server from the application server, for example, to meet security requirements.

Load balancing

▶ To increase performance, you can use several application servers in parallel (load balancing).

▶ You can combine different hardware and software components.

▶ Previously, complete functionality had to be covered by one single installation on the mainframe. Today, the client/server concept enables you to distribute business requirements across different systems — for example, to solve conflicts between country-specific software settings or assign specific functions, such as one installation each for financial accounting, production, and business units (e.g., system I for Europe, system II for Asia). The following chapters describe the wide range of options available when selecting the appropriate system topology, how many factors influence the decision-making process, and how important the right decision is for a globally active company.

Already, SAP R/3 implements various system topologies, depending on the specific requirements of the enterprise. Here, three different approaches comprise the basic structure, and are described and compared in detail in Chapter 3.

▸ Single Box: Global database with several application servers (see Figure 1.9).

▸ Decentralized Installation: Distributed, for example, across America, Asia, and Europe, without a shared database (see Figure 1.10).

▸ Distributed Systems: A central development approach includes the rollout of a template (see Figure 1.11).

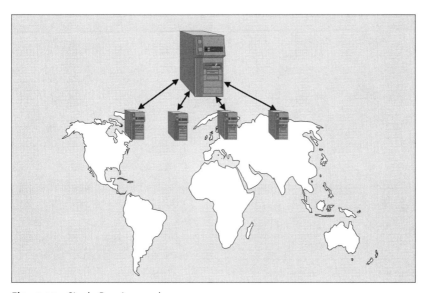

Figure 1.9 Single Box Approach

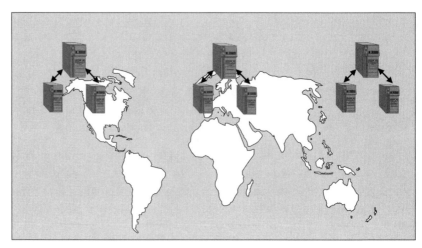

Figure 1.10   Decentralized, Distributed Installation

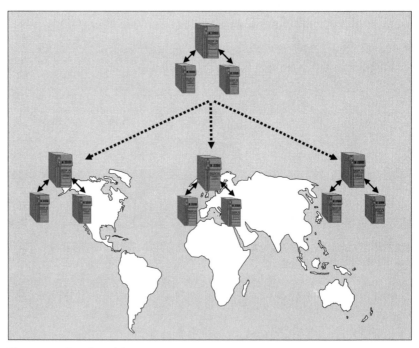

Figure 1.11   Distributed Systems

Application Link
Enabling

In the past, a central system could not always optimally standardize business transactions with integrated applications. Therefore, distributed systems were often implemented. Because this led to comprehensive data exchange, an integrated system landscape with applications was required that was loosely linked — that is, asynchronously and not via a shared database. That was when SAP introduced *Application Link Enabling* (ALE), which is based on the following:

▶ Architecture based on messages

▶ Business scenarios

▶ Communication technology required for data exchange

▶ Tools to synchronize data transfer

▶ Methods to implement the data distribution model in the system landscape

Furthermore, ALE required a considerably complex data-transfer synchronization due to asynchronous processing. It allowed for communication between applications of different release versions.

To smoothly transmit data between the distributed, non-integrated applications, a model was necessary that defined which data was supposed to be sent where and when, and whether a specific sequence had to be followed. Moreover, specific filters could be defined to channel the data flow. Figure 1.12 illustrates how different applications that run on different systems can be connected, using a logical model and comprising an integrated solution.

ALE distribution model

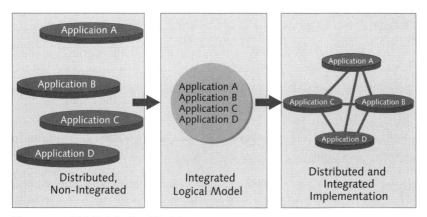

Figure 1.12 ALE Distribution Model

IDoc To transfer data, a specific format was introduced that enabled a simultaneous, structured entry of data that is relevant for a specific process or application. A container is provided for this purpose: the *IDoc* (Intermediate Document). The application then communicates with the ALE layer that created the IDoc, determines the recipient, and transfers the IDoc to the communication layer. After sending the IDoc via appropriate media, the steps are performed the other way around at the recipient's end. Then, the application can use the data as intended (see Figure 1.13). A transmission monitor supervises all transfers and ensures that data communication processes run smoothly.

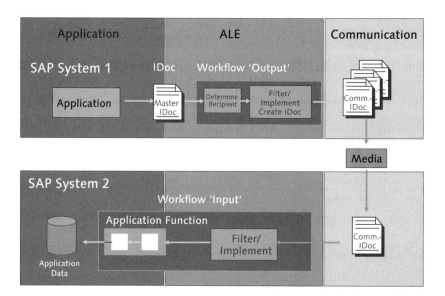

Figure 1.13 ALE Communication

Internet Although SAP R/3 enjoyed high acceptance by the enterprises, the next challenge was just around the corner: the Internet. In order to remain successful beyond the year 2000, SAP had to consider this medium in software planning.

BAPIs BAPIs (*Business Application Programming Interfaces*) were the first solution for this problem. They enabled the customer to access and work with SAP systems via the Internet from any location. To a certain extent, BAPIs were the precursor of today's well-known Web services. They exactly defined the interfaces of applications for processes and data that were implemented as business object methods, and allowed for uniform communication between different resources via different network protocols and interfaces, as shown in Figure 1.14.

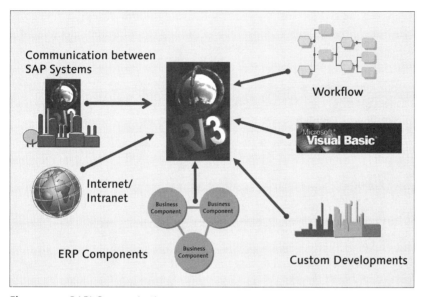

Figure 1.14 BAPI Communication

In May 1999, SAP announced a new strategy, *mySAP.com*, and initiated a complete reorganization of the enterprise and its range of products. mySAP.com linked e-commerce solutions with the existing ERP applications on the basis of modern Web technologies.

The new economy, which started with mySAP.com, was continued by mySAP technology, and then led to SAP NetWeaver. In 2004, SAP launched the first version of *SAP NetWeaver*, which formed the basis for Enterprise SOA.

SAP NetWeaver

With the integration across technological and organizational boundaries, SAP NetWeaver ensured standardized business processes and information, and thereby became the technology foundation for SAP customers and partners. Enterprise SOA, which was implemented at the same time, increased the flexibility and extensibility of business processes, and also supported a full interoperability with .NET and J2EE. Figure

1.15 illustrates the main components of SAP NetWeaver. Based on an ABAP (Advanced Business Application Programming) and Java development environment that is independent of the database type, business processes, enterprise data, and all other information are used. The users can access the relevant data in different ways. The same data is also available for the different applications. Integration with all other communication standards completes the ability to communicate with the outside world.

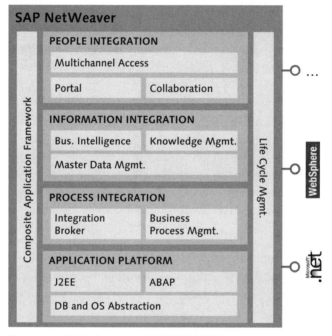

Figure 1.15 Main Components of SAP NetWeaver

At the time of this writing, SAP ERP 6.0, the latest enterprise software version, includes all of the developments that have been implemented by SAP to date. This introduction will not describe the functions in detail, because they are only slightly relevant to our topic: appropriate system topology.

Business process platform

What are the future prospects? Through 2010 SAP technology of the future consists of solutions that are based on new business process platforms and addresses large, as well as medium-size companies.

1.5   Summary

This introduction first introduced the general IT requirements in terms of globalization. Considering the rapid changes in international markets and the need to continually reduce costs, software must handle global and local processes at the same time, and still be flexible enough to accept changes.

To avoid potential conflict between IT, strategy, and business processes, models are implemented that include all parties and enterprise units, and reflect the defined needs for the company. These models (also referred to as *enterprise models*) clearly outline the relationships and responsibilities between business units and locations, and at the same time illustrate the implemented business processes. Basically, there are six steps to the completion of the enterprise model, which then must be analyzed according to the appropriate approaches.

Depending on the specific requirements of the enterprise, there are various system topologies that can be implemented for international installations. Three different approaches can be determined as the basic structure of these system topologies:

▸ Single box, global database with several application servers

▸ Decentralized, distributed installation without shared database

▸ Distributed systems with central development and template rollout

Since the smooth distribution of data between scattered systems requires a logical model and secure data transfer, these basic principles were also explained. The following chapters provide all the information needed to determine the system topology that is best suited to your enterprise.

The requirements of a multinational or global system are manifold. Consequently, system architectures must be able to optimally support and technically implement this complexity.

2   Business Requirements for Global Systems

A global IT solution contains both local and remote components. Some of the local requirements are mandatory (e.g., legal regulations of the respective country), whereas others can both be characterized on a local, regional, or global basis. This scope results from individual business processes and the enterprise model. In this chapter, you will first learn more about how SAP country versions and industry solutions facilitate system adaptation, and how the SAP Globalization Knowledge Base will assist you in implementation projects. We will discuss how languages are technically supported as well as the significant benefits of a Unicode-based system. Finally, the critical planning of interfaces will be explained, as well as how time zones are handled in an ERP system.

Global and local components

2.1   Covering Regional and Global Requirements

Generally, there are many different strategies for covering regional and global requirements. For example, a global player might almost exclusively use English as the companywide language, and only make use of local languages if absolutely necessary. Other enterprises, though, might develop distinctive language strategies that entail extensive translation projects for every country.

These different approaches can be found in all areas. Depending on the company's philosophy, either uniform or very diverse charts of accounts can be found for large installations; one company uses a single global currency, while another uses various local currencies and then consolidates one group currency.

Therefore, the question arises as to whether or not you want to organize your enterprise model with a local or global focus. This approach is not only determined by the business strategy, but also by the wishes and practices of the system users that have a local orientation. Their preferences must also be taken into account. For example, not only the menu's expected language must be considered, but also cultural aspects, such as the preferred payment method of various countries and their mappings in the IT system. In the U.S., the common means of payment is via check; in Germany, payment is generally through bank transfers.

Distribution of global and local functions

Basic processes must also be taken into account, such as payroll, purchasing, payment processing, and charts of accounts. For each of these aspects, you must check whether it is implemented globally or locally. Figure 2.1 illustrates this problem. The decisive question is: To what extent the dashed line in the center of the figure must be moved upward or downward; in other words, where do we draw the line between global and local implementation?

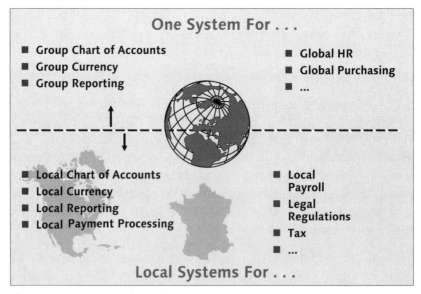

Figure 2.1 Distribution of Global and Local Functions

2.1.1 Legal Regulations and Regional Business Practices

Currently, SAP solutions have been deployed in more than 140 countries around the globe, and each country has its own set of legal regulations that change quite frequently. Moreover, they each have individual approaches and practices for general business processes. This applies both for standard functions, such as accounting, and the requirements of different industry sectors. For example, SAP ERP 6.0 provides different industry versions (industry solutions) with portfolios based on comprehensive knowledge of the industry-specific processes and requirements. Table 2.1 provides an overview of these specific applications.

Healthcare
▶ Universities and research institutes
▶ Internal and external security
▶ Public sector
▶ Insurance
Service Industries
▶ Services
▶ Wholesale
▶ Retail
▶ Logistics service providers
▶ Media industry
▶ Telecommunications
▶ Utility industry
Manufacturing Industry
▶ Automotive industry
▶ Construction, plant engineering, and ship building
▶ High-tech and electronics
▶ Consumer products industry
▶ Aerospace industry
▶ Engineering, tool building, and components construction
▶ Metal, timber, and paper industry

SAP Industry solutions

Table 2.1 Industry Solutions by SAP

Process Industry
▶ Mining
▶ Chemicals industry
▶ Life sciences
▶ Oil and gas industry

Table 2.1 Industry Solutions by SAP (Cont.)

SAP Country Versions

More than 10 years ago, SAP introduced Country Versions to cover local (and not necessarily industry-specific) legal regulations and provide functions that are required for country-specific business practices. The country versions enable customers to implement business activities in a specific country, using an individualized ERP solution, while simultaneously:

▶ Complying with essential legal regulations,

▶ Implementing country-specific functions that are required by most SAP customers,

▶ Carrying out country-specific Customizing,

▶ Using country-specific templates — for example, charts of accounts, tax calculation reports, and so on,

▶ Using a country installation program,

▶ Carrying out Implementation Guide (IMG) country-specific, and

▶ Receiving country-specific documentation.

As you can see, SAP Country Version isn't just a uniform software package; it contains an individual compilation of functions for each country that are required to smoothly implement productive business operations. Consequently, the scope of these country-specific versions differs considerably, and the type of provision is customized specifically for each country (e.g., templates, reports, etc.).

Country versions facilitate local implementation and operation

A critical aspect is that country versions do not comprise a software package that must be ordered separately (though there are exceptions, which will be discussed), but it is an integral part of an ERP delivery. As a result, you can simply use the version to facilitate implementation at the operating site of the specific country.

40

Each version includes general SAP ERP functions, *country-specific functions*, and a country template that can be used to set up the organizational units for the respective country. The country versions don't have specific application components; rather, they are part of various application components within the SAP system. The Financial Accounting component (FI), for example, contains both general FI and country-specific functions. These functions meet the legal regulations of the local legislation and/or the requirements of certain business practices. Country-specific functions include:

▶ **Localized versions of general functions**
  For some general functions, versions exist for different countries — for example, for travel expenses, payroll, or tax reports. Frequently, these versions (e.g., payroll) are required for individual countries or for one country only.

▶ **Functions provided for one country, specifically**
  A widely used example for these special functions is in the "cost of goods manufactured" list deployed in South Korea, which is not used in any other country.

The country template includes a number of settings within Customizing that are typical for a specific country. The country template is delivered with each standard country version. When you initially install an SAP system, you will also set up your own organizational units, which are very useful for country templates.

Country template

The most critical settings that can be implemented using the country templates are listed in Table 2.2 in the sequence in which they appear in the IMG. Detailed information on the template's settings can be found in the documentation for the specific country version at the SAP Help Portal *(http://help.sap.com)*, from which some of the examples in Table 2.2 have been derived.

Cross-Application Components (CA)
▶ Calendar settings (including holidays) of the sample holiday calendar and sample factory calendar.
▶ Address formatting for printing addresses in accordance with local standards.
▶ Regional settings — for example, the names of the regions in each country.
▶ Communication settings, such as international dialing codes.

Country template settings

Table 2.2 Country Template Settings

Financial Accounting (FI)
▶ Customizing settings for FI — for example, sales tax, withholding tax, account determination.

General Ledger Accounting (FI-GL)
▶ Chart of accounts: For countries that don't have any special legal regulations on the chart of accounts the INT general chart of accounts is provided.
▶ Balance sheet/P&L structure: Countries that work with the INT chart of accounts use the same balance sheet/P&L structure, which is also called INT.

Accounts Payable Accounting (FI AP)
▶ In FI AP, the country templates include the Customizing settings that are required for the payment program, including the most common payment methods of a country and the house banks — for example, Bank Accounting (FI BL). A limited number of country templates include national formats that support electronic bank statement.

Asset Accounting (FI AA)
▶ Each country template comprises reference charts of depreciation, depreciation areas, depreciation keys, and further transaction types, if applicable.

Controlling (CO)
▶ Each country template includes the following Customizing settings: cost types, standard hierarchies for cost centers, and standard hierarchies for profit centers.

Real Estate (RE)
▶ RE is covered by about one-third of all country templates. If a template exists for this area, it includes (with some exceptions) account assignments for all RE-related activities and settings for national tenancy laws, as well as rent adjustments.

Sales and Distribution (SD)
▶ Countries with costing sheets that deviate from the standard (e.g., due to tax types that cannot be found in any other country) are provided with a customized costing sheet.

Materials Management (MM)
▶ Settings for inflation accounting solutions are provided for the respective countries.

Project System (PS)
▶ The country templates contain examples for PS objects and PS functions that must be assigned to a controlling area. This includes sample settings for automatic and periodic clearing of revenues and results, as well as a sample value category.

Table 2.2 Country Template Settings (Cont.)

If you use a specific country version, you don't necessarily have to work in the language of the respective country. For further information on the use of different languages, refer to Section 2.2.1.

You must differentiate between three different types of SAP country versions that mainly differ with regard to their compatibility with other countries:

▶ **Standard country version**
The standard country version is most commonly used and features the following characteristics:

   ▶ It is fully integrated into the standard version of SAP ERP.

   ▶ It is compatible with other standard country versions and industry solutions, and can therefore be integrated into and used in a single system.

   ▶ It is delivered with every release update.

▶ **Add-on and/or modification[1] for non-standard country versions**
These versions are characterized by the following special features:

   ▶ You must thoroughly check compatibility with other country versions and industry solutions.

   ▶ They might not be included in every release update.

   ▶ Delayed delivery after release update is possible.

   ▶ Additional costs for use might occur — for example, for versions furnished by SAP partners.

▶ **Installation only (no full country version)**
"Installation Only" means that, for example, an ERP installation is operated productively in a country. The required legal regulations, however, were implemented for a customer in a special project in close cooperation with SAP or SAP partners. Consequently, it cannot be ensured that this solution also covers all legal regulations for other customers of this country. These versions are often deployed in African countries, for example.

---

1 Primarily for older SAP R/3 release statuses

The vast majority of country versions delivered by SAP are of the "standard" type and easily cover the requirements of those countries in which most SAP customers operate.

Non-standard versions are available for countries whose economic development is currently booming — for example, the former Soviet states. Many of these will gradually become standard country versions as ERP releases are updated and distributed. For more information, visit the SAP Service Marketplace at *http://service.sap.com/globalization*.

Figures 2.2 and 2.3 present an overview of the SAP ERP 6.0 versions available for the individual countries in the FI/CO areas and for Human Capital Management (HCM). They also indicate the degree of coverage on a global scale.

SAP Globalization Knowledge Base

The comprehensive documentation of country versions is supplemented by the SAP *Globalization Knowledge Base* (GKB), a tool for customers, partners, or consultants who introduce SAP ERP in different countries (also available for SAP Business One).

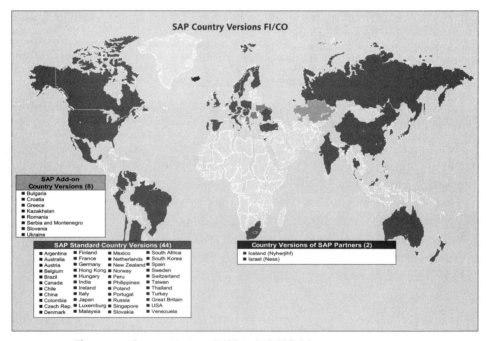

Figure 2.2 Country Versions FI/CO in SAP ERP 6.0

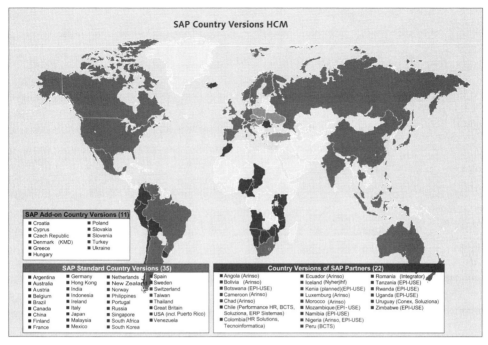

Figure 2.3 Country Versions HCM in SAP ERP 6.0

Even at the beginning of an implementation project, you can determine the implementation complexity for the respective country by using the SAP Globalization Knowledge Base. For all subsequent project stages, this tool provides extensive technical information about additional functions that are available for each country.

For 55 countries, the SAP Globalization Knowledge Base offers the following critical information pertaining to SAP ERP solutions for operations, financials, and Human Capital Management:

▸ SAP country information, including available solutions, and estimated complexity for implementation and maintenance.

▸ SAP language information — for example, legal regulations for language utilization, code page check, and translation.

▸ SAP Service Marketplace information, including links to related documentation.

In the detailed technical evaluation, you can also find specifics on the functionality provided by SAP for each country, such as:

▶ Country-specific master data,

▶ Country-specific business processes and functions,

▶ Country-specific reports, and

▶ Further technical details, such as additional tables, general remarks, User Exits, and SAP Notes on specific issues.

This tool can downloaded at the SAP Service Marketplace *(http://service.sap. com/gkb)* free of charge, this is particularly recommended if you want to create local working copies of Microsoft® Excel®-based files on your PC.

Working with the SAP Globalization Knowledge Base In order to begin using the SAP Globalization Knowledge Base, you must start a local copy, which means you must activate macro execution. The GKB Selection Sheet (which is only available in English) opens, as displayed in Figure 2.4.

Start country analysis On the initial screen, you can select the respective SAP ERP solutions and the countries planned for your project. Click on **Generate your view of country versions** to start the analysis. The start process may take between a few seconds and several minutes, depending on the selection and your computer.

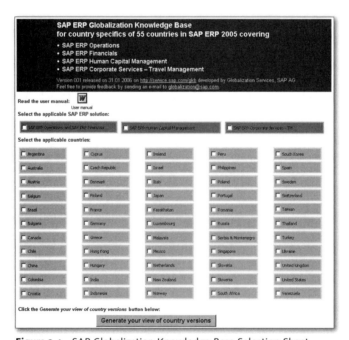

Figure 2.4 SAP Globalization Knowledge Base Selection Sheet

The calculation results are provided in three worksheets that provide comprehensive information:

▶ Country overview sheet, subdivided in two areas:

  ▶ High-level information, such as complexity analysis, availability, or language information.

  ▶ Functional aspects — for example, country-specific master data or tables.

▶ Country details sheet:

  ▶ Details on the references indicated in the overview sheet.

  ▶ Technical explanations.

▶ Additional info sheet:

  ▶ Explanations of the issues and terminology referred to on other sheets.

  ▶ Remarks and comments (general).

The following example illustrates how working with the SAP Globalization Knowledge Base can be practical:

Example for a GKB analysis

For planning a rollout to Brazil, Finland, and Germany, we select the respective countries on the initial GKB screen (all ERP solutions selected) and click **Generate your view of country versions**. Figures 2.5 and 2.6 show the results of the Country overview sheet and Country details sheet, which provide you with some critical initial information:

▶ **Country overview sheet:**

  ▶ All countries are part of the standard country versions and have been available as of SAP R/3 3.1.

  ▶ Brazil is the most complex country, because the interpretation of law documents is difficult, and the frequency of legal changes is very dynamic. You can expect a high level of effort for this project.

  ▶ All languages required are covered with a code page or Unicode.

  ▶ In Finland, it would be acceptable for users to work in English, but not in Brazil or Germany.

▶ **Country details sheet:**

    ▶ Unlike in Finland, various specific master data fields are used in Brazil.

    ▶ Implementation is significantly simplified by the detailed description and listing of these data fields.

Current
information on the
selected countries

If despite the comprehensive documentation of country versions and the facts contained in the SAP Globalization Knowledge Base you still have questions, or if you are confronted with apparently new legal regulations in a country, there is another efficient option to obtain help from SAP: Simply contact the *Country Advocates* responsible for the respective country. These employees of SAP Globalization Services will be pleased to assist you with your queries.

	B	C	D	E
		Brazil	Finland	Germany
General information		It you try to open any of the hyperlinks, you might receive the following MS Excel error message: Unable to open [URL address]. A security problem has occurred. Please re-try the link until the required information is displayed.		
1. Available solutions		World map of country versions and languages by SAP and Partner		
mySAP ERP Operations / mySAP ERP Financials				
1.1 Country version		Standard as of 4.0B	Standard before 3.1I	Standard before 3.1I
mySAP ERP Human Capital Management				
1.2 Payroll		Standard as of 4.5B	Standard as of 4.6C	Standard before 3.1I
mySAP ERP Corporate Services - Travel Management				
1.3 Travel Expense Management - Private Sector		No solution	Standard as of Enterprise Ext. 1.10	Standard as of 4.5B
1.4 Travel Expense Management - Public Sector		No solution	No solution	Standard as of Enterprise Ext. 1.10
2. SAP country information (recommendation by Globalization Services at SAP AG)				
mySAP ERP Operations / mySAP ERP Financials				
2.1 Complexity ranking		Very high complexity	Low complexity	Medium complexity
2.2 Frequency of legal changes		Very dynamic	Medium	Dynamic
2.3 Interpretation of law text		Very difficult	Easy	Difficult
mySAP ERP Human Capital Management				
2.4 Complexity ranking		Very high complexity	High complexity	Very high complexity
2.5 Frequency of legal changes		Very dynamic	Dynamic	Very dynamic
2.6 Interpretation of law text		Very difficult	Difficult	Very difficult
3. SAP language information				
3.1 Platform		Check if platform supports required language (locale) for SAP Code page		
3.2 Language compatibility check		The languages for the selected countries are supported by code page ISO8859-1 or ISO8859-9 or in UNICODE		
3.3 Official local language(s) delivered by SAP		Portuguese	Finnish	German
			Swedish	
3.4 Reporting required in which language		Portuguese	Finnish or Swedish	German
3.5 Language acceptance (experience by SAP)		Official language(s) only	English	Official language(s) only
4. SAP Service Marketplace information		Country contact	Country contact	Country contact
4.1 Consulting, training and shipment		Responsibility of respective subsidiary and / or partner		
4.2 Certified SAP translation vendor		Check out the translation partner certification program		
4.3 SAP Best Practices		Check out the SAP Best practices		
4.4 Available documentation		SAP Library	SAP Library	SAP Library
		Brazilian Glossary	-	-
		Brazil: CIAP documentation	-	-
		BR: Condition based tax calculation	-	-
4.5 Additional links		-	Service Area Travel Management	Service Area Travel Management
		-	-	Service Area TM (Public Sector)

Figure 2.5 SAP Globalization Knowledge Base, Country Overview Sheet

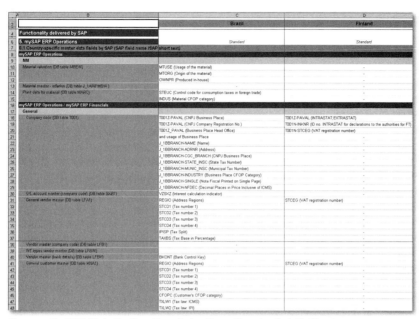

Figure 2.6 SAP Globalization Knowledge Base, Country Details Sheet

These contacts as well as SAP employees of the respective SAP subsidiary can be found in the SAP Service Marketplace under Localization for the selected country. Figure 2.7 shows, for example, the Website for Brazil.

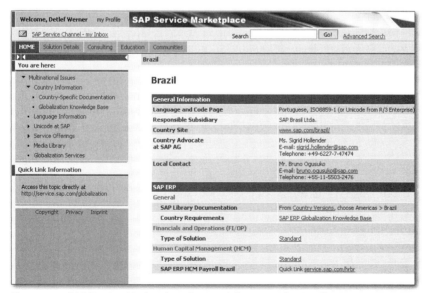

Figure 2.7 SAP Service Marketplace Country Information for Brazil

Overall, SAP ERP provides good coverage of the complex and manifold functional requirements of a multinational or global system. Therefore, each enterprise can be optimally supported for successful positioning as a global player through the suitable selection of basic system architectures.

2.1.2 Requirements of IT Users

We already established that users of IT systems are the driving force for deploying different languages in a global system, because they will want to use their native languages to enter/receive text and navigate the user interface. In fact, language is a central topic for planning software implementation. However, you must clearly differentiate between technology (the system must be able to display and save the characters of a language) and translation (menus or data are translated into the required language). These will be explained in this section.

Characters and character set

First we must explain what is meant by the terms "character," "character set," "code page," and other terms. A character, which is usually present in written form, is an abstract object with certain informational content. Characters can be letters (elements or printed characters of a language) and also numbers, punctuation marks, or symbols from mathematics, chemistry, music, and so forth. The *character set* contains all the characters that make up a coherent unit, such as a language. That set of characters can be displayed uniquely on a computer system without knowing their exact encoding. The character set LATIN-1, for instance, contains all the characters of the Western European languages — or more simply, the alphabet characters common to these languages.

Code point

In a computer system, a character is stored in binary or hexadecimal format as a sequence of bytes, which is referred to as a "code point." A code page contains every concrete code point for each character in a character set.

Code page

A code page is the digital binary or hexadecimal encoding of each character of a character set in the computer system. While the character set for a language is unique, in general there are multiple code pages per language; that is, the same character may have different encodings. In SAP systems, multiple code pages are necessary for the different system components, such as:

- The system code page for the application server;

- The front-end code page for the PC on which the user is working;

- The peripheral code page for the printer and communication with other systems (e.g., via RFC); or

- A database is technically configured by default in SAP single code-page systems using an ASCII code page (e.g., WE8DEC for Oracle). This is not relevant for languages in the applications, however.

In the following, we will be primarily looking at the system code page, which plays the central role. A basic prerequisite is that a unique conversion be possible between the system code page and the front-end and peripheral code pages, so that special characters can be displayed correctly in all possible cases.

System code page

From the very beginning, internationalization has been considered a very important concept in the development of SAP software. Table 2.3 provides a historical overview of translated languages. Western European languages were supported early on with SAP R/2 and SAP R/3.

Year	Release	Languages
1990	SAP R/2	Russian
1992	SAP R/2	Czech
1992	SAP R/3	Japanese
1993	SAP R/3	Japanese as standard in SAP R/3
1994	SAP R/3	Chinese (simplified, Mandarin)
1995	SAP R/3	Korean, Thai, Greek, Turkish
1996	SAP R/3	Chinese (traditional, Taiwanese)
1998	SAP R/3	Hebrew
2000	SAP R/3	Other Eastern European languages
2005	SAP R/3	Arabic (Unicode only)

Historical overview of translated languages

Table 2.3 Historical Overview of Translated Languages

Clearly, the use of a language with a complicated character set is not a simple matter. Even a layman can see the basic problems inherent in simple languages. If you log onto the Internet using a German PC, for instance, and happen to call up a Russian Internet page, or you receive a Russian email, unrecognizable characters will often be displayed, even if you can read Russian. That is because the PC is set for German, a language with the Western European character set. You can change your browser settings so that you see the Russian correctly. But, if you then go to a German Internet page, you will be surprised to see that the German characters such as ö, ü, ä, and ß will suddenly display as gibberish; you first need to set your browser settings back to Western European.

These problems are due to the nature of language, itself. Because German and Russian use different character sets and code pages, you have to set up your browser (in our example, Internet Explorer) accordingly using the menu entries, as follows: **View • Encoding**, and then select **Western European (Windows)** or **Cyrillic (Windows)**.

Internet pages often don't mention the language used
The Internet page, itself — that is, the URL — often reveals nothing about the language used. Therefore, in some cases, you really need to experiment before finding the right encoding for your browser.

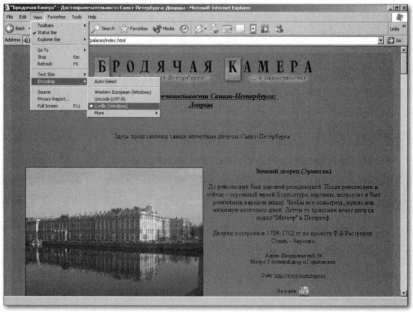

Figure 2.8 Russian Internet Page Viewed with Western European Browser (www.enlight.ru/camera/palaces/index.html)

This simple example demonstrates the general problems involved in multilingual applications, which are even more pronounced in the commercial use of SAP products for a global enterprise. The code page of the language used is a technical issue that is not directly visible in the application itself. The end user, after all, wants to use the application directly without having to worry about these details.

As long as an SAP system only operates with one character set and one code page (in this case we're talking about a single code-page system), the previously mentioned problems won't exist. On the other hand, that means that every system within a multinational enterprise would have to limit itself to languages that use that one character set in order to avoid the problems described.

Let's take a closer look at the code page ISO 8859-1 for the Western European LATIN-1 character set.

In the upper half of Table 2.4 (character range 0 to 127, shown in hexadecimal as 0x00 to 0x7F), all of the 7-bit ASCII characters are specified, including the English alphabet, numerals, and some special characters, while the range 0x00 to 0x19 is reserved for internal control characters. This 7-bit ASCII character set is generally also called the *common character set*, and is identical in all ASCII and ISO code pages.

Global character set

	0	1	2	3	4	5	6	7	8	9	A	B	C	D	E	F
0																
1																
2	SP	!	"	#	$	%	&	'	(	)	*	+	,	-	.	/
3	0	1	2	3	4	5	6	7	8	9	:	;	<	=	>	?
4	@	A	B	C	D	E	F	G	H	I	J	K	L	M	N	O
5	P	Q	R	S	T	U	V	W	X	Y	Z	[	\	]	^	_
6	`	a	b	c	d	e	F	g	h	i	j	k	l	m	n	o
7	B	q	r	s	t	u	V	w	x	y	z	{			}	~	

Table 2.4 Common Character Set

In the lower half of the LATIN-1 character set (character range 128 to 255, hexadecimal 0x8A to 0xFF, of which 0x8A to 0x9F are undefined), there are all the Western European special characters, like German umlauts, the French ê, and the Spanish ñ. As you can also see, the lowercase and uppercase letters have different encodings. The alphabet of a Western European language therefore contains a certain part of the global character set and some special characters from the upper range.

The alphabet of an Eastern European language with its special characters (including upper- and lowercase letters) — for example, the Czech Á á Č č Ď ď É é Ě ě Í í Ň ň Ó ó Ř ř Š š Ť ť Ú ú Ů ů Ž ž Ý ý — is not present in LATIN-1. For the Eastern European languages, therefore, another character set, LATIN-2, is defined.

Russian and Greek don't use Roman letters at all; they have their own characters and therefore need their own character sets. Even though one can usually guess the special characters with LATIN-2 languages (since the Roman letters are similar, except for the accents), with Russian and other Slavic languages, like Ukrainian or Bulgarian, there is a completely different alphabet.

Asian character sets Asian languages have several thousand characters and combinations of those characters. The languages supported by SAP — Japanese, Korean, and simplified and traditional Chinese — therefore need two bytes per character.[2] So, we use the term *double-byte languages* here. With two bytes, a maximum of 65,535 characters can be displayed uniquely, so that all the double-byte languages listed could basically be uniquely definable.

But this is unfortunately not the case; instead, each of these languages has its own code page due to its historical development, and the code pages have a large range of overlap. Only the common character set is identical for all of these languages.

The Thai language is an exception: Its character set contains 87 characters (elements), with consonants, vowels, and accents, from which about 2,000 combinations can be composed. A linguistically complete character

---

2 More precisely, we should speak of language character sets, as there are many Asian dialects that use the same character set.

is therefore a combination of multiple individual characters in the character set and can occupy between one and three bytes (in special cases, even 4 bytes). Therefore, here we use the term *multibyte language*.

Character composition

In Figure 2.9, you can see the Thai code page, which in the range 0x00 to 0x7F is also identical with the 7-bit ASCII character set (not shown), and in the upper range 0xA1 to 0xFB only describes the individual character elements. The linguistically correct character compositions must be performed by the software, such as when displayed in Microsoft Windows or when printing.

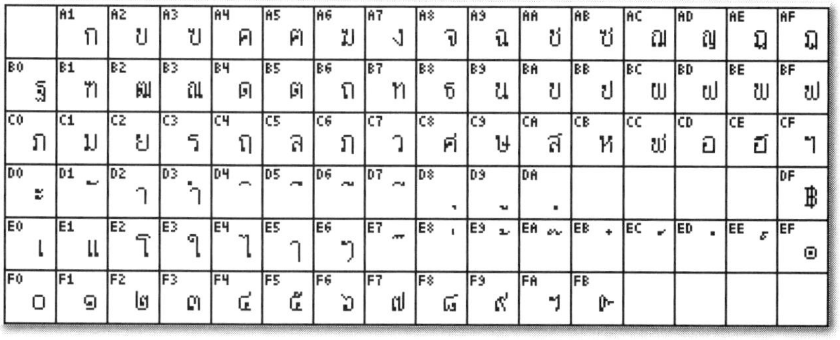

	A1 ก	A2 ข	A3 ฃ	A4 ค	A5 ฅ	A6 ฆ	A7 ง	A8 จ	A9 ฉ	AA ช	AB ซ	AC ฌ	AD ญ	AE ฎ	AF ฏ
B0 ฐ	B1 ฑ	B2 ฒ	B3 ณ	B4 ด	B5 ต	B6 ถ	B7 ท	B8 ธ	B9 น	BA บ	BB ป	BC ผ	BD ฝ	BE พ	BF ฟ
C0 ภ	C1 ม	C2 ย	C3 ร	C4 ฤ	C5 ล	C6 ฦ	C7 ว	C8 ศ	C9 ษ	CA ส	CB ห	CC ฬ	CD อ	CE ฮ	CF ฯ
D0 ะ	D1 ั	D2 า	D3 ำ	D4 ิ	D5 ี	D6 ึ	D7 ื	D8 ุ	D9 ู	DA ฺ					DF ฿
E0 เ	E1 แ	E2 โ	E3 ใ	E4 ไ	E5 ๅ	E6 ๆ	E7 ็	E8 ่	E9 ้	EA ๊	EB ๋	EC ์	ED ํ	EE ๎	EF ๏
F0 ๐	F1 ๑	F2 ๒	F3 ๓	F4 ๔	F5 ๕	F6 ๖	F7 ๗	F8 ๘	F9 ๙	FA ๚	FB ๛				

Figure 2.9 Thai Code Page

But the limits of a single code page system are already clear: Only languages in a single language group can coexist in a system and avoid technical problems. They must all use the same character set and one code page.

There are multiple single code pages from different manufacturers for the same character set. To be as standards-compliant as possible, and in order to support a number of platforms, SAP uses only ISO-8859 and uniform Asian for the system code pages of the application server. Table 2.5 shows the list of single code pages and assigned languages[3] in SAP systems.[4]

3 The languages are technically useable, even if there is no SAP translation available (e.g., Estonian).

4 For simplicity's sake, we will use the term "ISO code pages" for all languages.

Single code pages
and languages in
SAP Systems

Code Page	SAP Code Page	Languages Supported
ISO 8859-1	1100	Danish, Dutch, English, Finnish, French, German, Italian, Icelandic, Norwegian, Portuguese, Spanish, Swedish
ISO 8859-2	1401	Croatian, Czech, English, German, Hungarian, Polish, Romanian, Slovakian, Slovenian
ISO 8859-4[5]	1900	Lithuanian, Latvian, Estonian, English
ISO 8859-5	1500	English, Russian
ISO 8859-7	1700	English, Greek
ISO 8859-8	1800	English, Hebrew
ISO 8859-9	1610	Danish, Dutch, English, Finnish, French, German, Italian, Norwegian, Portuguese, Spanish, Swedish, Turkish
Shift JIS	8000	English, Japanese
GB2312-80	8400	Chinese (simplified), English
Big 5	8300	Chinese (traditional), English
KSC5601	8500	English, Korean
TIS620	8600	English, Thai

Table 2.5 Single Code Pages and Languages in SAP Systems

Clear limitations are placed on which language combinations are possible in a single code-page system.

To enable multilingual global systems before the availability of Unicode (see "Unicode Standard and ISO/IEC 10646,") limited specialized solutions were produced. MDMP (Multi-Display Multi-Processing), a combination of code pages in a system, made it possible to operate languages with more than one code page in parallel in a system.

With the availability of Unicode as the only technically correct solution in all SAP products, MDMP is no longer recommended and will no longer be supported as of SAP ERP 6.0. Single code-page systems are still supported, but may have limitations when using Java-based applications. Here too, Unicode is recommended. New SAP products and all new installations (as of 2007) will only be available in Unicode. Table 2.6

---

5 Baltic languages with some limitations (see SAP Note 198489)

summarizes technical SAP language support and recommendations. SAP language support is release-based and not time-based.

Code Page Technology / SAP Release	Unicode	Single Code-Page Systems	MDMP[2]	Blended Code Page Systems
SAP R/3 4.6C	Not possible	Supported	Supported, but not recommended	Limited support (no new installation)
SAP R/3 Enterprise[6]	Supported and recommended	Supported (for limitations, see SAP Note 838402)	Supported, but not recommended	Very limited support (no new installation)
SAP ERP 2004[7]	Supported and recommended	Supported (for limitations, see SAP Note 838402)	Limited support (SAP Note 47036, no new installation)	Very limited support (no new installation)
SAP ERP 6.0	Supported and recommended	Supported (for limitations, see SAP Note 838402)	Not supported (SAP Note 79991)	Not supported (SAP Note 79991)

Table 2.6 SAP Language Support

Note

For detailed information about "SAP language support" refer to the book *Unicode in SAP Systems* (see Appendix B), from which some of the information contained in this chapter has been taken.

Unicode standard and ISO/IEC 10646

What exactly is *Unicode*? The Unicode standard and ISO/IEC 10646 assign numbers to the characters of all important languages in a consistent and uniform manner, regardless of the system, program, or language. This procedure is very similar to the non-Unicode code pages previously

6 MDMP or blended code pages are no longer recommended; there are general limitations (golden rules) for MDMP.
7 Preferred Unicode conversion release.(Endnotes)

described. Put another way: In a Unicode-based system, there is only one character set — the "Unicode code page," so to speak. Different formats for the encoding of these characters provide the capability of defining millions of characters, so that historical scripts, symbols, and arrows can be used in addition to languages. Moreover, the Unicode standard also reserves number ranges for 'private' use, so that companies have the option of defining their own characters and symbols, and using the latter with uniform fonts, for example.

Unicode is a "real" standard

The fact that the Unicode is a real standard that encodes characters completely, regardless of hardware or software, gives it two great advantages over all other attempts to combine languages. First, Unicode data can be exchanged between IT systems without worrying about conversion algorithms or data loss. Second, characters from different languages can be combined together as needed — for example on the screen (and even in one line, as is illustrated in Figure 2.10) or when printing.

What is Unicode?

ما هي الشفرة الموحدة "يونكود" ؟   in Arabic

什麼是Unicode(統一碼/標準萬國碼)?   in Chinese (traditional)

What is Unicode?   in English

რა არის უნიკოდი?   in Georgian

Τι είναι το Unicode?   in Greek

यूनिकोड क्या है?   in Hindi

Cos'è Unicode?   in Italian

ユニコードとは何か？   in Japanese

유니코드에 대해?   in Korean

Что такое Unicode?   in Russian

Figure 2.10   Character Combinations with Unicode

Unicode character encoding

The Unicode standard doesn't just determine the uniform number of every character; it also defines different standards for the representation of those numbers in bits (Unicode encoding forms or schemes). Basically, a distinction is made between representation in bytes, words, or double words, corresponding to 8, 16, or 32 bits per character. Each format has its advantages and its disadvantages, and therefore, each can be used to leverage its particular strength. Conversion between the formats is easy. In short, these three formats can be described as follows:

▸ **UTF-8**
UTF-8 is a variable-length encoding — that is, a character can be represented by one or more bytes.

▸ **UTF-16**
UTF-16 uses byte pairs for the representation of characters.

▸ **UTF-321**
For UTF-32, every character is represented by a 32-bit code (only used rarely).

By now you can see that the number of bytes needed to represent a character is larger than in a non-Unicode system. This can result in potentially higher memory or processing-speed requirements, depending on the encoding and characters used, and this must be considered when planning a Unicode installation. (For more information, see "Conversion Roadmap" and its corresponding details at the SAP Service Marketplace, *http://service.sap.com/Unicode*.)

Memory requirements and processing speed

Unicode is not just a technologically perfect solution for representing world languages, but is in fact required for modern business processes and development platforms. Look at your own company; there are two areas where multiple languages are absolutely necessary: employee relations and master data. Many companies employ personnel from countries other than the one where they are based. Therefore, they need to store the names of all employees in the correct language and with the corresponding characters. This is a requirement that can only be met by using Unicode. For master data and for many other types of enterprise data that must be available globally, Unicode plays an important role. For instance, in a globally used ERP system, you must be sure that all fields are displayed correctly in any language on the input devices (even those locally installed) and can also be edited without errors.

Another reason for the rapid spread of Unicode installations is the increasing importance of the expansion of traditional sales and distribution channels over the Internet. If a smaller company with comparatively low overhead opens a Web shop, the products or services offered are automatically visible for Internet users around the world. When a customer orders something using that Web page, the back end must be able to store customer data (such as addresses and names) — an ability that can only be guaranteed by using Unicode. In other words, if a company operates a thoroughly interesting and well-presented Web store with the Western European code page, orders from Asia will never arrive, since the addresses will be stored incorrectly and cannot be interpreted. Failing to use Unicode in this case would lead directly to lost sales due to not only the loss of orders already placed, but new customers, too.

Unicode does not solve the translation issue

With a Unicode system, we are always ready (from a technical standpoint) to introduce any new language into a single global system. There is often the misconception that the introduction of Unicode will solve all language problems. Unicode is a platform that allows the technically perfect use of any combination of languages in a system, but it doesn't absolve you of the need to translate the application's text into each language. For instance, if Customizing text is created in English, it must first be explicitly translated before a Russian user can edit them in Russian. Indeed, there are currently some rather good tools for computerized translations, but they are useful only in very limited circumstances, if at all. Therefore, we will not spend any more time discussing them. Interested readers may refer to the special literature, such as *http://service.sap. com/languages*, or may contact SAP directly.

The SAP language package

A global solution must support the user interface, business data, and required legal documents — all in multiple languages, and their translations into different languages can start from different sources. For example, the business data — that is, the Customizing, master, and transaction data — is entered by users in the local language, while the translation of the user interface and some documents is available in the SAP Language Package, which contains more than 40 available languages (SAP ERP 6.0). To translate a custom development, documents, and forms, as well as other objects into all the languages used, intelligent translation tools are necessary. SAP provides these for customers, and they are a standard part of every SAP system. Thereby, the customer is capable of determining an optimum translation strategy and implementing it as efficiently as possible.

When examining the different objects and data necessary for a global system, the following groups can be identified as requiring translation:

- Development objects
- Business documents for printing
- Customizing and configuration data
- Master data
- Transaction data

While technical language support is essential in the global system, a company must determine its own optimum translation strategy. For instance, an enterprise that uses English as its primary company language in the country subsidiaries and with business partners may need translation less than an enterprise that primarily uses local languages in the individual countries. However, this should not lead to the common misconception that as long as you speak English, you can get by anywhere in the world. Local languages are legally required in most countries, so this alone is reason enough to configure local languages within the system and translate corresponding objects, even if only a few. But even without the legal aspects, in many countries it is simply impossible or not well accepted to force employees and business partners to use English. In Japan, for instance, business transactions generally cannot be completed without Japanese; and in Russia, the use of English is rare in many companies, even at higher education levels.

SAP provides different translation tools and procedures for the tasks listed above. A distinction is made between low-, medium-, and high-translation volumes. For small volumes, the text can still be translated and proofed manually. A high volume, such as the complete translation of your own, larger custom development, requires the full SAP translation environment. The central tool for the translation of text is the Translation Workbench (Transaction SE 63), which generates *work lists* that show the translators exactly what needs to be translated. Statistical reports show how much has already been translated, and a proposal pool contains all the terms translated. These are generated during the initial translation and can then be used uniformly for all later translations by other translators — a kind of 'semiautomatic' translation.

2.2 Languages, Time Zones, and Data Transfer

SMLT The SAP system supports a number of translated languages; SAP ERP 6.0 includes almost 40. The language with which a dialog user works is determined at logon by a selection on the logon screen, by a system default, or by a default setting in the user master record. For a logon in the desired language to be possible, it must first be loaded into the SAP system via language import. After a new installation of an SAP system, only German (DE) and English (EN) are installed. More languages can be loaded using Transaction SMLT.

When selecting a language (except for German, English, and Japanese), note that it is only partially translated. The language elements that are not translated must be provided a *supplementation language.* This supplementation language must, itself, be a fully translated language.

Language-Dependent Objects There are a number of different language-dependent objects (see Figure 2.11). Depending on the language, these are more or less completely translated.

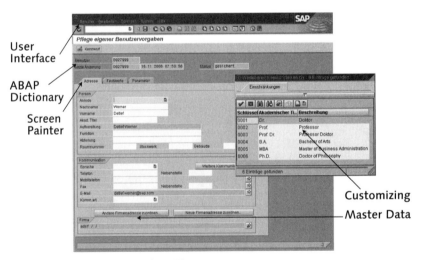

Figure 2.11 Language-Dependent Objects

The translations are completed by the supplementation language, but this only applies to delivered objects. If new language-dependent text is entered by the customer, then the entry applies only for the language version that corresponds to the logon language. That means that this input is not changed for other languages, which can lead to inconsistent data. For example, a user working under a different logon language may not even see the text. There may be an error message — perhaps: "Please enter all required fields" — for objects that have long since been entered. Individual objects, however, might behave differently:

► The text is displayed in an alternate language.

► Nothing is displayed.

► The user receives a warning or error message.

► The transaction can no longer be executed.

The translation strategy and volume most suitable for a global enterprise depends on many factors. Listed below are the most common global company language strategies, which differ in according to use and degree. The extent to which individual languages must be loaded into the SAP system and how completely documents/objects need to be translated depend not only on business conditions, but also political and cultural issues. User acceptance is an important aspect of this. A global enterprise is often forced to use an enterprise-wide language everywhere in the world (usually English); therefore, often, all text is not made available in local languages. This has led to the strategies described below, which outline the degree of translation in a global system.

► **Languages and translation: English only**
In this case, the SAP system supports only English as a logon language and for printing. All reports are generated in English as is all communication. Here, the problem of language-dependent objects is eliminated, and there are no translation costs. The question here is not just whether the user will have problems with the English language, but also whether English-language documents, such as annual reports, can be accepted from a purely legal standpoint. Therefore, this is a valid solution only for a small number of countries — those that already use English as their official language.

► **Language and translation: mostly English**
Here it is assumed that the users are fluent in English. They log on in English, and the menus and display screens are also in English. Reports, however, are generated in the local language, and language-

dependent objects are translated upon request. This requires some translation and customizing (e.g., for units of measure). The master data and communication are also available in the local language.

▶ **Language and translation: some English**
This solution can be seen as the ideal recommendation for global systems with many countries and different languages. The master language of the system is English, but beyond this, the users need not have a more-extensive knowledge of the language. They log on in their local languages and, therefore, also use the language-dependent objects, like menus, input forms, and so on. Communication and all legally relevant reports take place in the local language, and nontranslated text is displayed in the supplementation language, English. Depending on each language's degree of translation, there might not be translations available in some areas. Upon request, additional text can be translated, but in many internal areas this is unnecessary. In addition, there is a periodic language supplementation for newly generated text, and the standard tools are used for this task. Manual translations remain manageable.

▶ **Language and translation: no English**
Sometimes, the users have no fluency in English at all, or English is not accepted for political or cultural reasons. Here, the corresponding country language must be loaded and all text that is not delivered already translated must be manually translated. English is not possible as a supplementation language here — which means ongoing translation activity in the multilingual system. Even if the system is operated in only one language, this is still necessary, because every SAP support package and release upgrade will introduce new language-dependent text into the SAP system, which will need translation.

Translation Workbench The Translation Workbench (see Figure 2.12) is a tool for translating language-dependent text, with the support of a proposal pool. The Translation Workbench can also be used to continue the translation of partially translated languages. Call the Translation Workbench using Transaction SE63. Here you will find appropriate editors for different language-dependent text. Text can be translated using a work list (usually at high volume) that references a proposal pool, and text is either automatically stored, or text objects are translated directly (generally for low to medium volume). Translated languages — either delivered by SAP or customer translations — can be loaded into an SAP system using Transaction SMLT.

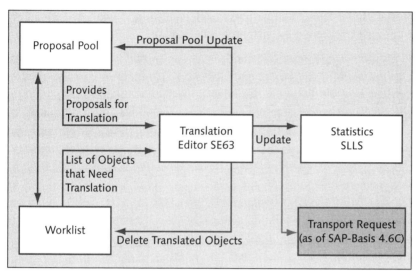

Figure 2.12 Components of the Translation Workbench

During an import or a language supplementation, the SAP system blocks language-management activities for the language affected. The system will deny all additional activities to be performed that use a locked language. Other languages are not affected by this procedure; therefore, parallel actions operating on different languages may be performed.

Language import

Support packages are provided to correct errors that occur in SAP transactions. SAP support packages can contain language-dependent data, like message text, ABAP text pool entries, or Dynpro text. After an SAP support package is imported using Transaction SPAM, the translated text for these objects are at the latest level in all languages existing in the system.

SAP support packages and translation

Problems may occur if another language is imported from the language CD-ROM and placed on a system where SAP support packages have been loaded. Because the language CD-ROM was created prior to the first SAP support package, and the SAP support package objects are only provided with translations to the languages already imported, the subsequent import of a language can put the objects contained in the SAP support packages into an undefined state, as far as translation is concerned. Text can either be obsolete (and therefore wrong), or it can be missing entirely (see also SAP Note 352941). Since SAP Basis 4.6C, you can load the language data contained in the SAP support packages at a later date in order to achieve a consistent language state.

Language import with SMLT

Language import takes place with Transaction SMLT (see Figure 2.13). An essential prerequisite of the language import is the technical support of the languages in the system. For instance, in a single code-page system, only the languages that match that code page can be imported. In a Unicode system, where all languages and character sets are possible, a new, non-SAP standard language must be configured prior to the language import.

Language import with Transaction SMLT is described in the individual installation guidelines, which can be found on the installation disks or at *http://service.sap.com/instguides*. The following sections describe some special features.

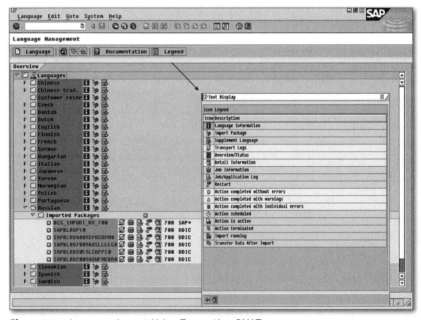

Figure 2.13 Language Import Using Transaction SMLT

Several languages can be imported in parallel. Depending on the capability of your SAP system, the simultaneous import of several languages may place a higher load on the system than the sequential import of languages. After importing the languages, you must still import the language data contained in the support packages. To do this, select the respective language in Transaction SMLT and then select: **Language • Special Actions • Import Patches**.

2.2.1 Language-Dependent Customizing

When importing a language with supplementation of the translation gaps, objects in the SAP standard are loaded and supplemented. For language-dependent Customizing texts, the supplementation is somewhat more complicated (see Figure 2.14). These texts may not have been translated into all languages and must therefore be supplemented; and don't forget that most Customizing texts are client-dependent.

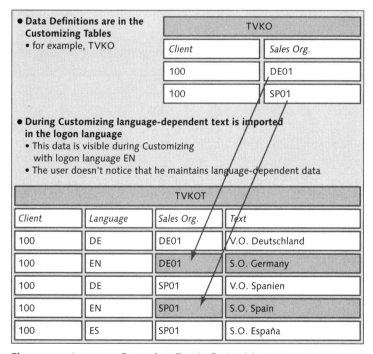

Figure 2.14 Language-Dependent Text in Customizing

Customizing data is only generated when the customer does so in the context of Customizing. This Customizing data of a customer client account is not overwritten during language imports or an upgrade. The import of data always takes place in Client 000. The reason is that Customizing places the responsibility for the Customizing data into the hands of the customer, and afterward it may not be overwritten by data from SAP. This applies equally to translations.

However, where translations are concerned, it is sometimes desirable for the customer to refresh the sample data and previous settings with the current translation from SAP. The clients should always be copied from Client 000 first, after it is supplied with all the languages needed. To update a translation language for Customizing of an existing customer client, you have two options:

► Use of tools

► Manual translation

2.2.2 Supplementing Customizing (Transaction SMLT)

To close the existing translation gaps in a language, language supplementation should always be started after a language import. The supplementation actions are client-dependent, and language supplementation is performed for the client in which you are logged on. If you use several clients, then language supplementation must be explicitly performed in every production client. You can access text stored in client-independent database tables from all clients at the same time. The pre-setting is selected in such a way that client-independent tables are supplemented when you are logged on in Client 000.

For the definition of supplementation logic, the following rules apply:

► Languages with translation level I (complete languages) cannot be supplemented. If this is still necessary, please consult SAP Note 111750, "Supplement German with English" (Customizing).

► You should specify a supplementation language for every language in the system (except for languages with translation level I).

▶ You can only supplement text from a language with translation level I, or from a language that has already been supplemented from a language with translation level I.

2.2.3 Special Tools

When supplementing Customizing texts using Transaction SMLT, the following options can be selected:

▶ **Combined with RSREFILL (Default Option)**
Three steps are performed in one operation: the retraction of a supplementation performed in the past, RSREFILL, and the supplementation. The RSREFILL step copies text from the Customizing tables in Client 000 to the current client. A reference language is required as further information, because only translation text that is the same in both clients (in the reference language) is copied from Client 000 to the logon client. Comparison with the reference language is used so that only semantically meaningful text lines are copied, and the translation remains consistent. The reference language is selected as the language in which Customizing will be performed on the target client, and it must be different from the target language. This mode can only be used in clients other than 000.

▶ **Combined with Client Maintenance**
Three steps are performed in one operation here, as well: the retraction of a supplementation, client administration, and supplementation. Client administration differs from RSREFILL in that there is no comparison with a reference language, so more text lines are copied in the target language from Client 000 to the current client. That introduces the risk that semantically incorrect text lines will be copied and that the translation will be inconsistent. This mode can only be used in clients other than 000.

▶ **Supplement Only**
Here, missing text lines are supplemented with the corresponding lines in the supplementation language. Table 2.7 shows an example of the supplementation of Customizing texts.

Client	Language	Text
000	EN	Company code
000	DE	Buchungskreis
000	Z1	Bucki
100	EN	Company code
100	DE	Buchungskreis
100	Z1	(Empty)

Table 2.7 Supplementing Customizing Texts

Supplementing
Customizing texts The language-dependent text for the Z1 language in Client 100 is missing and should now be supplemented (see Figure 2.15). The supplementation language is German (DE), and the reference language is English (EN). Depending on which option is selected, the supplementation works differently:

▸ **Combined with RSREFILL**
Because the reference language EN text in Client 000 is not identical to the language EN text in Client 100, the text from user-specific language Z1 is not copied from Client 000 to Client 100. Therefore, supplementation language DE text is copied from Client 100. The result is: "Buchungskreis."

▸ **Combined with Client Maintenance**
There is no comparison to a reference language, and the text of language Z1 is copied from Client 000. The result is: "Bucki."

TVKOT			
Client	Language	Sales Org.	Text
100	DE	DE01	V.O. Deutschland
100	EN	DE01	S.O. Germany
100	ES	DE01	S.O. Germany
100	DE	SP01	V.O. Spanien
100	EN	SP01	S.O. Spain
100	ES	SP01	S.O. España

Figure 2.15 Language Supplementation in Customizing

▶ **Supplement Only**
The text from supplementation language DE is simply copied from Client 100. The result is: "Buchungskreis."

2.2.4 Manual Translation of Customizing Texts

The link between the translation environment to the Change and Transport System makes it possible to create translated Customizing texts in a special system, mark it in transport requests, and then distribute it as desired through the system landscape. You translate the rest of the Customizing texts with Transaction SE63, mark the translation activity in transport requests, and finally distribute the orders using the Transport Management System (Transaction STMS).

2.2.5 Address Versions

Global application of SAP software leads to the use of different fonts for master data. Names and addresses of business partners should be available in the local language. International address versions (versions for short) are a property of Business Address Services, which enables the printing of addresses in country-specific fonts. In this context, "specific fonts" does not refer simply to country-specific details within character sets (like umlauts in German or accents in French), but refers to fonts that have their own character sets.

When printing addresses, note that the font of the addresses to be printed is often not determined by the current logon language or by the logon language when the address was created. Rather, International Address Versions offers the option of printing the same address in several different fonts, depending on certain parameters. For example, a Japanese address should be printed in Kanji (Japanese characters) if sender's country is Japan; in all other cases, address output should be in international characters (see SAP Note 316331).

Business Address Services

The default version of an address can, in principle, be entered in any allowed or existing fonts. In the interest of uniform reporting, however, it makes sense to enter all default versions of addresses in one installation, and in the same font. For a global system, English or the global character set is recommended.

In all applications that use Business Address Services, address versions are available that can be configured (see Figure 2.16). Because address versions must semantically match the default versions and only allow entering one address in different fonts, we must ensure that the entries for the address in the default version and associated address versions are consistent. For this reason, numeric fields in the address (e.g., house number, postal code, and telephone number) for the default version are offered as suggested values in the translated versions. Changes to these fields are written back to the default version of the address. Only text fields can differ in the different versions.

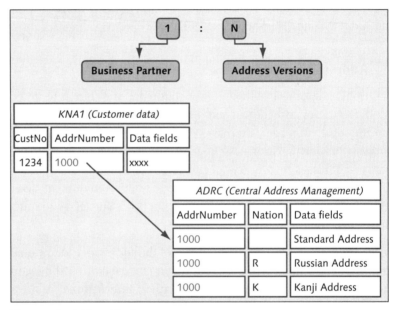

Figure 2.16   Address Versions

2.2.6   Time Zone Requirements for International Businesses

Time zone requirements for international business

In a global SAP system that includes transactions over several time zones, the respective local times are recorded. Theoretically, this can lead to errors, for example, when posting or conducting background processes. The time-zone function enables you to ensure critical synchronization of date and time. In general, this functionality depends on the respective application and can therefore be implemented in different ways.

The SAP system displays the time entered in two different ways: either as local time (*external time*) related to the given time zone, or as absolute time (*internal time*) that is independent of the respective time zone. Depending on the time zone, the local time can be, for example, Central European Time (CET), while the absolute time always refers to Universal Time Coordinated (UTC), also referred to as Greenwich Mean Time (GMT). UTC is always used as a reference if external times are converted to internal times for comparison. When recording the date, the time is often recorded, as well.

Displaying the time in the system

You can change the settings relevant to times zones in IMG — for example, the system time zone that must correspond to the operating system. For users and objects without any time-zone settings, a default zone is set. The user time zone is generally defined in the user address and is maintained by the end user. Figure 2.17 shows time-zone settings in IMG, and Figure 2.18 illustrates the user configuration. You can find more examples of using time-zone functionality at the SAP Help Portal (*http://help.sap.com*).

Time zone settings in IMG

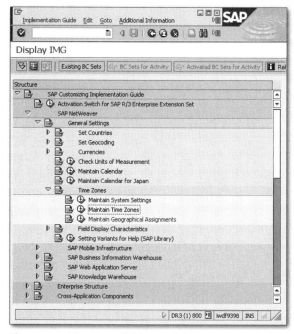

Figure 2.17 Time-Zone Settings in IMG

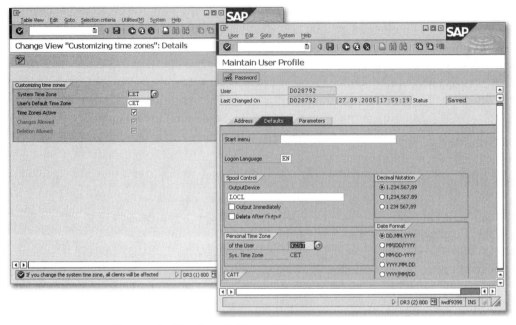

Figure 2.18 Time-Zone Settings of Users

2.2.7 Data Transfer Within an Enterprise and with External Systems

Communication and interfaces

Today, a global enterprise generally operates on a worldwide basis, or at least in several countries. Therefore, customers, suppliers, delivery firms, and other business partners are distributed across different countries and must exchange data between all of their computer systems. The Internet has created a significant technological breakthrough in this regard, so that business documents no longer need to be exchanged on paper, but can be exchanged electronically instead. It is expected, and even legally required, for these documents to be translated into the various national languages of the partners. Figure 2.19 shows a typical scenario in which SAP and non-SAP systems use the Internet and other communications media to exchange data between business partners with different roles.

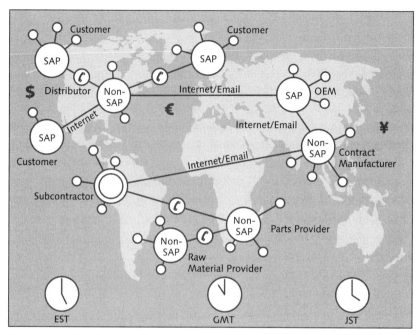

Figure 2.19 Global Data Exchange

The technology of communication and data exchange is a great challenge for IT systems. During the time of Big Iron, and even afterward, only a few, usually simple interfaces were the rule. Today, data exchange in all imaginable formats is a must. In addition to the existing challenges posed for data communication by different technologies, network protocols, data formats, and application protocols, now there is another challenge: If text from different character sets and languages must be exchanged (imagine a German automobile supplier expanding into China and therefore needing German and Chinese), then all text and languages must be correctly and unambiguously transmitted between the systems involved. Only two matching Unicode systems make this possible without limitation, given that non-Unicode single code-page systems can only process languages from a single character set. MDMP systems have a similar problem, as they only know languages of the code pages configured. Even more challenging is the fact that MDMP is only known in SAP systems, and there are significant limitations and even exclusions when communicating with non-SAP systems.

Global data
exchange

Homogeneous and
non-homogeneous
communication
For language exchange in a global enterprise, the ideal network would be one in which only Unicode-based systems from different manufacturers would communicate with each other (homogeneous communication). Unfortunately, this is a wish that will only be possible in the future. In reality, we generally now have networks in which Unicode and non-Unicode systems must communicate with one another (*non-homogeneous communication*). Using different encodings for Unicode and the non-Unicode code pages, text must be correctly and unambiguously interpreted and converted. Regardless of whether conversion happens in the application, middleware, or technical interface, non-homogeneous communication conversion can only be correctly performed under the following conditions:

▶ The code page of the non-Unicode system determines the characters that can be correctly transmitted.

▶ The code page of the non-Unicode system must be unambiguous and known to the Unicode system.

▶ The Unicode system must be able to determine the code page of the non-Unicode system from parameters or configuration data.

For the data transfer, conversion routines between Unicode and all non-Unicode single code pages used must be available:

Data transfer between the various non-Unicode systems is even more complex. For example, if you want to connect a European SAP system that includes MDMP with your Asian supplier's Java-based system, adapting the interface would incur a high cost. MDMP is only known in SAP systems, and Java applications work only in Unicode. Before the introduction of Unicode, many detailed questions had to be considered during implementation in order to effect data transfer without errors and with as few technically mandated limitations as possible. The following key questions must be answered:

Key questions on
implemeneting
interfaces
▶ Are code pages available for both the source and target?

▶ Do the code pages for the source and target use the same codes for all special characters?

▶ Does the medium support the code page correctly?

▶ Do I need any conversion programs?

▶ In the worst case, do business processes need to be changed (e.g., limiting them to English for specific data)?

So far, we have seen that a software application requires complex connections of different technologies for communicating with different system environments. Therefore, in the past few years, SAP has further developed the classic R/3 system to cover a universal communication landscape for multilateral data exchange between ABAP environment, Java/J2EE applications, and common Web technologies. The components provided by SAP for this purpose are summarized as the term *connectivity*, whereas all considerations are valid for both synchronous and asynchronous data transfers. Table 2.8 presents an overview of the most-critical communication options. For more-detailed information about the individual technologies, visit the SAP Help Portal *(http://help. sap.com)*. The examples in Table 2.8 can also be found there.

Classic SAP Technologies (ABAP)
▶ RFC interface (Remote Function Call)
▶ IDoc interface
▶ ALE and Electronic Data Interchange (EDI)
▶ BAPI
Communication Between ABAP and Non-ABAP Technologies
▶ SAP Business Connector
▶ SAP Java Connector
▶ SAP Java Resource Adapter
▶ SAP .NET Connector
▶ Internet Communication Framework
▶ SOAP Runtime for SAP NW AS
▶ Web service technologies in SAP NW AS

SAP communication technologies

Table 2.8 SAP Communication Options

At the end of this chapter, you still might be wondering: *Which hardware can be used to meet the requirements described in the previous sections?*

The answer is quite simple: At the time this book was written, all standard computer systems have the hardware, speed, and performance fea-

Hardward requirements and technical options

tures necessary to support all scenarios and topologies. Therefore, you only have to correctly select and plan the individual computer landscape, because there are no real limitations with regard to hardware.

2.3 Summary

In this chapter, we discussed the global IT solution's global and local components. Some of the local requirements are mandatory, whereas others can both be characterized locally and globally (or regionally). These components are not only determined by the business strategy, but also by the system's users, whose different requirements and preferences must be considered.

Industry versions

SAP provides different industry versions (industry solutions) with portfolios based on comprehensive knowledge about industry-specific processes and requirements. Country Versions (not necessarily industry-specific) is also available for covering local legal regulations, and for providing the functionality necessary for country-specific business and facilitating global implementation. Here, both the extensive documentation of the country versions and the SAP Globalization Knowledge Base (a customer tool), are very useful. For the very critical issue of diverse languages, you must differentiate between technical implementation (the system must be able to display and save the characters of a language) and translation (making sure remote offices get the text they need in the language required, and correctly).

Time zone functionality

The time-zone functionality is used for the necessary harmonization of date and time to ensure collaboration between users in different time zones. You were also provided with details on data transfer within an enterprise and the components offered by SAP for this purpose. All considerations apply to both synchronous and asynchronous data transfers.

In the following chapters, all of these issues will be taken into account and used to support our decisions when choosing the appropriate system topology.

This chapter provides an overview of the different architectures that can be used by global enterprises to integrate countries and solutions — from distributed decentralized SAP systems, to multinational single-instance installations with all countries and solutions implemented in one system.

3 Overview of Architectures

This chapter introduces the basic system architectures that are used most frequently and describes their concepts and properties, as well as the general advantages and disadvantages for global IT solutions. Due to their great significance for multinational enterprises, the focus is on central architectures. We then discuss complex system landscapes that are integrated with several SAP Business Suite components, which will illustrates that complex architectures often originate from a combination of basic architectures.

3.1 From Past to Future

The need for appropriate and optimal system architectures arose with the first distributed client/server systems — that is, after the end of the mainframe era. However, a real awareness of this subject did not occur until IT departments were forced to optimize entire IT structures because of growing worldwide competition and increased cost pressures.

When SAP launched R/2 on a mainframe system, only one approach for central architectures existed. Since applications on the mainframe are configured and used centrally, the mainframe, itself, only works centrally from both the hardware and implementation point of view. Implementations, however, could already be performed on a modular basis — for example, first financial accounting and then materials management.

SAP R/2 and Mainframes

SAP R/2 already contained the client concept, which enabled users to separate data for different clients. However, this concept was mainly used within projects, such as to differentiate between test and production data. In those early years, there was no great demand for efficient international and global implementations. If a multinational enterprise used R/2 in several countries, these countries were either geographic neighbors with similar legal regulations that could easily be implemented (e.g., financial accounting), or each country was considered an independent project that was implemented as well as operated on a single system with specific data.

Globalization with SAP R/3 and client/server architectures

When SAP R/3 and the underlying client/server architectures were introduced, the demand for appropriate system architectures changed quite quickly. The transition from a mainframe to client/server architecture was mainly technology- and hardware-driven. The age of networks and the Internet was dawning, making it considerably easier and cheaper to communicate across continents. Now, it was only a matter of time until the wave of globalization emerged.

It was quickly realized that now not only one architecture and procedure existed (similar to the mainframe), but a wide range of options and variants, which were all supposed to achieve the same result. Depending on the architecture selected, different options and variants were more or less suitable. This resulted in a new area in the IT world, where the optimal architecture was discussed not only for hardware and networks, but particularly for the architecture of implementations, as well as applications.[1]

In the early days of SAP R/3, many multinational enterprises took the approach of installing a separate SAP system for each country or business area. In the early 1990s, shortly after SAP R/3 was launched and after the end of the mainframe era, it was very 'modern' to exploit the new technical options for distribution and decentralization that client/server architectures provided. However, the significance for a large global enterprise's IT was not understood Moreover, organizations were structured rather decentrally in those years, which meant that project teams in different countries and business areas worked independently

---

1 We could use the term *application architecture* here, also.

of each other. But soon, many customers wanted to implement several countries on one system.

For this purpose, first it had to be determined whether multinational implementations were technically and economically possible. The other issue to deal with was whether the new client/server generation, as well as resulting new hardware and network capacities, could meet the requirements of central systems. At this point, we refer to the empirical rule by Gordon E. Moore (1965): Moore's law.[2] Moore determined that the number of transistors and other electronic components placed on an integrated circuit (IC) doubles approximately every 18 months, while the price remains the same. As Figure 3.1 illustrates, computer and hardware capacities consequently increase tenfold approximately every five years, while hardware prices remain the same. Although Moore's law came at the beginning of the age of computer technology, it is still applicable today.

Moore's law

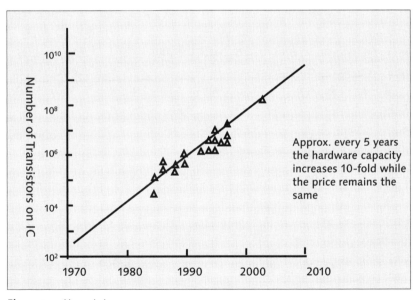

Figure 3.1 Moore's Law

2 See *http://en.wikipedia.org/wiki/Moore%27s_law* and *http://service.sap.com/sizing*, for example.

Networks Another very important criterion is network capacity, particularly the capacity of WANs (*Wide Area Networks*) that must be high enough to enable users from different countries, which are sometimes geographically thousands of miles apart, to work in an efficient dialog mode, using one central system. In this area, computer and database hardware development was considerably more differentiated. Today a common PC features the performance that yesterday's mainframe provided, but in many countries, the network infrastructure is still rather poor, particularly in areas with low infrastructure such as rural areas so that efficient connections to central systems are only possible to a certain extent, if at all.

In order to implement a central system approach, hardware and network infrastructure first had to meet technical requirements. From the early years of SAP R/3 to the mid-1990s, this was only possible in some cases. The capacities of database and application servers, as well networks reached their limits very quickly, or other restrictions existed (e.g., operating system software or databases), despite sufficient hardware capacity. Hence, enterprises had to wait until hardware and network infrastructures met the requirements to technically enable central, multinational systems with sufficient capacity. After the mid-1990s, servers, databases, operating systems, and network infrastructures were powerful enough — that is, large central systems with thousands of users, as well as databases in the terabyte range, could be implemented and operated.

Today, hardware provides nearly unlimited options and an environment only limited by costs, for example:

▸ Standard 64-bit architectures, which abolished many restrictions imposed by 32-bit architectures.

▸ New dual and multicore processors with clock speeds in the GHz range.

▸ A new generation of adaptive technology (*computing*) that enables you to dynamically change the assignment of hardware resources between different servers and systems during operation.

▸ Modern SAN (*Storage Area Network*) storage systems that can manage many terabytes of different server systems, and are characterized by high performance and low access times.

Network infrastructure can be divided into two areas. Within LANs (*Local Area Networks*) and internal company networks (*intranets*) at one (or close) location(s), transfer rates are high enough that capacity is no longer important. For remote connections to national organizations via rented/leased lines (third-party network operators), and (recently) also via Internet VPN (*Virtual Private Network*) connections, the capacities generally depend on how advanced the network infrastructure is and what local costs may incur. Particularly in the "new emerging market countries," such as BRIC countries,[3] network infrastructures are often limited and depend on the size of the location. You can compare this situation with that of private, home Internet connections. There are areas that still don't have DSL connections, even in big cities, due to lack of network provider expansion; whereas some remote, rural areas are provided with these fast connections.

Network latency is another limitation for remote connections that must be considered. Due to technically mandated waiting times in transmission nodes and routers between central systems and end users, network latency can lead to longer response times — despite a high network bandwidth. See Section 5.2.3 for more detailed information on this subject.

The fact that hardware and network meet the requirements for central systems does not mean that these systems can be implemented. Since SAP R/3 began, there have been other important technical criteria that directly affected the implementation of central/decentralized architectures, and that originate from the design and operation methods of SAP systems. Technical language support is an essential criterion that is still applicable today. Because SAP R/3 was designed for the simultaneous operation of languages with the same character set or code page, only one country (or a few countries with one language or a few languages with the same code page, a "language group") could operate in one SAP system. Consequently, globally set up enterprises had to implement multinational projects on several SAP systems and integrate these distributed systems with each other for uniform business processes — for example, by exchanging master data. This procedure

---

3 BRIC is a common, collective term for Brazil, Russia, India, and China.

required more effort and was used despite the demand for central systems.

But even in the mid-1990s, knowing that the hardware must be powerful enough, several global customers asked the critical question: How can multiple countries in a region, or even over multiple continents, operate together on a single SAP system, despite the technical restrictions of a single code page? Immediately, it was clear that the decentralized approach to operating an SAP system for each country or language group would not last. Customers quickly recognized that a global system with multiple countries is significantly more efficient and cost-effective for implementations and IT operations than one system for each country's language or language group.

At that time, the problem of how central systems could be operated with countries of several language groups was still unsolved whereas today, SAP Unicode technology enables the parallel operation of languages for all SAP products. At that time, numerous and sometimes controversial discussions were held concerning which architectural approach was the cheapest and best solution for implementing and operating multinational global projects: the centralized or decentralized approach. It was determined fairly quickly that there were recommendations, tendencies, and preferences for both approaches, but it was also determined that often a clear and perfect answer could not be found — and still cannot today, despite the removal of (technical) restrictions (which are described in more detail in Section 4.6). Therefore, there were (and still are) supporters for both approaches.

Numerous analyses and studies show that for a global enterprise, the single-instance system approach offers significant advantages over a decentralized distributed architecture including cost reductions. The single-instance, or single-box approach, refers to a central IT architecture with one global system and one database, on which all countries and languages of a globally active enterprise are implemented.

Today you can select from a wide range of architectures. Even though there are still important factors and criteria that apply to a limited extent for certain architectures (see Chapter 4), you can still select between several approaches in most cases. Therefore, a careful analysis must be performed that includes all aspects — from organizational to business, commercial, technical, and even cultural issues.

The latest SAP product generation, SAP NetWeaver 7.0, ERP 6.0, and SAP Business Suite 2005, heralded the new age of service-oriented architectures (*Enterprise SOA* — Enterprise Service Oriented Architecture). They open up entirely new worlds that may revolutionize previous IT.[4] Currently, we are still at the very beginning of Enterprise SOA, and it will take some time until a real transition is completed. At this point, we don't look at Enterprise SOA in great detail. But when dealing with this topic, you will realize that the typical criteria and issues will arise when discussing central or decentralized architectures and their concepts for global enterprises, even though, for example, the underlying technology may be completely different. Like "typical" SAP ERP systems, for example, each global enterprise must consider if and how its master data can be created, changed, or transferred between all processes and services involved, and do so in a standardized and consistent way, worldwide — even for decentralized data storage using central Master Data Management (MDM).[5] This involves all parties of an enterprise and its partners to the same extent — from strictly business-oriented analysts that are rather familiar with the business processes but not with IT, to technology specialists with IT expertise but little knowledge of business processes. Another important question is if and how you can use appropriate global templates for global implementations. These templates are an important prerequisite for the efficient implementation of business processes across corporate groups. Even though Enterprise SOA will bring many changes to the IT world, the typical challenges will remain the same when implementing global, multinational projects.

Enterprise SOA

The next sections describe in more detail the different architectures you can use to implement as well as operate SAP systems, and explain their properties and possible uses.

---

4 See *http://service.sap.com/esa.*
5 See *http://service.sap.com/mdm.*

3.2   Overview of Global (Central) or Distributed (Decentralized) Architectures

Topology   This section will first introduce the important term "system topology," or just "topology," to classify the different basic structures and patterns in which the various IT systems are arranged and linked in a system landscape. In the IT world, the term "topology" was used initially to classify network structures. We expand the term, as follows:

> **Definition**
>
> In system landscapes, system topology refers to structures and connections of several IT systems, to exchange data of shared and integrated applications and processes.

Figure 3.2 shows a selection of basic topological structures. The simplest topology is shown in the lower left, where the nodes (the IT systems in our example) are arranged on a line. Several more-complex topologies are also shown, such as the bus structure, where all systems are connected via a central track, or the hierarchical tree structure, as well as complete-connection (cross-bar) topology, where each system is connected to all of the other systems. Large system landscapes often contain combinations of different topologies.

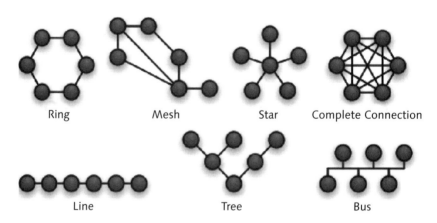

Figure 3.2   Basic Topologies

Regarding SAP systems, expanding this term to include application integration is particularly useful when several SAP systems run decentrally within a system landscape and, for example, are integrated via SAP ALE (Application Link Enabling) applications, or when several SAP Business Suite components are used that are connected to each other, such as in SAP ERP and SAP CRM systems. "Topology" is also useful defining the integration of SAP systems with non-SAP systems, as you will see later on.

Generally, various topologies and architectures, as well as the resulting system landscapes can be used for global implementations. Many variants of specific architectures also exist. If you carried out a survey among several multinational enterprises that use SAP systems, you would probably be surprised by the array of different procedures by individual enterprises, as well as by the number of systems used, their different topologies, and the complexities of the system landscapes.

Moreover, large enterprises often use several SAP Business Suite components for their entire global solution. For example, if you use SAP ERP and SAP NetWeaver BI components, there are several possible topologies for a worldwide solution (see Figure 3.3):

Complex system landscapes with SAP Business Suite

▶ Central ERP system and BI system

▶ Decentralized ERP system and central BI system

▶ Decentralized ERP system and BI system

▶ Decentralized ERP system and BI system, and an additional central BI system

The data transfer from ERP to BI is mostly unidirectional, so it is still a quite simple case. Many more combinations exist, for example, for the bidirectional case with SAP ERP and SAP CRM. The dashed lines between the three ERP systems in Figure 3.3 illustrate a loosely coupled connection — that is, the ERP systems only exchange data with each other occasionally.

In the first case, both components (ERP and BI) are centrally implemented. Therefore, only one system for each component exists, as well as one unidirectional connection from the central ERP to the central BI system. In terms of topology, this is a very simple case.

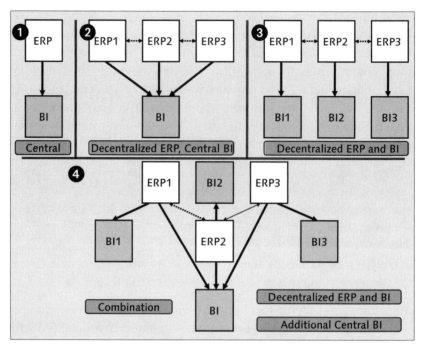

Figure 3.3 Possible Topologies for SAP ERP and SAP NetWeaver BI Systems

The second case is a little more complex. In a globally active enterprise, for example, there are three different SAP ERP systems that are divided into regions, by continents. System ERP1 for North and South America (America), ERP2 for Europe, Africa, and the Middle East (EMEA), and ERP3 for APA, including Asia and Oceania (Australia, New Zealand). This is common business practice. However, the BI system runs centrally. From a topological point of view, this is a tree structure.

In the third case, the ERP and BI systems are both decentralized and topologically form a grid like structure. Here we assume that the BI systems are set up systematically according to region by continent, similar to ERP systems.

The fourth case is a combination of topologies. In addition to the decentralized grid structure shown in the third case, there is another central BI system that is connected to the three ERP systems (case two), which is independent of the other BI systems. This can make sense if case two cannot be implemented with a single central BI system, and case three is not sufficient here because the BI system can only process regional data from the ERP system, but you require worldwide data processing.

Generally, numerous different system topologies and implementations based on those topologies are possible regarding central and decentralized data storage, business processes, and organization of enterprises. This book covers one very important aspect, however: the analysis and discussion of central, decentralized, and combined architectures. To better illustrate and analyze the relationships between technical, organizational, and business points of view (which are described at a later stage), and the structure of architectures for global solutions, we also use the more precise terms for those architectures — such as locally distributed (decentralized) architecture, regional (partly decentralized or centralized decentralized architecture, shared services) architecture, and global (completely central) architecture. These terms are used in addition to the comprehensive terms of the central and decentralized architecture.

3.3 Prerequisites and Definitions

Opinions often differ on which criteria and facts should be considered in a concrete discussion about architectures for a global solution. Also, there are often inconsistent definitions in literature. For example, an IT service provider that runs a data center and provides hardware infrastructure for SAP systems considers a "single-instance architecture" as a "single-server" or "single-storage architecture" — that is, he is referring primarily to the existing hardware infrastructure and its optimization. Of course, this aspect is very important, because large SAP systems only be used efficiently with good hardware. The following chapters illustrate that there are many 'strong' decision criteria for selecting and determining an optimal architecture, which depends on the underlying hardware infrastructure.

Architecture and hardware

Hardware must manage (very) high data and transaction volumes during continuous operation, and must also be expandable. There are often several thousand users active in single-instance systems. Network performance between different locations or countries and the central data center must be respectively high in order to achieve typical average dialog response times of approximately one second for each end user.

When determining the IT strategy and searching for the optimal architecture, appropriate hardware infrastructures and software/technical prerequisites must be considered. In addition, you must take into account all enterprise aspects — from business functions to the organizational environment, as well as the geographical, cultural, and political environment. Even if the hardware is powerful and cost-efficient enough for a single-instance solution, this might not mean that it is the optimal architecture for the enterprise.

When describing the different architectures and topologies, it is useful to determine the following definitions, requirements, assumptions, and common practices. This way, a useful foundation is established for comparing and valuing all technical, organizational, and company-specific aspects.

SAP Business Suite Components Analysis

The following sections will discuss architectures and topologies for SAP Business Suite components. The focus is on SAP ERP components (SAP R/3, SAP R/3 Enterprise, SAP ERP), because they constitute the greatest share of the SAP Business Suite components. All add-ons, industry solutions, and added country versions of these components are taken into account. The following further SAP Business Suite components include many specific or central functions that can only be used to a certain extent and in special cases; therefore, they should be dealt with individually when planning and designing the global IT solution:

▶ SAP Solution Manager

▶ SAP NetWeaver Process Integration (PI)

▶ SAP NetWeaver Portal

▶ SAP NetWeaver Master Data Management (MDM)

▶ SAP Text Retrieval and Information Extraction (TREX)

▶ Other specific SAP NetWeaver components, such as SAP NetWeaver Mobile

The Global Solution Transport Landscape

Transport landscape   Each SAP component in the system landscape contains a specific, standard, three-system transport landscape with one development system

(DEV), one consolidation or quality assurance system (QAS), and one production system (PRD). The transport landscape ensures that you can maintain and operate each component's production solution in an optimal manner. Additional systems might have certain purposes within the transport landscape, such as for integration, stress, or performance tests, or for multilingual, comprehensive translations, or for training. Figure 3.4 shows a standard system landscape with several SAP Business Suite components as well as the SAP Solution Manager and the SAP System Landscape Directory (SLD) as specific, central system landscape components which play an important role in the different phases and activities of a global solution's entire life cycle. Depending on the release status of the connected systems, these components might be mandatory.[6]

A specific system landscape that is structured individually for the enterprise's global IT solution is also referred to as a "solution landscape." **Solution landscape**

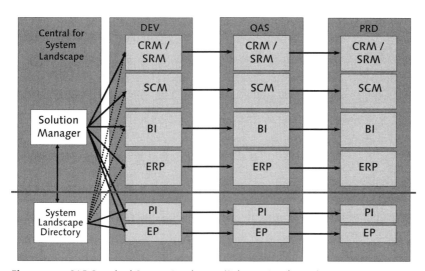

Figure 3.4 SAP Standard System Landscape (Solution Landscape)

---

6 SAP Solution Manager is mandatory for all SAP components that are based on SAP NetWeaver 2004 or higher and is recommended for all other maintained releases. SAP System Landscape Directory is an integral component of specific SAP components. It is particularly required for Java-based SAP applications — for example, the SAP XI PI component — because it centrally registers all system-specific data of each system within the landscape and provides this data to the XI system.

Architecture and Global Software Life-Cycle Processes

Numerous aspects have to be considered when selecting the appropriate architecture. For example, it makes a difference if the architecture is only considered for production operation, or if the software life cycle of the global solution is integrated as a whole. Analyses and architecture discussions usually reference all processes of the life cycle. To ensure transparency, it is useful to distinguish according to the following processes:

▸ **Implementation and development**
Because global projects are usually complex, planned at various locations, and implemented by different teams, the architecture focuses on how efficient planning, coordination, implementation, and development processes can be supported. Specifically, the proven use of global templates for the corporate rollout should be supported. In the global template approach, the major part of uniform data, processes, configurations, and developments is globally implemented. Only a small local part is individually adapted and changed — for example, because of legal regulations in the respective country. A global template approach can considerably influence the selection of an appropriate architecture. You can find details on the global template approach in Section 5.4.4 and further information about implementation at *http://service.sap.com/asap.*

▸ **Maintenance**
To keep a production system running in an optimized way, you require an architecture that enables you to stabilize and optimize operations, solve problems and program errors quickly, and implement important changes (e.g., legal adjustments and new requirements) with as little impact as possible on live operations.

▸ **Live operation**
For running operations, the focus is on architecture and infrastructure. Here, the essential emphasis is on the implementation of global solutions in appropriate IT and hardware infrastructures. The decisive factors are: sufficient performance of all hardware (such as database and application server), low response times for end users (which are distributed all over the world, and also during times of high loads), high availability and security, fast network connections, and other criteria that ensure smooth system operation.

SAP Client

In SAP R/3 and SAP ERP (as well as in several other SAP Business Suite components), an *SAP client* (also just "client") is defined in commercial, organizational and technical terms as a self-contained unit in an SAP ERP system with separate master records and its own set of tables. In organizational terms, a *client* is the highest level in the SAP system hierarchy. (This SAP client concept only exists for ABAP applications and selected SAP Business Suite components, but not for SAP Java applications.) Determinations made or data entered at this level apply to all company codes and all other organizational units. Apart from a few exceptions, all production data is stored, processed, and evaluated separately for each client.

Hence, an SAP client represents a self-contained unit that is logically separated from other clients. Clients cannot access the data of other clients. That means, client-dependent data, which includes customized, master, and transaction data (with a few exceptions), is separate for the various clients. On the other hand, client-independent objects, such as development and data dictionary objects, are the same for all clients. That is, generally speaking, it is a combination of shared central and separated decentralized objects. In an *SAP multiclient system*, which consists of several live clients, the master and application data is therefore generally separate. However, the development and data dictionary objects are shared. In the context of the architecture descriptions, we will again refer to this important aspect.

Logical and Business Systems

A logical system represents a unit that is independent of the underlying physical hardware. This unit provides all business data and application functions for enterprises or organizations. An SAP client is a logical system that is also configured as a logical system. An SAP multiclient system contains several logical systems with data that is separate from each other, even if it is technically stored in the same physical database or table.

Business systems are extensions of logical systems. Irrespective of the technical system data, they are designed to be transparently used by applications for a specific function. The term originates from the SAP Landscape Directory (SLD).[7] Business systems are particularly used when integrating external, non-SAP systems.

System Landscape

The existing logical systems are essential for analyzing a system landscape and discussing its architecture. That is, each SAP client represents an individual, logical system. This aspect serves as an important basis for determining if you should select a single instance or distributed systems.

Complex System Landscapes

Usually, discussions on the selection of the optimal architecture deal with SAP ERP systems (e.g., SAP R/3, SAP R/3 Enterprise, SAP ECC 5.0, SAP ECC 6.0). Global enterprises generally use a complex system landscape with several SAP Business Suite and SAP NetWeaver components, such as SAP NetWeaver BI, SAP CRM, or SAP SRM. Therefore, discussion about the optimal architecture as a whole enters a new level, since there are considerably more possible combinations for how central and decentralized components can be connected. Only logical systems are considered here.

External, Non-SAP Systems

If you want to include external systems in the discussion about architectures, it will become complicated. Therefore, we will omit these systems when possible, particularly when discussing central architectures, because external systems lead to decentralized scenarios. External systems are only considered if they assume an important task for global solutions. For example, if you use an external IT system to maintain master data globally, the system landscape and architecture discussion considers the system as another logical or business system. On the basis

---

7 SAP SLD is a Java-based tool within SAP NetWeaver, which centrally collects the characteristic data of all systems (SAP and non-SAP), as well as the components and services in a system landscape. For example, in SAP NetWeaver XI, it provides the foundation for configuring the interfaces (see *http://service.sap.com/netweaver*).

of these definitions and hints, we can now deal with the various architectures in more detail.

3.4   Decentralized Architectures

This section describes the concept and variants of decentralized architectures, as well as their advantages and disadvantages.

3.4.1   Structure

A decentralized architecture is distributed across several systems that are more or less integrated with respect to the enterprise's entire global solution. Depending on its design and requirements, these systems exchange varying amounts of data via specific interfaces. The decentralized architectures can be divided into the following variants, depending on the integration level:

Variants of decentralized architectures

▸ Locally distributed and completely decentralized systems (complete decentralization)

▸ Regionally distributed systems with shared services

▸ Combined configurations of central and decentralized systems (centralized decentralization)

Before analyzing these architecture variants in detail, we will first describe the criteria and strategies that you can use to distribute the global solution across individual systems. As mentioned at the beginning of this chapter, systems are often distributed by country and implemented at different times. Older SAP R/3 release software required this distribution because, for example, one system might be used only for one country due to restrictions in technical language support or problems with country version. Newer SAP products and technologies no longer impose these restrictions. For example, SAP ERP 6.0, NetWeaver 7.0, and all other SAP components that are based on SAP WEB AS 6.20 and higher support the Unicode standard for unrestricted, parallel operation of all languages (see Chapter 2 on Unicode). Consequently, in addition to distribution by country, there are other, sometimes more important criteria that govern the distribution of systems.

Distribution criteria and strategies

95

▶ **Distribution by corporate group**
Many global enterprises belong to a corporate group that consists of various organizations. The organizational structure of a corporate group changes as company sales, takeovers, acquisitions, and mergers take place, which today occur almost daily. This directly affects the IT infrastructure. For example, in a takeover, the company that has been taken over is supposed to be integrated into the existing IT infrastructure of the corporate group. If this process is too complex or too costly, an individual system is often used for the new enterprise.

The fast pace of mergers and acquisitions

The fast pace of mergers and acquisitions is another increasingly important trend; groups resell the companies they took over, and rather quickly. For IT, this means that the data and processes of a sold company, which were integrated into the system with a great deal of effort, have to be removed from the global system. Tools and services of the SAP SLO (*System Landscape Optimization*) support the consolidation and splitting of systems, but these can be quite complex.[8] Therefore, it is useful in these cases to implement the company that has been bought on a separate system, rather than integrate it into the existing system.

▶ **Distribution by country and region**
Systems are very frequently distributed by country and region. Several aspects must be taken into account. Software-related restrictions, particularly of older SAP releases, did not allow for the combination of several countries and languages in one system. Consequently, specific systems had to be set up for certain countries or regions. Some countries have very complex legal regulations as well as complicated tax structures, such as Brazil and India. These regulations cause many deviations and exceptions, and therefore make it difficult to operate in parallel with other countries — a good reason (at least for these countries) for configuring specific systems. An enterprise usually does not introduce and implement a global solution simultaneously in different countries or regions. Generally, the process spans several years. The procedures, methods, templates, and global processes are often different for each country or region. Consequently, different systems must be implemented.

---

8 See *http://service.sap.com/slo*.

▶ **Distribution by location**
In some cases, geographical distribution by country or region isn't sufficient, or the enterprise has an organizational and functional structure that makes it sensible to use specific systems for certain locations. This, combined with other distribution criteria, can also be taken into account — for example, distribution by business area or industry.

▶ **Distribution by business area**
Enterprises often implement IT in different organizations gradually. Several years may pass before all business areas use the new IT. Since the areas usually work independently of each other, specific systems are used by the respective business areas that implement them. On global systems, the subsequent harmonization and consolidation of these systems can be very complex or difficult due to organizational reasons.

Gradual
implementation

▶ **Distribution by function and industry**
If an enterprise can be assigned to several industries, the business processes, practices, processes, and data may be very different among them. Therefore, the various industries use specific SAP systems. If an enterprise uses SAP Industry-Specific Solutions (IS Solutions), the software imposes the restriction that only one IS solution can be activated on one SAP system.

▶ **Distribution by business process**
Distribution by business process considers aspects similar to those of distribution by industry. For various reasons, some enterprises prefer to run different processes on different systems. For example, financial accounting and materials management processes run on different systems. Very often, financial accounting, sales and distribution, and logistics departments are separate from human resources. Consequently, two different systems are required. The reason is often for security reasons: Sensitive personnel and payroll data should be managed on a separate system in an isolated network.

To further elaborate on the SAP world and our general discussion about IT architectures, we also deal with the concepts of horizontal and vertical integration. These terms are derived from similar architecture topics used in computer science.

Horizontal and
vertical integration

▸ **Horizontal integration**
Horizontal integration connects different IT applications, processes, and data, which already exist separately in parallel or are newly created. It optimizes existing business processes and develops new processes. Horizontal integration leads to synergies. For example, if a global enterprise has implemented similar or identical IT solutions separately in several countries, horizontal integration can optimize these solutions.

▸ **Vertical integration**
Vertical integration maps business processes, services, and data efficiently on an IT basis through vertical architecture layers. It therefore enables transparent and uniform integration of applications in external systems. For example, an SAP SD business process that runs on a separate SAP system should be completely integrated with an SAP FI process running on a different SAP system. For this purpose, you can use the SAP ALE solution. (See also the discussion on ALE in Section 1.3 and Figure 1.14).

If we transfer these concepts to the integration of distributed systems in a global solution, the criteria for organizational and geographical aspects lead us to horizontal integration (*horizontal distribution*). On the other hand, functional and process-related criteria favor vertical integration (*vertical distribution*). Furthermore, we can also assume that horizontal integration requires less data exchange, and vertical integration requires more data exchange. Therefore, horizontal integration is also referred to as "loose coupling," and vertical integration is also called "strong coupling." This is can be easily explained: A global SAP solution that is distributed by country or region has its own database and generally implements all typical ERP applications, if necessary, including country-specific adaptations. It only sporadically requires the data exchange with other systems — for example, month-end closings or product range updates.

Vertical system integrations are often distributed by processes — for example, financial accounting, as well as sales and distribution processes run on one system, while materials management runs on another. Since materials management is closely linked to sales and distribution as well as financial accounting processes, almost every transaction must run on both systems. Consequently, more data is exchanged in a vertical integration than in a horizontal integration. Figure 3.5 shows an overview of the distribution criteria.

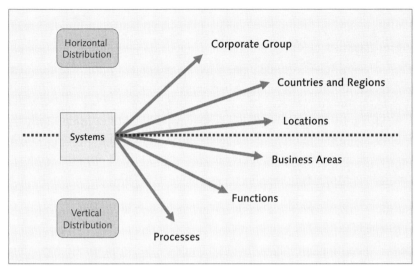

Figure 3.5 Distribution Criteria for Decentralized Systems

3.4.2 Local and Completely Distributed Decentralized Architecture

This architecture distributes the global solution of an enterprise on several systems according to the previously described criteria. The individual local systems (clients as logical systems) work separately and independently of each other.

Each individual system has its own database. The systems communicate with each other only to a certain extent via individually defined interfaces. Each system and solution running on the system can be considered independent of other systems and solutions. The implementation and operation teams work independently of other teams. Please note that the local system hardware can, though, be located in a central data center in this architecture. The development and configuration processes are locally controlled. A global template can, but must not be used.

Advantages and Disadvantages

The following aspects support a local and completely distributed decentralized architecture:

Advantages ### Local Freedom

Decentralized architectures provide the easiest way to integrate new projects, applications, or countries, because they provide freedom in implementing functions, schedules, and solution approaches. You can quickly implement new requirements and functions without worrying too much about the existing solution. Often, the decentralized approach is tempting and preferred first, considering its implementation speed and cost savings over the short term.

Local Independence

Local independence is another advantage of this architecture approach. Various IT teams can work relatively independently of each other and only need to coordinate to a certain extent. In decentralized architectures, the data centers are usually in different locations or countries. Consequently, the IT teams work independently of each other for hardware planning and procurement, installation, maintenance, and system operation.

Network infrastructure
The limitations of the technical network infrastructure between locations (between the base data center/offices and the remote solution system) should not be underestimated, so that a decentralized architecture with systems at different locations might be the only architecture allowed. Despite the latest communication technologies, remote connections that are fast enough and affordable cannot always be implemented, particularly in politically isolated states or developing countries that are just now part of global enterprises because markets have opened up. This topic is described in detail in Section 5.2.3.

No Integration Effort During Implementation

This architecture does not require much integration with other projects when implementing. You can quickly plan and implement a new application without worrying too much about the existing solution. At first this may seem to be a considerable advantage, because the (shorter) time factor represents a clear competitive advantage. However, the effort required to integrate the new solution into the existing one is often underestimated or even overlooked. For example, the central maintenance of the enterprise's master data or global group reporting, which evaluates data from all decentralized systems, must be taken into account.

Easy Implementation of Country- and Industry-Specific Features

You can easily implement country-, application-, and industry-specific features. This is an important criterion that will be discussed in detail in Sections 4.6.4 to 4.6.6. If the existing system runs on an SAP release that does not support, or insufficiently supports a new country (which is important for you), or does not support a specific industry solution, you must consider either an upgrade to a higher SAP release or install an SAP add-on before the new country or the industry solution can be implemented. With a central approach this may require a great deal of effort, the only option is to follow the decentralized approach and implement another new system on which the new country or industry solution can be implemented.

A direct consequence is in ongoing maintenance during live operation. Like standard software, SAP add-ons and industry solutions must be maintained. Thus, legal changes or important corrections require the import of SAP patches and support packages into the system. Add-ons and industry solutions often have specific maintenance strategies that deviate from underlying SAP standard software. For example, add-on-specific corrections that are provided as add-on patches or CRTs (Conflict Resolution Transport)[9] can only be combined with certain SAP standard support packages.[10] This is usually no problem for decentralized systems with one add-on or industry solution.[11] Problems may occur when several add-ons are combined in a system, or when the add-on maintenance

Ongoing maintenance

---

9 CRT is a specific add-on patch or add-on support package that is required to synchronize or recover add-on-specific modifications of the SAP standard after an SAP standard support package has been imported.

10 See *http://service.sap.com/patches*.

11 In a system, SAP supports only one industry solution as the add-on or activated solution within the SAP ERP 6.0 switch framework architecture by default. SAP does not support various add-on or switch framework industry solutions in one system.

strategy cannot be applied for the underlying standard software. Chapter 4 describes this in greater detail.

Release Independence

Independence when selecting the release can be considered a generalization of the previously mentioned maintenance issue. If the global system is very large and complex, and if it has several modifications, an upgrade is quite time-consuming. Cases have occurred in which the status of the existing global system and its implementation led to the consideration of a completely new implementation with legacy data transfer. Here, it is more efficient to set up another decentralized system with a higher SAP release to implement the new project.

The Unicode aspect

Particularly interesting is when an SAP Unicode system is required for the new project, but the existing system runs without Unicode (e.g., because Unicode is not available in SAP release 4.6C or older). For the new project, you should then implement a decentralized system as a Unicode installation on the latest SAP release — for example, SAP ERP 6.0. Of course, you must take into account the integration with existing systems, which can become time-consuming, depending on their requirements and scenarios. Non-homogeneous communication between existing non-Unicode systems and Unicode systems is nearly always a specific challenge, because the technical processing of multilingual texts differs considerably between them.

Easy Software Life Cycle: Development, Configuration, and Customizing in One Local Development System

The software life cycle can be easily managed if you use the decentralized approach. When a decentralized local system is introduced, a three-system transport landscape is usually also implemented for the local system. Therefore, development and customizing are locally managed, first transferred to the local QAS system, and then to the PRD system via the local transport track. This enables development and customizing to be independent of existing systems. The transport runtimes can also be kept short; consequently, so can the entire project's — from design to implementation to go-live processing. This might at first seem to be an advantage, but the integration with existing other systems and solutions is a great challenge that must be considered from the very beginning.

Easy System Operation

In contrast to global systems that operate 24/7 over many countries and time zones, decentralized systems can be easily operated. Downtimes can be scheduled on short notice, because the system is often not used at night or on weekends. Data backups and other maintenance processes can run in appropriate time windows, preferably at night (local location). Corrections can be implemented on short notice and without any great efforts for prior announcements or planning.

Downtimes are easy to schedule

The following describe some of the disadvantages of implementing local and completely distributed decentralized architectures.

No Synergy Effects Between the Different Teams

Disadvantages

In the decentralized architecture, specific teams responsible for the implementation and operation of the system are often used for each system. If the teams work independently of each other, which is usually the case, uncoordinated and redundant activities can occur, particularly in the areas of development and configuration.

Whereas a smooth-running system operation requires recurring activities, such as data backups, this is usually not desirable for the development and configuration of identical solutions on different systems (which is often the case in global enterprises). If the different teams don't collaborate, the development and configuration effort and costs will be repeated several times (redundant). A global template approach, in which the major part of the corporation-wide solution (customer developments and configurations) is centrally developed and rolled out only once, cannot be used in decentralized architectures — or it will require a great deal of effort. Redundancy generally increases as team collaboration decreases. This is particularly the case when decentralized systems and their teams are located in different countries.

Redundant Systems in the System Landscape

Usually, each decentralized system requires specific hardware, particularly when the systems are based in different locations and countries. This still applies if all servers for the decentralized systems are located in

Specific hardware for each system

a worldwide, central data center. Although modern computer technologies and server generations currently exist that provide ideal prerequisites for consolidating servers saving hardware costs (blade systems, for example),[12] there will still be several redundant decentralized systems. These include, for example, the different databases and the required hard disk space for each decentralized system.

Hardware Infrastructure and Operation Effort

The effort and cost of the hardware, itself, is not a factor; rather, the expenses for infrastructure, continuous operation, and maintenance can consume a major part of the total IT hardware budget. If decentralized systems are based in different locations, a specific data center with corresponding infrastructure and its own staff must be implemented for each system — and of course, consequently increase the total costs for the enterprise's IT. High-cost network connections in a single, central data center can be avoided only to a certain extent in this case: Due to the required integration between decentralized systems (or at least between some of them) and the numerous connections to offices where end users are based, networks with remote connections are always necessary — and incur costs. A worldwide, central data center that includes all decentralized systems would probably reduce operating costs. However, additional effort is required to operate and maintain each decentralized system.

Incompatible Systems and Interfaces

Big to enormous effort

System-interface incompatibility is a very critical aspect. In a decentralized architecture, individual solutions are independent of each other only in rare cases. They must be integrated at least partially, because they provide the enterprise's base for global business processes. Generally, this requires numerous interfaces between different systems — and not only from a technical standpoint. Interfaces are used to transfer data and integrate complex, distributed applications across system boundar-

---

12 A blade system consists of a basic unit that includes "blade servers." Each blade server is a self-contained server with its own CPU and working memory. Optionally, you can include a hard disk in the blade server or use SAN hard disk memory. For details, see http://en.wikipedia.org/wiki/Blade_server.

ies. If decentralized systems have different SAP release versions, or if different industry solutions and add-ons are installed, or if there is a mix of Unicode and non-Unicode configurations, adjusting these interfaces technically or developing programs for their integration represent an enormous effort.

Different System Release Versions

Different system release versions may have advantages on the one hand; but on the other hand, they can also have considerable disadvantages. In general, different release versions always result in considerable extra effort[13] — effort that continues throughout the life cycle of the enterprise's entire IT solution. Different maintenance activities with different releases must be performed for all live systems. All corrections, bug fixes, patches, support packages, and respective activities must be maintained for all existing releases. Due to the systems' different release versions, functional differences must be taken into account. Interface programs might require considerable effort to effect technical transfers, particularly for integrations between decentralized applications.

Redundancies During System Implementation and Maintenance

Usually, the decentralized approach contains a specific, three-system landscape on which the entire project, from design to implementation to live operation and maintenance, is performed by one team. This leads to redundancy in both the system and project. For example, data redundancy exists for the enterprise master data, which must be distributed and replicated on all decentralized systems.

Redundant data retention

If a decentralized architecture is selected, particularly because of horizontal distribution criteria (e.g., distribution by country), very similar business processes are often implemented on all decentralized systems — processes that differ only slightly, such as for legal functions of individual countries for each system. Consequently, independent teams often perform the same project work, from design to live operation and maintenance.

---

13 See *http://service.sap.com/upgrade*.

No Collaborative and Coordinated Development and Configuration

Redundant customer developments
Missing collaborative and coordinated development and configuration processes are an immediate result of the redundancies that occur when you implement and maintain the systems. Because project and operating teams for each decentralized system usually work independently, and with little collaboration and coordination, customer developments and configurations (e.g., customizing) are managed individually. Consequently, enterprise-specific functions that are not provided in the SAP standard, and thus must be developed, are often developed almost identically several times — once for each decentralized system. This high number of duplicate customer developments must all maintained, periodically extended, and upgraded during their life cycles. Obviously, this causes a lot of development and configuration work and consequently incurs high global enterprise costs.

When you consolidate all or several decentralized systems into one central system or less-regional systems (centralized decentralized or shared services systems; see Section 5.5 for details), master and transaction data, as well as configurations such as customizations, are consolidated, but customer developments are often consolidated only to a certain extent, if at all, because of missing or insufficient documentation, or developers that can no longer be contacted. In these cases, all customer developments must be copied. They mount up to many thousands of programs with similar functions.

No or Only Restricted Applicability of the Global Template Approach

Because decentralized systems are often very different (e.g., due to different SAP release versions) and project teams usually work independently in each decentralized system, it is possible to use the global template approach only to a certain extent, if at all. This approach has proven itself for the entire IT life cycle of a global solution and is successfully used by many global enterprises with a central architecture.

The primary objective of the global template approach is to centrally define, develop, implement, and roll out shared data, processes, developments, and configurations, corporate-wide. Moreover, local adaptations should only be made decentrally, if required — for example, due to legal regulations in specific countries. This approach requires an existing lead system for the global template, and a lead system is not provided in a completely decentralized architecture.

Figure 3.6 illustrates a completely decentralized architecture. It includes an overview of most-important advantages and disadvantages.

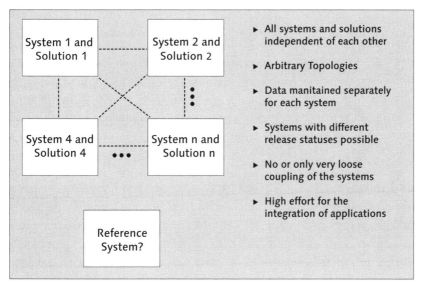

Figure 3.6 Completely Decentralized Architecture

3.5   Regional Architecture with Shared Services

This section describes the concept of regional architectures with shared services, as well as their advantages and disadvantages for global IT solutions. Regional architectures with shared services are often also referred to as "shared services" architectures. We will use this term as a synonym.

3.5.1   Concept

All systems in completely decentralized architectures basically work independently. They often require access to shared data and services in order to better coordinate and integrate the distributed applications. This

Shared services

leads to a regional architecture with shared services that can be considered a special extension of the decentralized architecture. Here, a decentralized approach with globally used, shared processes, applications and data on the 'shared' services systems is deployed.

As is the case for local and completely distributed decentralized architectures, systems are distributed according to enterprise criteria. They also have their own databases and work independently of each other. However, to better support the global solution as a whole, specific applications, data, processes, or shared services are created, which you implement on a central system with a central database and connect to the distributed systems, which can then integrate shared services. Shared services are central or global applications, functions, or processes with mostly central data, which are an integral part of the global solution — from development and configuration, to maintenance, to central master data maintenance.

Shared services systems

It is important that this architecture is considered hierarchical; shared services systems are the lead systems, to which the subordinate, decentralized systems are connected. The decentralized systems exchange data only to a certain extent, if at all. This differentiates them from completely decentralized architectures in an important way. Take a closer look, and you can see that these architectures can be called "partly" centralized architectures; shared services systems implement global services, applications, processes, and data on a hierarchical basis, distributed across the decentralized systems. If you apply this to the definitions of horizontal and vertical integration of distributed systems (see Figure 3.5), it can be seen that these architectures are primarily suited for horizontal distribution of a corporate group across different IT systems. Vertical integration with distributed applications and processes for each decentralized system cannot be implemented without data exchange. Consequently, hierarchical architectures are generally not well or only conditionally suited for vertical integration. Horizontal distribution, where the systems are frequently distributed by country or location, is particularly well suited for this architecture, because it usually allows shared services systems to provide decentralized systems with data, centrally and hierarchically.

The following describe two specific, shared services systems in greater detail:

▶ **Global development system**
In this variant, all global developments and configurations (i.e., customizations) are managed on a global development system and distributed across local systems. In the distributed systems, you create no customer developments (or only if required) and only adjust global developments — for example, if necessary because of legal regulations in the respective countries. The development system supports the use of templates to develop and configure the global solution.

▶ **Global master data maintenance system**
Central master data maintenance is a very important part of global solutions, and every enterprise wants to centrally maintain its master data. The global master data maintenance system has a central database that manages master data. The master data is centrally created and changed in the system, and then distributed to local systems.

Extensions can be managed in the local system, if necessary, but they don't conflict with central data. For example, if master data is created centrally in English, translations can be managed in local systems in order to process master data names and addresses in the respective local languages. Since translation into the local language is only required in the local system, this procedure makes perfect sense.

Today, master data systems are often SAP ERP systems, such as SAP R/3 Enterprise or ERP 6.0/ECC 6.0, which are only configured for master data maintenance. Master data is then typically distributed across local systems via SAP ALE scenarios. If you must process master data between several SAP Business Suite components, for example, between SAP ERP and SAP CRM, you can consider using the SAP NetWeaver MDM component.[14] As a part of SAP NetWeaver, MDM enables consistent maintenance and distribution of master data between heterogeneous systems. Therefore, you can use this architecture to integrate into the global solution not only SAP R/3 and ERP systems, but also SAP Business Suite components, and even systems external to the system landscape. This decentralized approach contains globally used, shared services and, typically a shared development and master data system, and combines the benefits of completely central or completely decentralized implementations.

SAP ALE and SAP NetWeaver MDM

---

14 See *http.//service.sap.com/mdm.*

3.5.2 Advantages and Disadvantages

The following advantages and disadvantages pertain to the use of a regional architecture with shared services:

Advantages of Completely Decentralized Architectures are Retained

These architectures mainly retain the advantages of the decentralized approach — namely, system independence, as well as the independence of applications and processes that are implemented on the systems. There is the option to use different release versions, as well as flexibility and speed when changes are made.

Relatively High Independence for Business Processes

Like the decentralized approach, regional architectures with shared services are also characterized by decentralized systems, which can be distributed according to similar criteria. These can be either horizontal distribution criteria (e.g., geographical) or vertical (i.e., application- or process-relevant). You can use the criteria to locally implement and operate different applications and business processes, independent of each other.

Avoiding Redundant Functions:

A common disadvantage of the decentralized approach is the fact that specific functions and activities are redundantly managed on each system in nearly the same way, even if the implemented applications and processes are different. This includes not only master data maintenance, but also customer developments — for example, cross-corporate or cross-application reports that don't have to be developed separately for each decentralized system. You can avoid these redundancies by providing shared services systems for central master data maintenance and central development.

Central Development and Configuration

The development of specific global IT solution applications and configurations are important aspects for worldwide enterprises. Development, in particular, causes effort and costs, and must therefore be managed as efficiently as possible. However, the configuration of global solutions is supposed to be managed without redundancy, if possible — that is, as many systems as possible should be configured only once. Regional architectures with shared services enable central development and configuration, and that means central customizing.

Global Template Support

While the use of global templates for a completely decentralized approach is only possible to a certain extent, they are well suited to regional architectures via the shared services system. All suitable template objects are usually created on the shared services system in the corporate headquarters by a central, global team, then combined into the global template of the corporate group, and finally distributed across the decentralized systems, where local extensions and adjustments can be made, if required.

You are provided with various tools to distribute global templates. The different SAP release versions are often a challenge you may have to face when using this architecture in real life. At this point, you should note that SAP Solution Manager provides a specific function to support the creation and distribution of global templates across distributed systems within a group rollout.[15] Therefore, it makes sense to use SAP Solution Manager together with the shared services system for this purpose.

SAP Solution Manager

Reducing Redundant Implementation and Maintenance Costs

Shared services systems reduce total implementation and maintenance costs by avoiding multiple developments, configurations, and data maintenance, as can occur with a completely decentralized architecture. They do, however, incur new costs (e.g., central applications must be implemented and integrated with decentralized system); but usually, these

---

15 SAP Solution Manager supports the entire life cycle of IT solutions — from business blueprint to configuration to live operation. SAP Solution Manager provides central access to tools, methods, and preconfigured content that can be used during evaluation, implementation, and live operation of the systems. Within the scope of project support, SAP Solution Manager enables you to work with templates for corporate rollouts, which are well suited for a global template.

costs will pay for themselves after a time and soon guarantee ROI (return on investment) — that is, the total costs are reduced compared to a completely decentralized solution.

Selective Scenarios with Global Processes and Data

Although regional architectures with shared services may be structured decentrally, shared services systems make an important contribution to the implementation of specific global processes and global, integrated data solutions. Standardized and harmonized master data maintenance is invaluable for every large enterprise. The costs of using inconsistent or redundant master data were often (and still are) overlooked by enterprises. In completely decentralized architectures, there is a high risk that master data identical to a business partner's product will be created several times, and with different data attributes. Consequently, it is impossible to create accurate company-wide analyses, reports, financial statements, and so on based on this master data. Often, a great deal of detailed work is necessary to obtain desired results. These architectures also enable the implementation of other important global processes, such as central development, configuration, and customizing during implementation, or central availability checks as an integral part of logistics business processes, which are then distributed across the decentralized systems.

Good compromise between decentralized and central architecture

In summary, this architecture can be seen as a compromise solution that retains the advantages of completely decentralized architectures and reduces the disadvantages by providing the option to use selective global processes, scenarios, and data. Therefore, it can be used if a completely decentralized solution is not suited for an enterprise, but a central global approach cannot be implemented.

Disadvantages

No Real Integration of Business Processes

Despite the option to implement selective global processes, scenarios, and data via shared services systems, the majority of applications and processes are still distributed across decentralized systems. Like completely decentralized architectures, this architecture also only provide the option to loosely couple processes and applications without much effort. It would require enormous integration work to create a *strong* coupling. If only loose couplings exist, the distributed services, processes, applications, and data may increasingly diverge from the initial shared global template approach. Consequently, overall, the existing global shared services are less integrated.

Example: Global Master Data Maintenance

Let us take a look at a global master data maintenance example to clarify the disadvantages in business process integration. Master data is centrally maintained in English in the shared services system and distributed across the decentralized systems, which are distributed by country. Because the decentralized systems in our example don't run under Unicode, the master data can only be translated into the local language in the decentralized systems that are configured for that local language's code page (non-Unicode). English always uses the global character set that is compatible with all (non-Unicode) code pages. Consequently, the master data is globally distributed in English. Now, the master data is locally translated in the distributed systems and must be stored in the local database of the decentralized system — but in English and the local language. Therefore, the master data is stored several times and not harmonized.

Despite global shared services master data management, data redundancies occur that cause behavior similar to that seen in decentralized systems. You could solve the redundancy problem by running all decentralized systems under Unicode. However, redundancy can occur for other reasons, too — for example, when new fields are locally added to master data due to legal requirements. This would also result in a non-homogeneous replication of master data.

Conditional Suitability for Vertical Integration

If the decentralized systems are distributed by applications and processes, the integration must meet considerably high requirements regarding functions and data volume, which are usually higher than those for horizontal integration. For example, if financial accounting applications run on a decentralized system, and sales and distribution applications run on another system, most SD activities must exchange data with the corresponding FI application. The FI applications could also be implemented on the shared services system; however, due to the close connection between FI and SD, this would lead to disproportionately high integration work. For vertical integration, this architecture has the major disadvantage that decentralized systems exchange data only to a certain extent, if at all, and data exchange is particularly required for vertical

High requirements for integration processes

integration. In this architecture, the shared services systems are especially suited for implementing global services, applications, processes, and data — separately and easily. For this purpose, you should distribute the decentralized systems horizontally, instead.

Need for Interfaces with Resulting Effort and Problems

Shared services architectures generally have the same or slightly higher number of interfaces when completely decentralized, because these interfaces are in addition to those of the decentralized systems.[16] Therefore, a great deal of effort is required to adapt and maintain the various interfaces. If the decentralized systems have different release versions, additional effort is required to keep the interfaces, including their programs and applications, compatible.

Non-homogeneous interfaces

Non-homogeneous Unicode and non-Unicode system interfaces are also a problem, particularly when the shared services system runs under Unicode and the decentralized system does not.[17] Also, do not forget that the interfaces must be high-performance in order to avoid bottlenecks when large quantities of data are transferred. This is considerably easier if you use loose couplings. In summary, we can say that the problems regarding interfaces are as (or even more) complex than those of completely decentralized architectures.

Almost no Harmonization or Standardization
Between Distributed Systems

Decentralized systems remain dominant

In this architecture, the shared services systems provide global services, applications, processes, and data, but these often only cover a small part of the enterprise's entire global IT solution. The decentralized systems

---

16 In practice, it is possible to equip one or a few selected decentralized systems with shared services functions in addition to local applications. When doing so, you must strictly separate local processes, shared services processes, and their respective data. However, this is not always possible.

17 This non-homogeneity can often be found in real life when the shared services system is up to date and has the latest SAP release. Due to global language support, it runs with Unicode, while the decentralized systems often have an older release version that does not support Unicode, and which cannot be upgraded as quickly as desired.

often remain dominant and mainly autonomous. Over time, the applications and processes diverge from the initial shared standard. Local teams coordinate with the central team only to a certain extent, if at all. Across the entire system, many local changes are made, so the global level of standardized applications and processes, as well as harmonized data, is low to nonexistent.

This architecture conceptually provides good options for standardization and harmonization. But often in real life you cannot implement them, because the degree of decentralized freedom and independence is relatively high, as with decentralized architectures. Figure 3.7 illustrates the shared services architecture with an overview of its most important advantages and disadvantages.

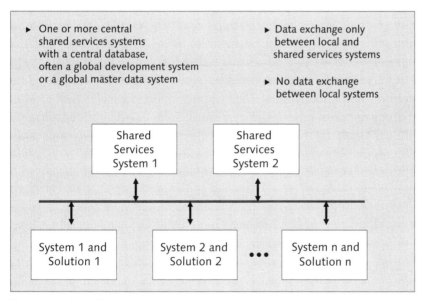

Figure 3.7 Shared Services Architecture

3.6   Centralized Decentralized Architecture

This section describes the concept of centralized decentralized architectures, as well as their advantages and disadvantages for a global IT solution.

3.6.1 Concept

Centralized decentralized architectures are an extension/generalization of shared services architectures in which the distributed systems communicate with each other, and can integrate applications and processes in a many ways. This is particularly important if the systems are distributed vertically, and dedicated applications and business processes run on individual distributed systems. That means if several distributed systems are connected, integrated, and consolidated via business processes, this is called *central decentralization*. It is a combination of central and decentralized concepts, and therefore categorized as a very complex architecture.

Process integration
It is particularly important how the processes can be integrated on distributed systems. For this purpose, you can use horizontal and vertical integration. Often, you cannot find one clear solution for an optimal integration. So, the question arises as to whether the distribution of processes is useful at all, as well as whether the integration is efficient and easy to maintain, as well as accepted by the end users. To keep the architecture simple and manageable, it makes sense to use a shared services architecture as the base, use as many shared services solutions as possible for the architecture, and gradually use as few integration scenarios as possible for the architecture.

3.6.2 Advantages and Disadvantages

Centralized decentralized architectures provide the following advantages:

Flexible Reporting

Advantages
In addition to the shared services architecture, the decentralized systems can exchange data with global services, processes, applications, and data by themselves. This fact provides nearly unlimited options for distribution and integration. However, it also increases complexity.

This aspect opens new options for the global reporting processes of the corporate group. The corporate headquarters can call data from each distributed system at the click of a mouse or has the option to create consolidated reports with a high degree of accuracy across the group. Shared services systems provide advantages here.

Specific Integration with High Complexity

On the one hand, data can be exchanged between distributed systems, and on the other hand, data can be exchanged between the global services, processes, applications, and data of shared services systems. Therefore, you can efficiently create specific integration scenarios with a somewhat high degree of complexity in centralized decentralized architectures without having to accept the disadvantages of decentralized systems. Because this architecture allows for vertical integration — that is, different processes and data can be distributed across different systems — they must also be efficiently integrated. The following real-life examples illustrate how the architecture can be used adequately.

Complex integration scenarios

Example

An enterprise runs all SAP ERP applications with a global, centralized decentralized architecture in many countries, but wants to locate payroll and HR processes (SAP ERP HCM) on a specific decentralized system in order to separate it from financial accounting applications (SAP FI), as well as sales and distribution, and logistics applications (SAP SD and MM), due to high security requirements. The central master data management, which also includes HR master data, is implemented on the shared services system. This leads to the following selected integration requirements:

▸ Master data exchange between shared services, and FI, SD, and MM system.

▸ Master data exchange between shared services and HCM.

▸ Posting the payroll data from the HCM to the FI system.

This means that the procedure requires data flow between all systems supported in this architecture. You can select proven procedures to integrate the applications — for example, the SAP ALE function, which supports an exchange of master data as well as integration between the distributed SAP HCM and SAP FI applications. At this point, it is worth mentioning that modern approaches based on Web services can also be used as integration solutions. They are based on the new IT generation of (enterprise) service-oriented architectures (SOA and Enterprise SOA).

Flexible Options for Change

Changes to applications or processes on decentralized systems — for example, due to changes in legal regulations — can usually be made quite quickly and efficiently by adjusting only the system on which the application runs.

Special Case: Simplifying the Shared Services Architecture

Let us take another look at regional and shared services architectures. Because distributed systems exchange data only to a certain extent, if at all, further shared services systems are always required on a higher hierarchy level. The question is: Must one of the distributed systems simultaneously assume the function of the shared services systems? And the answer is "No." However, it can be implemented if you use a centralized decentralized architecture. For example, a dedicated decentralized system additionally assumes the task of a global master data system when sharing services with all other distributed systems. Consequently, a separate master data system is not necessarily needed. This approach is particularly interesting if there are only a few decentralized systems.

Centralized decentralized architectures have the following disadvantages:

Disadvantages **Limited Global Control**

Because unlike in shared services architectures, the tree-like hierarchy is not used, new options arise for system distribution, but the level of centralized global processes and data may be also reduced. Centralized decentralized architectures risk getting too close to the entirely decentralized architecture, and therefore tolerate its disadvantages. You must always ensure that the level of distribution across decentralized systems remains moderate and controlled, and that the global processes, data, and teams retain their lead position in these architectures.

Complex Network of Business Processes and Data Between Systems

Due to the distribution options that the centralized decentralized architecture provides, it also enables vertical integration (in contrast to shared services architectures) — that is, you can implement various applications and processes on decentralized systems. Although this aspect is usually desired, it may lead to complexity that can, in turn, causes problems with the integration of processes and data. If too many processes and data are distributed across decentralized systems without shared services, the effort required to integrate and consistently synchronize distributed applications, process, and data can increase considerably, as was the case in our previously discussed decentralized architectures.

Not the Best Solution from a Global and Local Point of View

As was mentioned, centralized decentralized architectures allow for the distribution of processes and data across decentralized systems, as in completely decentralized architectures. However, the presence of lead global shared services — such as central processes and data, as well as global teams for implementation and operation processes — eliminate the advantages of completely decentralized architectures.

Let's assume, for example, an ABAP program is supposed to be changed in a specific country, because you want to implement a certain business practice. This program has been developed by the corporate headquarters and is part of the global template. Assuming that this architecture sets up the development processes as shared services with global control of the decentralized systems, the desired change must be requested and approved within a corporate-specific change process. It may be that the desired change is finally only implemented on the respective decentralized system, because it is a very special function that is only required in that one country. Usually, in decentralized architectures, the development processes and the teams would be set up in a decentralized structure, which allows for a direct implementation of the desired change. This example clearly illustrates the dilemma between global control on the one hand and local flexibility on the other hand. Figure 3.8 illustrates the centralized decentralized architecture with an overview of its essential characteristics.

Global control versus local flexibility

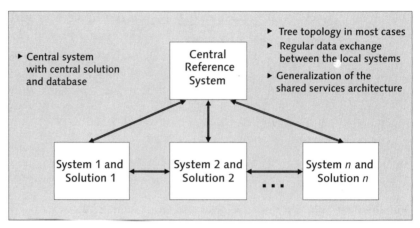

Figure 3.8 Centralized Decentralized Architecture

3.7   Central Architecture

This section describes the concept of central architectures, as well as their advantages and disadvantages for a global IT solution.

3.7.1   Concept

The central architecture consist of a single central system on which all enterprise applications and data are implemented on only one database and run in live operations. Therefore, it is a quite simple architectural solution. However, the enterprise and its IT department/partners must meet high requirements regarding planning, implementation, and (particularly) smooth operation of the architecture. In a central architecture, a distinction is made between two cases:

Two cases of central architectures

▸ Single-instance systems or central single-client systems, and

▸ Central multiclient systems.

The completely central approach, which is applicable for global IT solutions by all manufacturers of ERP software in the nearly same way, is the "single-instance or single box case," which can be also referred to as a "central single-client system." SAP ERP ABAP systems provide the specific multiclient function, so another variant of the central architecture can be used, which we call the "central multiclient system"; it is topologically a combination of a central and decentralized architecture.

The multiclient system is quite popular in many global enterprises because it uses the same hardware, shared development, and data dictionary objects of an SAP system (centralized aspect), but different data for each client (decentralized aspect). However, a multiclient system can only be used on SAP ABAP systems that support several clients — that is, on SAP R/3-based ERP systems that exclusively run ABAP applications, or in some limited cases, also on SAP CRM and SRM systems. Other SAP Business Suite components, such as BI, SCM, and PI, as well as all systems that use Java-based SAP NetWeaver components, are single-client systems. Consequently, you can only use the central single-instance approach.

3.7.2 Single-Instance System: Central Single-Client System

In central systems, all applications and countries are implemented and operated on one system in one client. These are 'real' central systems, often called *central single instance, single-instance ERP,* or *single-box ERP systems* in literature or the IT world. There is only one live client on which all processes, applications, and interfaces are centrally processed for all countries, and with all customized, master, and transaction data.

One production client

In large enterprises, these central systems often run 24/7, and all national organizations of an enterprise, worldwide, access the system via remote connections. The systems are often operated in one single computer data center together with one Disaster Recovery Center (DRC) at another location for emergencies. You can see that the reliable, efficient, and secure operation of such central systems must meet particular requirements. However, the entire life cycle of the IT solution that the enterprise uses requires careful planning and procedures when designing, introducing, and implementing the central systems because each design, development, and configuration must be carefully adapted to all applications and countries. See Sections 5.3 and 5.4 for more detailed information on this subject.

In summary, we can say that the single-instance approach is becoming increasingly popular, particularly when enterprise business processes

Increasing popularity

and data are identical or at least very similar in the different countries, and only differ in the various legal regulations of the countries.

3.7.3 Central Multiclient System

In multiclient systems, enterprises use a specific solution or purpose for each SAP client. Due to the data separation of the clients, but shared development and data dictionary objects, multiclient systems are not central or single-instance systems, but also not completely decentralized systems, because clients share development and data dictionary objects, and system and hardware resources. Therefore, it can be seen as a variant of the centralized decentralized architecture, where the client-based separation represents the decentralized component, and the use of shared development and data dictionary objects, as well as system and hardware components, represent the central and/or shared services component. We refer to this architecture as "central multiclient system."

Complete centralization means mapping all business process and data in one single system — in this case, one single client. Multiclient systems are not completely centralized, because the clients act almost like independent systems, since client-dependent data and customizing processes are separate for each client. Multiclient systems use identical hardware (i.e., the same application servers and database), and their entire SAP ABAP development objects, as well as data dictionary, are client-independent. Therefore, this reduced centralization is referred to as a "central multiclient system."

Restrictions for multiclient systems

In SAP ERP systems, ABAP applications support SAP multiclient systems. For this purpose, SAP CRM and SRM may be used only to a limited extent. They aren't supported or useful in other SAP Business Suite components. If Java applications also run on an SAP ERP system that requires the SAP Java stack, multiclient concepts cannot be used or need specific solutions, because the SAP Java architecture is based on a single-client concept.[18]

---

18 Since SAP ERP 2004/ECC 5.0, SAP ABAP, and Java applications can be operated on one instance and database simultaneously, use the dual-stack architecture by installing the SAP Web/NetWeaver AS Java required for Java operation as an add-in instance together with SAP Web/NetWeaver AS ABAP; see *http://service.sap.com/ netweaver*.

Central multiclient systems can be used in the following cases:

▸ **One country or a few countries for each client**
This architecture is a suitable approach if you are not (yet) able to use the single-instance architecture, but also don't want to use decentralized architectures with several systems, and if you can manage shared developments for all clients. This architecture is also suitable if an existing decentralized architecture with distributed systems is supposed to be consolidated in a central single instance, but a 'big bang' is not possible. Then, the central multiclient system represents an intermediate step within the consolidation, and the transition from the multiclient system to a central single instance is the next step.

▸ **Separate applications for each client**
Under certain conditions, it may be useful to operate specific applications in different clients — for example, HR in one client and financial accounting in another. However, the issue of integration then arises; that is, in this case, the distributed applications must be integrated between the clients. This is technically identical to the decentralized approach, with the difference that sender and recipient are represented by the same server.

▸ **Separate production data for each client**
Holdings often demand that their subsidiaries use similar or identical applications, but can access shared datasets only to a certain extent. In this case, multiclient systems can be used, because they allow for a high centralization level, and meet security and integration requirements by using separate data for each client.

▸ **Development, implementation, and tests with several clients**
Multiclient systems are particularly suited to the different steps in the software life cycle of the IT solution, such as implementation, development, testing, and training. Several clients are set up in the development, quality, and training systems (as well as other systems for different reasons). All of the systems access the same development objects and generate separate data. Section 5.4 describes this in greater detail.

Figure 3.9 illustrates a central architecture, with an overview of its essential characteristics.

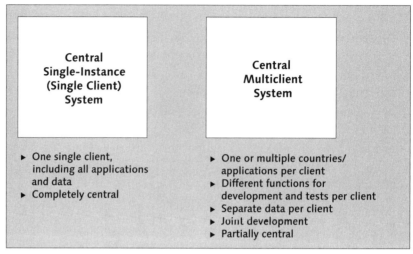

Figure 3.9 Central Architecture

The complete central architecture, in particular, provides the technical and organizational prerequisites for a controlled global IT solution, from planning to implementation to operation. It is certainly difficult and time-consuming to implement this architecture across the entire enterprise, especially if the enterprise's IT has not used a central architecture approach from the very beginning.

3.7.4 Advantages and Disadvantages

If you take another look at the advantages and disadvantages of the architectures that have already been presented, and which are more or less decentralized, you will see that the question again arises: How can you centrally plan, coordinate, and control your entire global IT solution? In practice, it has often proven to be insurmountably difficult to create an efficient global solution.

The technical aspects usually don't require the big challenge of a central control. However, you must take a look at the 'upper' management of the enterprise — that is, the people responsible for the business processes of the enterprise. Only if the central business processes are planned and implemented on a uniform basis can the IT implement these. Today, a global enterprise is generally set up with locations in many countries worldwide. In the individual countries, the local managers of the global enterprise often want to determine or influence the enterprise strategy and its IT implementation by coordinating with corporate headquarters only to a certain extent, if at all. The consequence is a divergence that starts at the business processes and data end of the enterprise and then usually leads to a decentralized IT architecture. Consequently, there is no actual global, uniform IT solution in the enterprise as a whole, but only a collection of isolated individual solutions.

The central architecture particularly provides the following advantages:

Central Global Team

Advantages

The team that creates the entire global solution for the enterprise, from planning at the business process level to detailed implementation of the IT solution, has a central global structure — central, because it manages the entire solution, both implementation and operation; global, because it collaborates with different organizational units worldwide, such as national organizations.[19] The team does usually not work in one single location — for example, at the corporate headquarters. It is a team whose members work at different locations worldwide and collaborate as one 'virtual' team. One core team works at a central location. The global team makes decisions regarding analyses, planning, new requirements, and changes, according to a defined process in the entire life cycle of the global IT solution. This means that local individual decisions are made only to a certain extent, if at all.

The technical options available today enable good communication between team members collaborating worldwide. However, it often makes sense to have a central core team that works at a specific location (e.g., corporate headquarters) and assumes a lead role in the global IT solution. Setting up regional centers (e.g., in America, Europe, and the Asia-Pacific region) has proven effective for enterprise IT. In regional cen-

Core team

---

19 In practice, there are several global teams for the individual project areas. You can also outsource individual areas. For example, you can commission an external IT service provider to operate the data center, including the entire IT infrastructure for the global solution, according to defined service agreements. Application management to support the end users, for example, can be handled by an IT subsidiary that has been outsourced.

ters, team members work on global solutions 24/7. In this way, a global enterprise can also easily manage the problems regarding time zones.

Central Planning and Central Change Management

As a central architecture enables the implementation of all IT-based activities in a central global system, the prerequisites are met to plan and implement the entire IT solution of the enterprise centrally. Of course, the technical aspects of a central system are sufficient on their own. A lot of project and organizational work must be done to set up an appropriate global team and define the processes — that is, how the team is supposed to collaborate within the enterprise, worldwide.

Central change management

This approach also enables central change management, which is particularly reflected during running operations. The different organizational units forward each change request (whether it is a change in legal regulations or business processes) to the central team according to a standardized process. The team then prepares an appropriate solution that can be integrated into the existing global IT solution with as few problems as possible. However, a change request can also be rejected if it is not deemed required — for example, if a specific country requests change that is not considered a statutory requirement or business-critical, but rather "nice to have."

Central Development and Configuration

A very important aspect of the central architecture is that all customer developments and configurations are made in a single central development system. Therefore, the prerequisites for creating an efficient global IT solution are met. Section 5.4 provides more information on this aspect.

Of course, the technical aspect alone doesn't ensure that this centralization can really be achieved. It is more important that customer developments and configurations are planned, designed, and implemented centrally as well as globally. For example, if a corporate report must be developed for all countries (instead of one report for each country, which in practice is often done in a global architecture), it is useful to develop a single generic program that implements the corporate logic and covers country-specific properties via configuration settings. Consequently, future maintenance of this single program is considerably easier than maintaining a program for each country.

Central Data

All master, transaction, configuration, and other data are processed only once in the central database. There is no distributed data and no risk of redundancy over different structures. You don't have to develop and maintain complex interfaces that communicate with other databases in decentralized systems. Consequently, you can avoid potential difficulties with non-homogeneous communication between decentralized Unicode and non-Unicode systems. This combination is used in enterprises that operate worldwide or are geographically far apart and use several languages with different character sets, as well as decentralized systems that have not (yet) converted to Unicode.

Central database

Any user in any country creates a date. This date is immediately available for all other users. No synchronization or replication is required, as in decentralized databases. If no further SAP Business Suite components or external systems are operated that actively change the global system's enterprise data of the global system, the system automatically becomes the shared master data system.[20] Please note that a central database can become large rather quickly. Therefore, specific requirements must be met when running operations. Sections 5.2 and 5.3 explain this aspect in detail.

Central Operations

Central architectures enable the operation of global systems in a single data center, worldwide. SAP database and all application servers, as well as other central server components, are located in one data center

---

20 Example: An SAP NetWeaver BI system (Business Intelligence) analytically processes data provided by the SAP ERP system and other data sources, but doesn't change active master and transaction data. Depending on the configuration, an SAP CRM system can, for example, change business partner data (e.g., customer and supplier data) transferred from the SAP ERP system. Therefore, a CRM system can actively change data.

that has the entire infrastructure for maintenance, backups, high availability, disaster recovery,[21] and other operation activities. All organizational units and countries are connected to the data center via remote connections. The local hardware and software components required are installed at the work centers of the end users, which enables them to work with the global system.

Windows Terminal Server (e.g., Citrix) Alternatively, access to the global system can be provided via server-based Windows Terminal Server solutions — for example, Citrix.[22] Here, only limited client software is installed on end users' PCs. Via the software, the user can log onto Citrix and start work. There may be other specific devices set up in the individual offices, such as printers, which are remotely connected to the global system. In contrast to decentralized architectures, operating the system must be centrally performed at one location and with one team. Even if you locate and operate all servers at a single location in a decentralized architecture — which is often done today and can be considered 'data center consolidation' — the total amount work is considerably reduced due to hardware components and their maintenance, which are required only once for the entire system. An important aspect is that the bandwidth is sufficient and availability of remote connections worldwide is ensured. This is described in more detail in Section 5.2.3. There are no disadvantages allowed here, such as the frequent failures or too-slow network response times that make the efficient operation of a central system almost impossible or even fail.

Integrated Reporting in Real Time

Another advantage can be immediately derived from the central data storage in this architecture. All enterprise data is centrally stored and consistently available in real time, so requirements for corporation-wide reporting can be easily met. Standard or customer-specific reports that

---

21 To be protected against possible total failures or even the destruction of the primary data center, we recommend setting up a so-called "disaster recovery center." The DRC mirrors the live system in a physically remote, secondary data center according to various procedures. If a total failure of the primary data center occurs, live operation can be switched to the DRC system after an agreed-upon period of time.

22 See *www.citrix.com.*

consistently access data can be used anytime. You don't have to retrieve data from other decentralized systems via interfaces that may have to be prepared with a great deal of effort.

Now, you can create the group reporting that has often been requested from corporate headquarters — that is, the corporate management/organizational unit can be see prepared data from any country, region, or enterprise area at the click of a mouse, and in real time.

Group reporting

Easier Maintenance and Usage

In this architecture, all life-cycle components of the global IT solution are managed centrally — from planning to design to development and configuration, as well as operation, maintenance, continuous optimization (hardware and software), and other modifications. Each activity requires a certain amount of effort. In contrast to decentralized architectures, each implementation is needed only once, which makes maintenance much easier.

This leads to many simplifications for end users; they don't have to log on to several decentralized systems and process several sessions simultaneously, which can easily lead to errors. Data entry or searches for orders and customer numbers need only be done once. Global systems generally lead to improvement in usability for end users. This advantage is also provided if you use the SAP NetWeaver Portal. End users no longer have to manage the login process on the different systems, because the portal assumes this task; but they still have to work with decentralized systems — for example, due to missing master data, searching in both systems for an identical business partner with two different customer numbers for a global order.

Simplifications for end users

Harmonization and Standardization

In general, the central architecture offers (perhaps very) good prerequisites for a high level of harmonization and standardization within the enterprise's entire global IT solution. As was mentioned, the central architecture provides the technical base and infrastructure. However, these, alone, are not sufficient.

Harmonized
business processes

You must also create project- and organization-specific requirements in order to gain company-wide harmonization and standardization — from designing and modeling business processes that will be implemented in the global system, to supporting end users worldwide. If you can set up a central global team or organization that can define these processes, and plan, design, implement, operate, and support them from a business point of view, and if you can protect them from the resistance of local organizational units and countries, then you can achieve the desired goal without problems. The following are disadvantages to using central architectures:

Disadvantages

Global Complexity

The advantages of a central architecture with a single-instance system are certainly promising, and in practice, almost every global enterprise that uses a decentralized architecture for its ERP solutions is trending toward a central architecture, sometimes with considerable effort for consolidation projects. Although the increased effort in a decentralized architecture is obvious, particularly for integration between systems, the central architecture is or can become highly complex when it comes to global solutions. This can be best explained by a couple of selected scenarios:

For example, the management decides to modify the sales process in a specific country, so the IT team must implement the modification in the central system. Depending on the configuration and existing functions, implementation can be very easy or very complex. If required, the system must be shut down. The activation of the modification must be planned and announced in advance, because the central system usually runs 24/7. If the central system requires an upgrade that also involves functional changes, this process must be planned years in advance, because it often takes quite a long time to prepare worldwide users for the new release, implement the functional changes, and perform sufficient tests and training.

Complex upgrades

Often, only one weekend a year can be considered for upgrades or other main changes. For example, Unicode conversion on large central systems can cause long downtimes. If the scheduled dates cannot be met, you must wait another year.

Higher Risks

The central architecture provides new risks that don't occur or are reduced in decentralized architectures. A considerable risk occurs if the worldwide end users or enterprise organizational units don't accept the global project.

This is not a technical problem, but rather a social, cultural, or political one. Especially in large enterprises that have been historically established in different countries on a continual basis, managers in the countries often determine local events, and influence planning and implementation processes of the IT solution, which can be quickly implemented decentrally. Now a global project will be implemented in which the central global team will assume control. Consequently, local managers may lose their influence and, as a result, challenge the global project and have a negative influence on end users. This issue requires particular sensitivity. For example, it is useful to include local managers in the global team and assign them respective functions in which they can use their influence.

Sensitivity required

Missing or insufficient support is another organizational risk. To support a global IT solution with 24/7 operations, support organizations must meet especially high requirements. They must be available at all times, follow guaranteed service agreements, and communicate with the end users in their local languages, if required. It is often erroneously thought that end users will accept English, even if it is defined as the corporate language. In addition, the support teams must have sufficient expertise at all locations.

Sufficient support

The technical risks are also higher than those in the decentralized case. A global central system with a single database generally represents a Single Point of Failure (SPOF). If the database fails, the entire global system is not available, which would affect the systems of all end users. In a decentralized architecture, however, only one system and the respective users would be affected.

The risk of hardware failures (e.g., hard disk failure) are usually less critical, because modern high-availability solutions ensure continuous operations in these cases. Human failure is the important risk factor: For example, if a deletion report that erases important master or transaction

Human failure

data is started due to human error, the entire global system is affected, and there is no easy way to solve this problem. In the worst case, the global system must be reset to the status it had before the deletion report was executed. This may result in considerable losses.

Network The network is another technical risk; it must be protected against failure, which often involves high costs. In addition, the network must be fast enough to support reasonable response times for end users. Further risk factors are described in the following chapters within the scope of discussing architectures.

Differences in Local Business Processes

One of the greatest questions to answer is how a historically grown global enterprise can model its business processes, and roll them out in all organizational units and countries on a global basis. In our case, we assume that the applications are identical — for example, FI or SD — and there are no industry-specific differences. The technical aspect, again, is not as important as social and cultural ones. Legal regulations are mandatory in the countries and must be integrated into the global solution without further discussion, and SAP country versions as well as the global teams support this integration within the scope of the global project. The business practices of the respective countries, which have been locally proven over the years, are of more concern.

Local and global business processes The global team will usually try to consider local requirements as much as possible. They will, however, often impose restrictions if the requirements are not really necessary ("nice to have") or too many adjustments and modifications must be made. However, if the local requirements differ considerably from the global solution, there's no other solution than implementing a decentralized system for the country.

Local teams do not cooperate It has often been proven that a global solution didn't fail because requirements could not be met, but because the local teams didn't cooperate or agree to reduce local requirements, and actively work on a global solution. Therefore, it is very important that local employees in countries work actively on the global solution design and are included in the global team. Therefore, the global team must have members with expertise on each country and in all business processes.

Lack of Local Acceptance of the Global Solution

A global solution with this architecture is often planned and implemented at a specific location — for example, in the corporate headquarters. At the beginning of the global project, users in the different countries are often involved only to a certain extent, if at all. The solution is therefore planned on the drawing board.

Depending on the employees' experience and knowledge, you may see a 'surprise effect,' more or less. The solution may be formally correct, but unusable for the end user. They don't accept the solution, dislike their work, or find tricky workarounds to perform their daily tasks.

Employees don't accept the solution

An integral part of the global project, therefore, is to carefully prepare the enterprise's IT organizations, worldwide, for the global solution — involve them in the project, and support them with training. A quick, 'big bang' approach[23] is often only successful for new ERP installations and implementations, because in this case, the central architecture has been selected at the very beginning, and is globally planned and implemented, including end-user training.

Performance and Database Size

In addition to network problems, the database size and performance of a global central system is a risk factor, mostly from the technical point of view. Since a global system can have several thousand active end users and database growth rates of two- or even three-digit gigabytes worldwide each day, the system must meet extreme requirements.

Hardware is becoming more powerful (see Figure 3.1). Manufacturers are building increasingly powerful servers and disk systems, and the adaptive computing technology opens new dimensions of computer

Adaptive computing

---

23 We define the "big bang" approach as follows: The global project is exclusively planned and implemented by a strong central team. All decisions are (almost always) made from the corporate headquarters for the countries, and the solutions are quickly implemented. Within the scope of one project or project phase, several countries or applications are rolled out simultaneously and put into production on a key date.

performance and dynamical utilization. Central systems can still reach certain limits, which can be exceeded only by accepting considerable disadvantages.[24] Usually, database size and the related disk space are no big problems; performance and load are of more concern. Performance is also an important criterion for the acceptance of the global solution, and the following example explains this.

Example Let's assume that the average dialog response time of a transaction is approximately 0.5 seconds in a decentralized system, 1.0 seconds in a global system, and quite a few spins of the 'working' hourglass for network delays. An end user with a lot of system activity will probably be unhappy with this global system's performance, and therefore work less efficiently. Long-running background jobs are another problem: There are no nights with low-level system activity in a global system with operations around the world, all running 24/7. There will always be normal working hours on one of the continents, and the systems run in dialog mode. Consequently, specific measures must be taken to manage long background jobs efficiently and in parallel with dialog mode. Network connections have an important influence on performance for end users. They must have sufficiently high bandwidth (guaranteed by the network provider), latency must remain in the tolerance range, and a fast-enough backup connection must be available in case of failure. Chapter 5 describes all of these system aspects in greater detail.

3.8   Variants and Combined (Hybrid) Architectures

This section first provides an overview of variants for the architectures presented so far. It will also discuss combined architectures, which are often used in real life.

3.8.1   Overview

Overview of combined architectures The previous sections introduced the elementary and basic system topologies, and architectures for a global IT solution that uses SAP Business Suite software components, including their properties, advantages, and

---

24 See Gunther Schmalzhaf, *SAP Adaptive Computing — Implementation and Application,* SAP PRESS 2006; and *http://service.sap.com/netweaver.*

disadvantages. The following sections describe how real-life system architectures are structured, keeping in mind that they are often not used in simple, basic forms.

In reality, complex system landscapes that consist of up to several systems are used, and at first glance, have only little to do with the basic architectures previously described. However, complex architectures are often combinations or variants of several basic architectures. Therefore, the entire architecture can be logically broken down into basic architectures and their combinations.

In practice, large global enterprises may have a system landscape with a high number of systems and don't seem to use one of the architectures described, although a decentralized architecture is always suitable. Often, the reason is that for many enterprises, the architecture discussion only started a few years ago. At the beginning of ERP implementation, the 'historically decentralized approach' was mainly used — that is, one specific system installed for each organizational unit, each country, each business area, or each application module, and then all the systems connected together.

Non-identifiable architectures

Only since enterprise IT departments had to adhere to budgets did most of them start to plan their system landscapes as efficiently as possible. As soon as they determine which basic topology can be used — particularly, whether it is should be central or decentralized — they design the system landscape, define the number of systems and their roles, and specify the different connections. Since enterprises and their IT departments are subject to continuous change, this also affects the system landscape. Consequently, architectures often change over the years, particularly if it consists of decentralized systems.

A complex system landscape is often a combination of several basic architectures (which we already described) in a similar or modified form. Therefore, they are often also referred to as "hybrid architectures." We distinguish among the following cases:

Hybrid architecture

▶ Variants of the basic architectures

▶ Combination of several architectures in one system landscape

▶ Integration of several SAP Business Suite components with different architectures

3.8.2 Variants of the Basic Architectures

In decentralized architectures, there are no actual variants, but any number of decentralized systems can be set up, and each system can be connected with any other system. Therefore, the degree of freedom for this system landscape is not restricted. However, large global enterprises often use architecture combinations — for example, one part of the system landscape consists of decentralized systems that belong to one region, and the other part consists of a central system that is assigned to another region. This combination is described in the next section.

Variants of the shared services architecture

Shared services architectures probably have the most variants and deviations of basic architectures. For example, they contain systems that don't directly fit into this kind of architecture and have a decentralized, or 'isolated' character. The following two examples illustrate this aspect (see also Figure 3.10).

Master data system as a shared services system

> **Example**
>
> A global enterprise wants to implement a shared services architecture and selects the system for its global development and configuration. Now it realizes that one development system, alone, cannot be implemented due to the multiclient concept used, because a specific system, DEV1, is required to develop and maintain the enterprise-wide global template. DEV1 must be tightly coupled to the global development system, DEV2. On the other hand, the various regions, for which separate systems are planned, are not supposed to have their own development system. A similar, frequently used scenario exists when a specific country or application cannot (yet) be globally developed due to high complexity,[25] and therefore requires its own development system.
>
> A master data system as a shared services system provides another scenario. A corporate group wants to implement the shared services architecture worldwide, and realizes that the business processes and master data in corporate headquarters (PRD1) differ considerably from the processes and data in the worldwide national organizations (PRD2 and PRD3). Consequently, in addition to geographically distributed systems, another specific system is set up for the corporate headquarters. All of these systems are connected to the global master data system as shared services.

---

25 For example, this applies to the BRIC countries (Brazil, Russia, India, and China). Particularly Brazil and India have very complex legal regulations that require very specific solutions with adjustments and modifications. Consequently, these countries might be required to operate on specific systems.

Figure 3.10 provides an overview of shared services architecture variants

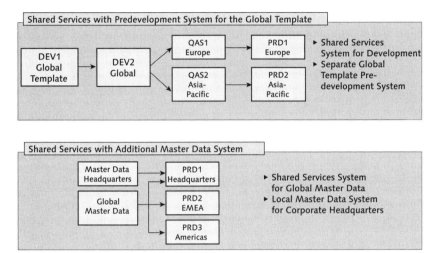

Figure 3.10 Variants of the Shared Services Architecture

3.8.3 Combination of Several Architectures in One System Landscape

Like the enterprise itself, IT is usually subject to continuous change and development, even if it is not restructured due to business changes. Consequently, the entire global solution landscape doesn't have a uniform architecture, but consists of several historically grown system landscapes with different architectures, which are either basic architectures or variants of them.

Combination of several architectures

However, this is not surprising when we consider, for example, how an international enterprise in Europe has started to gradually implement IT for a global solution years ago. First, a decentralized system was installed and configured for each application or enterprise area in the country where the corporate headquarters are based. Then, specific systems were set up for each country in Europe with one system for Eastern Europe with an SAP CEE add-on (Central and Eastern Europe).[26] Now, the enterprise has gained important experience and decides to implement regionally central systems when expanding to America and the Asia-Pacific region. Countries of respective continents and their applications are integrated into these regional systems. Finally, a worldwide master data system is introduced that supplies the decentralized systems in Europe as shared services, as well as the continentally centralized systems in America and the Asia-Pacific region. Therefore, this example is a combination of the following basic architectures, as shown in Figure 3.11:

▸ Decentralized architecture, structured by corporate headquarters applications

▸ Decentralized architecture, structured by countries in Europe

▸ (Continentally) central systems in America and the Asia-Pacific region

▸ Worldwide shared services architecture with a central master data system

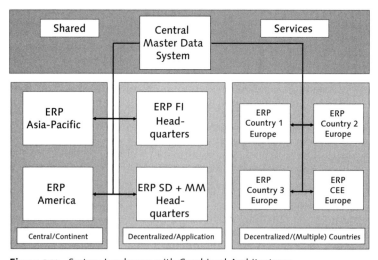

Figure 3.11 System Landscape with Combined Architectures

---

26 The SAP CEE add-on contains the SAP ERP country versions for several East European countries and Russia, up to ERP 2004 (SAP standard from ERP 6.0) for the Ukraine and Kazakhstan, and for Greece from ERP 6.0. Details on the SAP CEE add-on are provided in the SAP Notes 520991 (Core-CEE) and 572252 (HR-CEE), as well as their references.

3.8.4 Integration of Several SAP Business Suite Components with Different Architectures

Today, nearly all system landscapes of global enterprises use different SAP Business Suite components that are integrated with each other. SAP ERP components (e.g., SAP R/3, SAP R/3 Enterprise, SAP ERP) are mainly used. However, you can frequently find other components, which must also be structured in an appropriate architecture. From a historical point of view, in several cases, the SAP ERP solution was (and still is) first implemented and operated by the global enterprise before further SAP Business Suite components were introduced. Consequently, first architecture and topology of the SAP ERP solution was determined, and then the system landscape was set up.

When determining an architecture for new SAP Business Suite components, the easiest approach may seem to be a rebuild of the SAP ERP architecture. This is possible, but not always useful, and may even lead to considerable disadvantages.

Architecture for new SAP Business Suite components

Let's assume, for example, that several decentralized systems are operated for the SAP ERP solution. Now, the enterprise wants to implement SAP NetWeaver BI and SAP SCM. If the same decentralized architecture was used for BI and SCM — that is, one BI and SCM system for each ERP system — the total number of systems and additional connections between each decentralized ERP, BI, and SCM system in the system landscape would increase threefold. Obviously, you should look for alternatives in this case.

You may change the ERP architecture, for example, and consolidate several decentralized systems in one central system, but this often requires a great deal of effort and is therefore less suitable. This aspect is described in detail in Section 5.5. Since in our example new SAP BI and SCM components are supposed to be implemented, it makes sense to consider a central approach for BI and/or SCM. The solution landscape may then be a combination of decentralized ERP, and central BI and SCM systems.

Technical restrictionsIn some cases, combined scenarios within a system landscape, in which one SAP Business Suite component is supposed to be central and the other decentralized, are subject to technical restrictions and can therefore not be implemented without problems. The middleware between SAP Business Suite components manages connections between the systems, and acts as an integration layer between the technical and respective interfaces. It must support systems that have several connections — for example, the connection of an SAP NetWeaver BI system with several SAP ERP (back-end) systems, or of an SAP ERP system with several CRM systems. A central SAP NetWeaver BI system can be combined with several SAP ERP systems (nearly) irrespective of the number of connections. SAP CRM/SAP ERP combinations, however, impose technical restrictions that must be analyzed for each individual case.[27]

Numerous combinations

There are numerous different architecture combinations in an SAP Business Suite system landscape. Figure 3.3 illustrates a sample combination of a system landscape with one SAP ERP and one SAP NetWeaver BI system, including various central and decentralized cases, as well as a variant of an additional BI system that can be considered a global shared services system. It clearly shows that the system landscape complexity depends on the number of decentralized components: The higher the number of components, the more complex the system landscape.

Formula for estimating required systems and connections

Table 3.1 will assist you in estimating how many systems and connections you need for a role in your system landscape, such as production, as a maximum or minimum. It does not refer to hardware, but logical systems and connections. Now, we make the following, simple assumptions: The architecture of the system landscape consists of either only decentralized systems (maximum case) or central systems (minimum case). The shared services and centralized decentralized architecture can be categorized as between these two extremes. Moreover, we assume two specific cases for how the systems can be connected: either only within a decentralized system group, each consisting of one SAP Business Suite component; or each system connected with all of the others (*cross connection*). All other connections belong to a category between these two cases.

---

27 Multiple connections between SAP CRM and SAP ERP systems (both directions) represent a "MEP/MBE" (Multi-System Exchange Project/Multiple Backends) case, whose feasibility must be analyzed in close collaboration with SAP; see SAP Note 853430 and references for details.

Table 3.1 lists the formulas for estimating the maximum and minimum numbers of systems and connections in a system landscape. The following variables are used:

n = *Number of SAP Business Suite components used*

m = *Number of decentralized systems*

	Maximum (Decentralized)	Minimum (Centralized)
Number of systems in the system landscape	$m \times n$	n
Number of connections: systems connected only within a decentralized system group	$0.5 \times m \times n \times (n-1)$	$0.5 \times n \times (n-1)$
Number of connections: all systems interconnected	$0.5 \times n \times m \times (n-1) \times (m-1)$	$0.5 \times n \times (n-1)$

Table 3.1 Number of Systems and Connections in a System Landscape for Different Architectures

Table 3.1 clearly indicates that the number of systems results from the product of the number of decentralized systems and SAP Business Suite components. The number of connections increases quadratically as the number of systems increases. If a cross-connection exists, it increases double quadratically. If all SAP Business Suite components are used only centrally, the number of connections decreases considerably, even if a cross-connection exists.

3.9 Summary

This chapter described all topologies and architectures of global SAP solutions in detail. Four basic architectures can often be found and have been proven in real-life projects:

- ▶ Decentralized architecture
- ▶ Regional/shared services architecture

Four basic architectures

- ▶ Centralized decentralized architecture
- ▶ Central/Global single-instance architecture

The central architectures are particularly significant. A multinational enterprise can use it to implement a worldwide IT solution on a global single-instance basis in a uniform manner, as long as the prerequisites are met. In decentralized architectures, the question arises over which criteria should be used to distribute applications on various decentralized systems and how the distributed applications can be integrated.

For this purpose, applications can be distributed horizontally by organizational unit, location, country or continent; or vertically by application, function, or process. You can also combine these two approaches. In shared services architectures and centralized decentralized architectures — which are a combination of completely decentralized and central architectures — central, globally used applications and processes are defined that are used by all decentralized systems.

Global master data management as well as central development and configuration, combined with the global template approach within the software life cycle of the global solution, are particularly well suited to be used as shared services. Complex system landscapes with several SAP Business Suite components include variants and combinations of various basic architectures. The more significant the decentralized architecture is, the more complex the system landscape is when it comes to the number of systems and connections.

Each enterprise has its own criteria that influence the selection of the system architecture. For example, business and organizational issues must be considered, as well as software and hardware specific aspects.

4 Factors Influencing System Architectures

An enterprise's individual situation considerably affects the selection of an appropriate system architecture. The three-dimensional globalization model includes all aspects leading to an appropriate and tangible target architecture. In this chapter, we'll describe the three globalization dimensions *process*, *organizations*, and *products*. Moreover, we'll introduce facts, methods, tools, services, and recommendations for different system architectures.

4.1 General Considerations

Before the IT department of a large global enterprise can determine an appropriate system architecture, numerous prerequisites must be met. Generally, it is not sufficient if this task is only assigned to the IT department of the company or an external IT service provider. Rather, globalization concerns the entire enterprise, from top management to end users, because ultimately, they have to work with the global IT solution.

Globalization of enterprises

Therefore, the enterprise as a whole must support a global solution. Normally, it is not enough (or even doomed to failure) if only the IT department actively promotes a global project without the support of management and the employees. This often depends on the global structure of an enterprise — whether the individual countries and departments work independently, and make and implement their decisions on a local basis, or whether the business processes and its IT implementation have been globalized right from the onset. Take a look at the current situation, and a wide variety of scenarios can be seen: You can find enterprises that are real 'global players' with distinct global organizations. Their applications and business processes are modeled and implemented globally to enable central coordination and implementation of the individual requirements coming from different countries and departments.

But you can also find large international enterprises that have completely different organizations. Even though they operate globally in many different countries, their individual systems are mainly independent of each other. These enterprises also have global business strategies with economic backgrounds; however, the modeling of global and harmonized business processes, and the IT implementation hardly exist, if at all. In the individual countries or departments, the managers and local employees focus on local implementation and optimization of businesses. Communication and planning with corporate headquarters is mainly limited to business-relevant aspects, such as sales, market penetration, and promotional activities. The globalization of the enterprise and IT take a back seat.

Meaning of globalization for enterprises

How do enterprises understand the term "globalization," and how do they approach it? This is very interesting. Interpretations and explanations can differ considerably, as you can see in the following answers from a survey, in which employees of different international enterprises explain their personal concepts of globalization:[1]

► "For us, globalization means to buy and sell enterprises in order to be a global market player."

► "For us, globalization means to implement business processes on a global scale. In Japan, incoming orders should be processed in the same way as in California."

► "Globalization means to be able to deploy employees at any global location without requiring training. Business processes are supposed to be identical at all locations."

---

1 See *http://service.sap.com/globalization*.

▶ "For us, globalization means to operate a central, single-instance system, and to provide all business data in a central and standardized manner."

▶ "For us, globalization is to reduce costs by introducing shared service centers — for example, a call center for support or a shared service center for financial services."

As you can see, enterprises can have different focuses with regard to globalization. Interesting answers cite "globally identical business processes" and "central single-instance systems" as a suitable architecture for global IT solutions. The other answers also tell you that globalization in all areas of an enterprise makes sense — that means both in business-relevant and process areas, and organization and employee areas, as well as in IT. In order to achieve a successful global IT solution, including an appropriate architecture, the enterprise and all its areas must be ready for globalization. This means that the IT department can't develop the global IT solution and its system landscape architecture independently, but must collaborate closely with the persons responsible for applications, processes, and human resources, as well as top management.

Often, it has been generally assumed that it's IT's sole responsibility to plan, implement, and operate the global IT solution of an enterprise or to implement the required changes of an existing IT solution and architecture. This can be the case, and often leads to improved efficiency and reduced costs, for example, by consolidating and reducing systems.

Collaboration between business and IT

Ultimately, the IT department is, however, often not able to influence the business processes determined by the company. These processes, however, are decisive for the efficiency and costs of an IT solution. If a process within an enterprise has inefficient modeling — for example, orders are processed differently in every country, although only minor legal differences exist for the various countries, which means different approaches are not mandatory — overall costs for the enterprise are high, and these costs cannot be significantly reduced, even if the best IT team and hardware are available.

In this case, a higher-ranking intervention is required within the framework of change management. Here, you first must globalize and optimize the unfavorable process (e.g., order processing) by introducing a

Change management

company-wide, uniform process. Then you can enable country-specific changes before it is integrated into the IT solution. It goes without saying that uniform order processing is easier to implement in a central architecture than a multiple distributed one.

Global players have already implemented central SAP system landscapes in many countries and departments across many time zones, and are familiar with the SAP system challenges posed by globalization — and they know how to overcome these challenges. But which solutions are used by other international enterprises that have not yet obtained globalization on a high level — companies whose processes are highly diversified, and whose teams in various countries work independent of each other?

Standardization of business processes and data

Obviously, the major challenges for international corporations are not IT and software, although this is still a general assumption. Imagine the following real scenario.

> **Example: Introducing a new country**
>
> An enterprise wants to introduce a new country with a new language, or change from a decentralized to central architecture with multiple countries and languages. The management consults IT experts to obtain information. For example, the existing or consolidated system must be converted to Unicode, because this is required for parallel operation of the various languages with different character sets. (See Chapter 2 for details on Unicode.)
>
> After management decided on the Unicode conversion (and if applicable, system consolidation), the project managers and users assume that this process is complete and start planning for Unicode conversion. At a later point, they find out that master data, including names and addresses, are not automatically translated as originally assumed. End users in the 'new' country complain about the lack of support, and that, without any new development, it is not possible to create quarterly reports that include sales figures for the newly introduced country. In this case, the necessary Unicode conversion was technically implemented correctly by the IT department. Now the problem is that the users assumed that Unicode automatically translates the master data for the applications — which of course is not the case. They also forgot to improve the support organization in conjunction with the introduction of the new country. Neither was there any global report that could simply be extended for the new country; this resulted in extensive new development.

In addition to IT-specific questions about hardware and software, you also have to consider process modeling, project management, change management, organization of global rollouts, and support, as well as how to combine all these aspects into one solution.

4.2 Three-Dimensional Globalization Model

We can conclude that three main aspects or *dimensions* are crucial for enterprise globalization and must therefore be taken into account: product-relevant aspects, organizational aspects, and aspects relating to business processes. The efficiency of a global IT solution depends on how these dimensions are globally defined within the enterprise. This, in turn, affects the selection of an appropriate system architecture.

4.2.1 First Dimension: Product

The first dimension of globalization describes all product-relevant aspects of the deployed software in combination with the IT environment. Here, the focus is to what extent the software product can support different countries and languages, as well as general functions of internationalization and globalization. Depending on the scope of functionality this results in different aspects that influence conception, system architecture, supported hardware, and additional IT-specific issues. For a global IT solution, the software must support applications, processes, data, and business practices for global implementation and operation, and provide sufficient functionality to support legal regulations and business practices of the individual countries.

Product-relevant aspects

SAP ERP[2] and other SAP Business Suite products support this dimension by providing an integrated software solution that meets these requirements. In addition to global and international aspects, such as Unicode for supporting all languages in the system, uniform maintenance of business data, central reporting, but also global tools and infrastructure, e.g.,

---

2 See *http://service.sap.com/erp.*

a central ABAP development and customizing environment, there are multiple country versions available (see Section 2.11) that support legal regulations and business practices of the respective countries, and which can be fully integrated into a global software solution.

4.2.2   Second Dimension: Organizations

Global enterprise organization

The second dimension describes the global organizations of an enterprise and defines how these are globally established for different activities. The organizations comprise different teams within the enterprise, including management, process supervisors, project teams, support teams, IT operations teams, service providers, and end users. The global project teams plan, design, and implement global IT solutions with a centrally oriented approach (ideally the global template), and closely work with other teams that are responsible for modeling business processes and their changes. The global teams can integrate the individual local conditions and requirements of the countries into business processes and the global IT solution by collaborating with local or virtual teams.

The support teams play a very critical role within a global IT solution. They are responsible for smooth 24/7 support and operation around the world. Teams with global expertise are established to optimally exploit the skills of globally active employees and distribute it within the enterprise. These experts work, for example, in the research and development department or are responsible for training.

4.2.3   Third Dimension: Processes

Modeling and changing of business processes

The third dimension describes all aspects concerning modeling and changes in an enterprise's business processes. A global IT solution is only practical if the company can harmonize and standardize different local processes and data.

This sound simple, but in practice, this is probably the most complex dimension, because the changes affect business processes and practices of the entire enterprise and cannot, in most cases, be implemented easily.

Imagine a global company that produces consumer products that are manufactured differently in every country and have different product attributes. The business processes concerning these products or goods, however, are very similar in every country — for example, the sale or purchase order of goods. Therefore, you can model a global process, despite the obvious differences, and at the same time leave sufficient leeway for local specifics.

Change processes, such as restructuring and process-related changes, considerably influence business activities. Here, it is of major importance to coordinate changes globally. As we already mentioned, local situations and specifics of respective countries must be taken into account and implemented as required. Global IT processes are critical within a global IT solution. They include user support and data center operation, which is frequently outsourced to third-party service providers.

Change processes

For smooth operation you must ensure that sophisticated company-wide processes are defined, and *service level agreements* (SLAs) must be established if you outsource processes to service providers. SLAs help you determine how fast and to what extent problems or service requests must be handled by the service provider. For planning, implementing, and developing global IT solutions, ideally you have global IT processes and procedures that enable central development and configuration of new projects, as well as maintenance of existing production systems. This is directly linked with the system architecture, because the central architecture or shared services architecture promotes central development of these processes. Of course, this process must offer options for implementing local adaptations or individual applications without any effects on the global solution.

Figure 4.1 shows the three-dimensional globalization model.

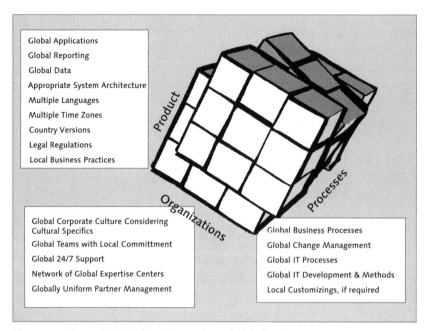

Figure 4.1 Figure 4.1 The Three Dimensions of Globalization

4.3 Business Processes

Globalizing business processes

In addition to IT issues, project management, and change management, the *modeling of business processes* is another critical topic for the globalization of a system landscape. You can't just implement efficient enterprise globalization within IT; you must also consider optimized business processes supported by management. This specifically applies to the optimal selection of the global IT solution architecture. Technical and IT-infrastructure aspects play a critical or even decisive role for selecting the architecture, but only at first glance. IT technology, hardware, worldwide networks, security, and availability have become very sophisticated and powerful, providing enterprises with all architecture options. In the past, arguments were often cited that related to the technology, like "We can't introduce central single instance, because the network connection to the end users is too slow, and we need the entire night for the online backup in our U.S. data center so that the users in Asia are impaired."

These views might still be valid in some cases, but are no longer the general rule.

If no specific architecture is absolutely required due to product-related factors (we will detail this later), processes and enterprise organizations play a decisive role in finding a common solution that relies on close cooperation with the process and IT experts and teams. Here, a process-oriented approach makes sense.

First you must analyze and model the business processes of the enterprise, ideally using appropriate modeling tools that can be implemented using graphics software, like Microsoft® Visio®, or software products specifically designed for modeling processes, such as ARIS. At this point, it has not yet been determined (and is not yet relevant) how the processes will be implemented using IT technology, which software components will be used and how often, or which systems will be deployed. The business strategy and process architecture of the enterprise can be described centrally and holistically. This is particularly important for large global enterprises and can be considered a prerequisite.

Today, however, there are conflicts of interests between the various departments of an enterprise, particularly between business-related and application-oriented or process-oriented teams on the one hand and IT teams on the other. This results in the following problems, which often lead to interference with, or even failure of an efficient global IT solution, and consequently the optimal architecture:

▶ **Problem Number One: Design and modeling of business processes**
The process experts and managers don't speak the same language as the IT teams; consequently they don't collaborate. They often have different opinions regarding the same targets. Frequently, process managers and IT teams use different concepts and incompatible tools; in short, they work at cross-purposes. Consequently, you can lose a lot of time and money in implementation projects, because internal coordination, which is also referred to as an alignment between system and IT, can only be partly achieved or not at all. The more locations and departments are affected, the more these factors multiply in a global enterprise.

Business process modeling

Problems with buseiness and IT collaboration

151

▶ **Problem Number Two: Process configuration**
Often, there are only minor or no connections between process flows and logistics, and technical IT implementation. Frequently, the company-wide methodology, transparency, and uniform process documentation is missing. For new requirements or changes, suitable solutions or parts thereof are not reused; standardization and corporate governance is lacking. In addition to Problem Number One, this is the most frequent reason why a global enterprise is not able to use a central single-instance architecture, even though the technical prerequisites are available.

▶ **Problem Number Three: Process integration**
There are often many different systems and interfaces, due to a highly decentralized architecture. For the integration of distributed applications, no standardized approaches exist. Each interface and respective solution is individual, which results in numerous specific solutions for A2A (*Application to Application*), B2B (*Business to Business*), and industry-specific solutions. There is neither a joint process repository or process management for cross-system and intercompany applications.

▶ **Problem Number Four: Process ownership**
Often, employees of the business departments don't have the experience or skills to automate processes. Local business departments are not flexible enough to align the global enterprise without changing the entire process. Required changes and problems with process flows are often passed on to the central IT department, whose employees are not able to solve them all.

Enterprise architects as a bridge between business and IT

Enterprise architects are essential in global enterprises.[3] They play a key role in designing business processes and IT, because they act as intermediaries. Here, they take an active part in the development and optimization of business models and flows, and participate in the design process for the optimal IT architecture. They form a link between business and IT, and provide comprehensive know-how on business processes, applications, data, and technology. In this way, enterprise architects support the approach of globally designing business processes and help the

---

3 For further information on enterprise architects, refer to Paul Kurchina, "*Design the present and future of IT.*" SAP Info, German, Home, E-Paper No.144.

company find appropriate IT solutions with the optimal architecture. Figure 4.2 shows a model for collaboration within a global enterprise. In order to combine IT and business, the business experts and analysts on the business side and the enterprise architects on the IT side form a special team and central contact point to actively promote collaboration between IT and business. This ensures that business and IT always work together to find joint solutions, and at the same time can concentrate on their core tasks.

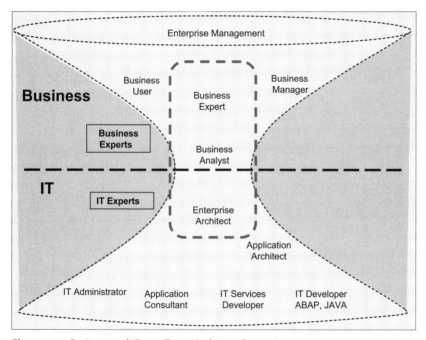

Figure 4.2 Business and IT as a Team Within an Enterprise

To ensure that this joint team can collaborate efficiently, appropriate tools and methods must be provided to link business process modeling with IT solution implementation. For this purpose, you can deploy *SAP Business Process Management (BPM)*, which is well-suited for a global enterprise. We'll present BPM in the following section.

4.4   Business Process Management

The connection of business processes with global enterprise strategies and IT implementation is of high significance for the management of new and ever-changing business areas. Business process management constitutes a continuous and flexible adaptation of business processes, their organization, and the IT landscape to market requirements. With BPM, enterprises can continuously adapt and optimize their business processes and scenarios to new requirements.[4]

The necessity for Business Process Management

To find and implement the optimal architecture for a global IT solution, harmonization of IT landscapes constitutes a great challenge for enterprises. The problem with many IT landscapes is their growing, increasingly complex structure. In the worst case, a high number of decentralized systems exist that are integrated only to a limited extent. Enterprise mergers and splits pose great challenges for IT departments. Within a short period of time, IT systems and their architecture must be adapted and optimized to the new business structure. Identifying business-critical systems becomes more complicated, and consequently, efficient cost reductions can only be achieved with great difficulty or not at all. This situation is improved for the long term and IT development and maintenance costs are sustainably reduced only when business teams and IT aligned with global targets and business processes work closely together. Business process management is a well-suited and efficient instrument to achieve this difficult IT target. BPM ranges from analysis and optimization of business processes to implementation in software, and to automatic control and measurement of processes by means of key figures. Therefore, BPM is a self-contained cycle.

Using BPM

BPM comprises the following basic steps. After the business strategy has been determined and described, the business processes are designed (modeled) and implemented in the IT department, as well as measured and analyzed using key figures, also called "key performance indicators" (KPI). Weak points can be quickly determined, and optimization can be derived

---

4 See *http://service.sap.com/bpm* and IDS Scheer Expert Paper, "Business Process Design as the Basis for Compliance Management, Enterprise Architecture, and Business Rules," (*www.aris.com*, May 2006), on which some of these explanations are based.

through analysis and monitoring during operation. Using these optimization potentials is iterative and is not supposed to be a one-time activity. Over time, only a self-contained cycle enables sustained and long-term advantages. We can therefore consider this a real business process life cycle. The success of BPM depends on the general willingness of an enterprise, the process orientation, and the continuity with which it is operated.

BPM particularly assists you in modeling business processes that include users with different roles and tasks — especially outside IT — and in optimizing communication with IT experts. The business process models can be created at different abstraction levels — that is, business process level, configuration or implementation level, as well as execution level. Various integration options are provided. You can model and configure company-specific, internal business processes as well as the critical end-to-end processes between separate, heterogeneous applications and systems, as well as those beyond company boundaries. Figure 4.3 shows an overview of BPM.

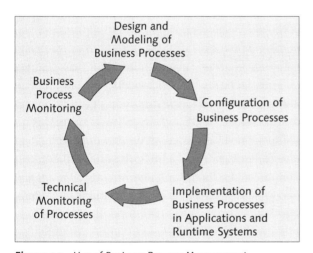

Figure 4.3 Use of Business Process Management

4.4.1 Tools for Business Process Management

You are provided with numerous tools and methods for business process management. We'll describe how BPM can be usefully deployed in a global SAP system that is based on the SAP NetWeaver platform to achieve an optimal global IT solution. We'll present the *ARIS for NetWeaver platform* as a special tool that enables you to use holistic BPM for a global SAP solution.[5]

ARIS platform

The ARIS platform provides you with tools for the entire business process management's required periodic changes and improvements. This enables you to manage not only your operative business processes, but also the entire BPM process, itself.

ARIS for SAP NetWeaver

ARIS for NetWeaver supports integration of business process modeling with the implementation of global IT solutions on SAP Business Suite components.[6] Because this software is aligned for the analysis and description of business processes and their feasibility on SAP Business Suite components, it is well-suited for supporting the third dimension of globalization, which is beneficial for finding the appropriate architecture for the global IT solution. ARIS for NetWeaver includes a description of the (business) process architecture — from business models to executable processes, and beyond system boundaries, based on SAP NetWeaver process infrastructure (PI).[7]

ARIS process levels

ARIS for NetWeaver works at three process levels:

1. At the top-most level (process architecture model) you can create a rough overview of the company from a business point of view — that is, without any technical context. Based on this overall process architecture, the process strategy is determined; in other words, you don't take the concrete system landscape and IT architecture into account yet. By designing the process architecture, however, you can set the course for the company's determining a completely global process, such as central purchasing or distributed processes.

---

5 The ARIS platform (Architecture of Integrated Solutions) provides integrated software products to support enterprises in the continuous improvement of business processes. (More information is available at *www.aris.de.*) All phases of a BPM project are covered, from strategy definition to process design and migration of the models to IT, to controlling the executed processes.

6 See IDS Scheer, "*ARIS for SAP NetWeaver. The Business Process Design Solution for SAP NetWeaver.*" White paper, October 2006, *www.aris.de.*

7 See *http://service.sap.com/xi.*

2. At the next level (process configuration model), processes are described that were designed especially for customizing and configuration. SAP Solution Manager provides the required reference processes. You can synchronize these process models between ARIS for NetWeaver and SAP Solution Manager. Because SAP Solution Manager knows the functions and processes of the individual Business Suite components, and provides them via the reference processes, you can map the modeled processes from ARIS on the given IT landscape at this level. Here, you functionally define the architecture of the system landscape.

3. At the process-execution model level, SAP components and non-SAP components communicate via SAP NetWeaver PI. SAP NetWeaver PI offers a standardized *Business Process Execution Language for Web Services* (BPEL4WS), which enables you to display business process logic in a standardized manner in XML format and integrate it in the runtime environment. For our architecture discussion, this is not very important, because third-party systems are integrated only to a minor extent, if at all.

Figure 4.4 shows an overview of BPM and ARIS for NetWeaver.

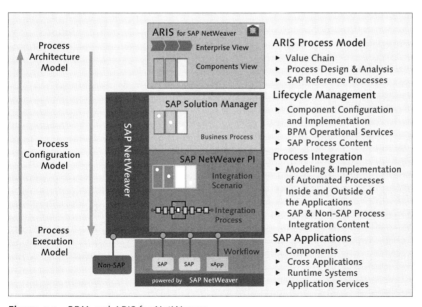

Figure 4.4 BPM and ARIS for NetWeaver

ARIS and SAP Solution Manager

SAP Solution Manager supports the integration and implementation of SAP Business Suite projects.[8] It provides integrated content, reference processes, tools, and procedures that reduce the project effort, and are required for both efficient implementation and productive operation of an SAP solution. At the operative level, for example, SAP Solution Manager offers a central Business Process Management (BPM) tool for monitoring global SAP solutions; which you can use to follow both technical system data and business processes flow via different systems and interfaces. Additional functions of SAP Solution Manager include a support desk with local note database, automatic forwarding of serious problems to SAP Global Support, and other functions for supporting the entire life cycle of an IT solution. SAP Solution Manager offers roadmaps for SAP Business Suite reference processes, which enable you to introduce efficient BPM for the entire IT solution or parts thereof. For further information on SAP Solution Manager you can refer to *http://service.sap.com/solutionmanager* and to specific documentation in *http://help.sap.com* • SAP Solutions • Solution Manager.

Reference processes in SAP Solution Manager

In order to efficiently exploit process-oriented procedures with SAP Solution Manager and BPM you must establish a relationship between global business processes and SAP solutions. Because a pure modeling tool like ARIS only works at an abstract level (i.e., it does not establish any connection to the actual IT solution), you must carry out another step after the modeling process to map the business process model on the existing IT components. For example, you can implement a company-specific sales process on an SAP ERP, SAP CRM, or a suitable non-SAP component. ARIS for NetWeaver provides such a tool that enterprises can use to select the modeled business scenarios and processes that they want to support using the SAP solutions. For this purpose, SAP Solution Manager offers reference processes via business roadmaps that can be customized during implementation, and used for operation and business process monitoring.

Synchronization between ARIS and SAP Solution Manager

To efficiently use this tool, you must exchange or synchronize the modeled processes and additional configuration content between ARIS for

---

8 See *http://service.sap.com/solutionmanager, www.aris.de;* and Marc O. Schäfer and Matthias Melich, *SAP Solution Manager*, SAP PRESS, 2006.

NetWeaver and SAP Solution Manager (see Figure 4.5). Here, the SAP reference models are integrated with the ARIS process architecture, and customized according to customer requirements and business processes. These are then incorporated in a detailed requirements specification or business blueprint, which then forms the basis for a SAP Solution Manager project. There, the technical implementation and model customizing is done.

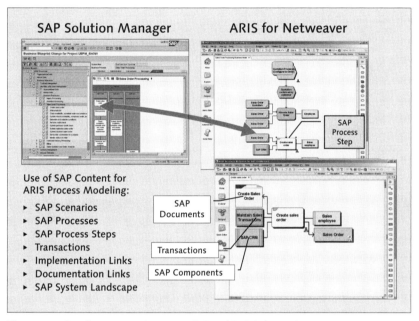

Figure 4.5 Synchronization Between ARIS and SAP Solution Manager

This ensures that the IT solution is geared toward the company's business processes as closely as possible and not the other way around. On this basis, you can align the SAP standard processes and functions with existing enterprise processes, and adapt them, if possible.

Central Customizing using SAP Solution Manager

From the adapted business process (which should be implemented by the IT department, and which was created by aligning the adapted ARIS business process model with SAP solutions and scenarios in SAP Solution Manager as a business blueprint), you can directly configure and customize the deployed SAP components. This means that there is no direct connection between an enterprise's process world and IT world. SAP Solution Manager enables direct navigation for the customizing functions of respective SAP Business Suite components via the business blueprint. You can also make settings that are processed in the three-system landscape via the SAP components transport system. This central function is particularly beneficial for a global IT solution that uses many different components, and assists you to support global projects and rollouts efficiently. We'll discuss this in Section 5.4, where we'll also explicitly detail the global template approach for a corporate rollout, which Solution Manager is very useful for.

Figure 4.6 shows a concrete example of how an FI application process (which can originate from an ARIS model in the business blueprint) is connected directly with the implementation guide of the linked SAP ERP system. This is required to carry out configuration or customization (Transaction SPRO) of account groups.

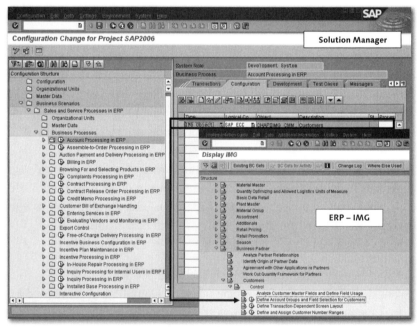

Figure 4.6 Process-Oriented Configuration from SAP Solution Manager

4.5   Organizations

Depending on the degree of globalization of an enterprise you can implement a global IT project more or less efficiently. Many global players recognized the necessity for globalization a long time ago, and they knew
how to successfully implement their enterprise objectives by using a
global IT solution. Particularly companies and enterprises that have
worked locally or independent at different locations recognize the current need for globalization.

Often, medium-sized companies that are suppliers for large, multinational enterprises are forced to follow the globalization trend, for example, due to expansions in China, where a plant is opened for manu-
facturing car spare parts. Consequently, the existing IT solution must
be extended. In our example, an existing SAP implementation must be
introduced in China.

Depending on the enterprise's degree of globalization, this project cannot be solely implemented by the IT department. Initially, the processes
must be modeled in such a way that the business activities can be performed efficiently in China and implemented in the IT department. For
this purpose, you can use the procedures and tools described in the
previous section. Equally important, or even essential, is the presence of
appropriate, organizational units of the enterprise, which can successfully
implement global projects and activities — from planning to implementation, to operation and support. Therefore, organizations must include
global teams that collaborate on a worldwide scale and bring together
both remote and local expertise. But how can this be achieved?

4.5.1   Corporate Governance

High demands are placed on the top management of a global enterprise.
Frequently, global enterprises are large and listed on the stock exchange.
To ensure success on the international market, management must promote the trust of its global employees as well as its investors, customers,
business partners, and the general public. In this regard, definition of
and compliance with sound corporate governance is a good instrument.
This is particularly important for a global enterprise, because the entire

strategy, plans, and objectives must be implemented globally. A high degree of standardization and harmonization must be achieved, while simultaneously, all local organizations and employees must be taken into account.

Definition Corporate governance generally comprises all international and national values, and basic principles for a sound and responsible corporate management that is valid for both employees and top managers. Corporate governance doesn't comprise internationally uniform rules, but only some acknowledgement of basic international principles, country-specific concepts, and responsible management. In addition to country-specific corporate governance provisions, there also exist some cross-national, industry-specific regulations.

Corporate governance features a multilayer structure, and includes mandatory and voluntary measures: compliance with laws and regulations, adherence to acknowledged standards and recommendations, and development and adherence to company-specific guidelines. Another aspect of corporate governance is the definition and implementation of management and control structures. Typical characteristics of sound corporate governance include:

Characteristics of a sound corporate governance
- A functioning management;
- Protecting the interests of different groups — for example, the special interests of employees in the various countries;
- Target-oriented collaboration of management and management supervision;
- Transparency in corporate communication;
- Appropriate handling of risks; and
- Management decisions with an orientation toward long-term added value.

Sound corporate governance ensures responsible, qualified, transparent management oriented toward long-term success. It is supposed to provide a basis for not only the organization, its members, and owners, but also for external interest groups. Corporate governance concerns not only management, but all managing teams within the organizations of an enterprise, also.

One special aspect of sound corporate governance can be applied to globalization: the way global central interests of a corporate group are harmoniously combined with the local interests and objectives of individual countries. This can be achieved with a sound global corporate culture, which we'll explain in the following section.

4.5.2 Global Corporate Culture

For a global enterprise that comprises locations and divisions around the world, it is a major challenge to establish an organization that can support the globalization of the enterprise in all areas. Only if the enterprise and all of its employees and business partners are prepared to follow the globalization path can all prerequisites be met to efficiently implement global strategies and objectives. This requires a global corporate culture that is accepted and implemented by all employees at all locations. It doesn't matter from which perspective you look at the globalization of an enterprise. You will see that the aspects of centrality, consistency, and harmony always take center stage.

This requires establishing global, centrally acting teams and processes. On the other hand, each location and country must have teams and processes with sufficient scope for decision-making processes at the local level. For example, there could be legal regulations, or more or less mandatory business practices in a country that must be respected by the corporate headquarters.

Global teams with local employees

But not only the business-relevant or technical facts are critical. In fact, corporate employees must be integrated with the global enterprise. But this will only be successful if they don't have to give up their values, cultures, or ways of living. Consequently, corporate headquarters and global teams must show good manners by respecting culturally influenced behaviors, traditions, and so on of specific countries and regions, and integrate them into their organizations accordingly.

A special issue is the language used within a company. Obviously, communication within the organizations of a global enterprise should be in one language; in most cases it is English. Of course, local teams can communicate in their respective languages. In some countries, even this can lead to problems regarding local acceptance. In Japan or Russia, for

Company language

example, English is hardly ever used among the general public and is only spoken by people with higher education. These local and cultural specifics affect the procedures and decisions of employees. Therefore, global teams that comprise international members have to observe certain rules with regard to communication and collaboration, both in meetings and in telephone or videoconferences.

Respect for sociocultural specifics

On the other hand, respect for local behavior and traditions must not become too intense. In other words, the formation of local teams that hardly pay attention to global targets and projects of the enterprise, and (only) consider local interests when making decisions or solutions should be prevented. 'Local kings' in various countries or regions are not suited for a global enterprise. This can occur particularly if an enterprise and all of its organizations have shifted from a decentralized independent structure to a global structure.

When it comes to IT, this can mean the IT infrastructure is comprised of several local data centers and teams that are merged into one central data center at the corporate headquarters. But this also means that the local IT teams must change their tasks or even lose their positions. This is a very sensitive issue that must be handled carefully to be successful. The employees concerned must be assigned appropriate tasks and positions, and be integrated with the new global teams, especially because they have local expertise that is essential for the new global team. But if the local teams are taken by surprise, the transformation will not be accepted, and the global IT project will not be supported constructively.

Balance of global and local teams

Summing it all up, it can be said that you have to keep a balance of global and local teams within the organization of a global enterprise that represents and implements global interests and standards. At the same time, these teams should respect the local regulations and customs of the individual countries. Figure 4.7 illustrates how these concepts relate to the IT of an enterprise.

At this point, we want to give you some tips and tricks that were tried and tested in many complex global IT projects. The problem is, on the one hand, you must focus on harmonization and standardization with regard to global solutions. On the other hand, you must remain flexible and adaptable enough to quickly and efficiently integrate deviations from the standard and local specifics. In the following list, we provide recommendations for a global standard.

Global Corporate Culture

- Process Harmonization
- Global Data Standards
- Consolidation of Infrastructure
- Global Reporting Tools
- Common Corporate Culture

Local Culture in the Countries

- Localized Processes
- Specific Local Data
- Respect for Cultural Traditions and Behavior

You have to find the right balance:

- The focus should be on the common corporate culture while simultaneously respecting and considering local specifics
- Groups of "local kings" don't work for a global enterprise

Figure 4.7 Balance of Global and Local Organizations

Recommendations for Global Standards

Global standards

▶ First, focus on the business processes, then on IT (in many cases, it's the other way around).

▶ Get support from top management.

▶ Create small teams with process owners (steering committees).

▶ Implement decisions as soon as they are made.

▶ Determine clear limits for standardization.

▶ Stick as closely to the standard as possible.

▶ Special requests are only permissible via the steering committee and for positive business cases.

▶ Implement small steps and quick successes for large projects.

▶ Be very patient.

Support and data center teams play a very significant role for successful global IT solutions. If you want to operate the IT solution centrally as a single instance, you must specifically prepare these teams and their organizations on the running operation, as well as for the support of the central solution. But also regarding any other IT architecture operated by a global enterprise, specific requirements and prerequisites must be determined for its support and data center. We'll describe these requirements in the next section.

4.5.3 Requirements of the Support Organization

Global service and support

Operating a global solution demands high support requirements with regard to the specification of service and support processes.[9] Only if the entire support organization or a third-party service provider of an enterprise is structured globally can the global solution operate successfully. Here, the emphasis is not on the architecture of the system landscape, but on qualified training of the support team, its global teamwork, and the efficient functioning of all support processes.

The support organization has to face the following challenges: It must be organized on a global scale, and subdivided into a first level for ender-user contact in case of problems, a second level for complex issues, and further levels for specific problems. A great challenge for a globally active enterprise is to provide support to every single user in any part of the world, with the same quality and at the same expertise level. But how can a global support organization efficiently provide global, 24/7 support?

Regional support centers and 24-hour operation

For global enterprises, centralized regional and continental support centers have proven successful. For example, in America, EMEA (Europe, Middle-East and Africa) and the Asia-Pacific region, support works during the daytime of the respective region, and transfers support to the next support organization during an overlap phase to provide efficient, 24-hour operation. This is also referred to as the "follow-the-sun" model (see Figure 4.8).

---

9 See Gerhard Oswald: *SAP Service and Support*, SAP PRESS 2006; Marc O. Schäfer, Matthias Melich: *SAP Solution Manager*, SAP PRESS 2006; Andreas Schneider-Neureither: *Optimization of SAP System Landscapes*, SAP PRESS 2004.

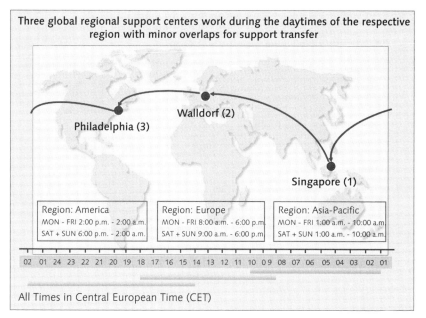

Three global regional support centers work during the daytimes of the respective region with minor overlaps for support transfer

Walldorf (2)

Philadelphia (3)

Singapore (1)

Region: America	Region: Europe	Region: Asia-Pacific
MON - FRI 2:00 p.m. - 2:00 a.m.	MON - FRI 8:00 a.m. - 6:00 p.m.	MON - FRI 1:00 a.m. - 10:00 a.m.
SAT + SUN 6:00 p.m. - 2:00 a.m.	SAT + SUN 9:00 a.m. - 6:00 p.m.	SAT + SUN 1:00 a.m. - 10:00 a.m.

02 01 24 23 22 21 20 19 18 17 16 15 14 13 12 11 10 09 08 07 06 05 04 03 02 01

All Times in Central European Time (CET)

Figure 4.8 Global 24-Hour Support of a Global IT Organization

The following illustrates the requirements expected of a global support organization:

Requirements of Global Support Organizations

Global support organizations

▶ Global support must be available 24/7.

▶ Global teams must be able to collaborate without any geographical or cultural boundaries.

▶ All members of the support team must be trained well and must be able to integrate themselves into a global team.

▶ The support organization must be able to support the IT solution in the given architecture. If this architecture changes — for example, due to system consolidation from decentralized to central — the support team must adapt itself quickly to the new system landscape.

▶ There must be no barriers with regard to language; the enterprise should determine one global enterprise language (in many cases, English) in which all members are fluent.

▶ For optimal support of local end users, the support teams must provide sufficient local experts who can communicate with the end users in their local languages, and who know the local specifics well.

4.5.4 Data Center Requirements

Own or third-party data center

The safe and efficient operation of the data center is a critical area for an enterprise. Here, all vital processes based on sophisticated information technologies come together. Many enterprises have to determine whether they want to run their own data center or if it is more efficient to outsource applications, systems, and processes — in other words, transfer the responsibility for the operation and infrastructure to service providers as a whole or in part. The general trend is to outsource IT and data center operation to owned IT subsidiaries or to external data center service providers.

Outsourcing means to employ the *hosting services* of a specialized data center service provider. These services must be exactly adapted to the requirements of the enterprise. Hosting services must be able to keep pace with the global orientation and future growth of the enterprise. This requires a service provider with the appropriate know-how, experience, modern technological infrastructure, and ability to respond to changing requirements.

The data center that operates the global IT solutions, whether company-owned or third-party, must meet the following requirements:

Data center service provider

Requirements of Data Center Service Providers

▶ Flexibility regarding changes — for example, in case of restructuring, company mergers, or splits, and the resulting changed system landscapes.

▶ High performance.

▶ Fast and secure global network connections from/to the data center for all enterprise locations.

▶ High security and availability of global IT solutions.

▶ Data security.

▶ Alternative data center in case of emergency (disaster recovery center), including fast switchover times.

▶ Transparent costs.

▶ Professional services and support: there are various service categories, depending on the SLA — from purely technical, basic support to different variants of application support.

▶ Compliance with service standards, such as service level agreements and ITIL (IT Infrastructure Library).

It is very important that both the support organization and the data center comply with customary IT service standards. This is particularly essential (even decisive) for large global enterprises that have a complex, global IT solution for selecting the optimal architecture. Because running global solutions without interruption demonstrates the success of the implementation, you must ensure an appropriate high level of service and support. Therefore, the following sections will describe two selected service standards that have gradually established themselves.

Compliance with IT service standards

4.5.5 Service Level Agreements

An SLA comprises clearly defined and measurable service and performance agreements spelled out between a service provider (in this case the IT subsidiary of the enterprise or an external data center of a hosting partner) and the service recipient (here, the global enterprise).[10] Due to its detailed nature, the service has a clearly defined obligation. Most service level agreements address typical services for information technology, such as computing power, network bandwidths, and support

---

10 See *www.itil.com;* and Vital Anderhub, *Service Level Management — The ITIL Process in SAP Operation,* SAP Press Essential 25, SAP PRESS, 2006.

hotline availability. These factors are of utmost importance for an enterprise's global IT solution and architecture. If, for example, an enterprise operates a central single-instance system, the service level agreements must define the global network bandwidths. These services are critical to success, and consequently, their quality is defined in the SLA.

By means of precise, comprehensible definition of services, the service level agreement has the following effects on a global enterprise:

SLAs

Service Level Agreements
▸ Expenses can be assigned by cause to the areas that incur the highest costs, according to the quality received and quantity required.
▸ Transparency with regard to services and costs result in a more sensible handling of the services provided.
▸ Both the services and distribution of tasks is clearly defined, and therefore, frictional losses can be reduced.
▸ Services are compiled according to the requirements of the internal customer; therefore, you can optimize the respective process chains and reduce costs.
▸ (Partial) services can be separated and outsourced.

Whether it is a single task or an entire process, you should always specify the basic principles and scope of services in these agreements. This way, both parties (service provider and recipient) have a sound basis for checking the services rendered:

▸ **Required availability of the service**
For the service recipient, this means that employees can work efficiently, for example. For the service provider, this means the computers must be operational. In any case, it is crucial to define the service levels. You require a contractually documented description of the activities, and reaction or response times for specific services. You must also specify all critical aspects, and all issues that are excluded from the service.

▸ **Measurement methods**
You also have to define and establish measuring tools and methods to check compliance with the SLAs.

► **Response time**

This is the time between user action of the user and the system response, including all processing and reaction time. In a central single-instance system, the response time is the entire runtime between input of an end user at any location and the system response at the local PC of the respective end user — in other words, the total network runtime and the system time for the user's activity.

► **Support reaction time**

This is the time between support's receipt of an incident and problem message and reaction to that problem, within a specified scope.

► **Sanctions**

These are determined in case of insufficient performance. Here, sanction-relevant and sanction-irrelevant services (service levels) must be clearly distinguished within the scope of the contract. You also must consider that different SLAs can be allocated with different sanctions.

► **Environmental conditions**

These define which services are to be rendered by the service provider within the scope of the SLA and how they can be checked.

► **Flexibility**

Changes in the basic conditions must be taken into account. If, for example, the number of work centers changes due to expansion in new countries, or if the hardware of a system landscape (architecture) changes, you must adapt the SLAs accordingly.

When compiling an SLA, you must first define its scope and specify who is supposed to render which services. You must determine the *service level requirements* and define the key figures. For global IT solutions, you can determine several SLAs, which can result in insufficient transparency for complex business processes and applications. Therefore, you shouldn't created very complex SLAs, but only the most critical. In some cases, 'simple' service level agreements are sufficient. For example, you can agree that the support team of the service provider is supposed to respond to the error message within a specified period of time, regardless of what the problem is or from where it was sent.

Service level requirements

Another critical standard for IT services is the IT Infrastructure Library, which the service organizations of a global enterprise should make use of.

De-facto standard

4.5.6 ITIL Standard

The *IT Infrastructure Library* (ITIL) is an internationally acknowledged, de-facto standard for professional IT service management, which describes IT codes of practice as a manufacturer-independent set of rules.[11] Its objective is to establish quality management for IT services to enhance the efficiency and profitability of IT in support of enterprise objectives and business requirements. In addition, risks in providing IT services are to be minimized, and best-practice procedures are to be implemented efficiently. Consequently, ITIL enables targeted, process-oriented, user-friendly, and cost-optimized provision of IT services. Figure 4.9 shows an overview of the ITIL standard structure, including various defined areas.

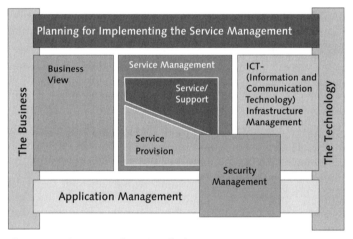

Figure 4.9 Overview of ITIL Standard Structure

Contents of the ITIL standard

The ITIL is a set of rules (standard or IT library), comprising a series of modules, or disciplines, that enable enterprises to improve their use of

---

11 See *http://en.wikipedia.org/wiki/Service-Level-Agreement* and Vital Anderhub, *Service Level Management – The ITIL Process in SAP Operation,* SAP Press Essential 25, SAP PRESS, 2006.

IT resources and ensure better-quality IT services. A critical aspect in this matter is the reference to core businesses of an enterprise or the organization and the concentration of IT services on the best-possible support of business processes. IT service management means that you can monitor and control the quality and quantity of IT services in a targeted, business process-oriented, user-friendly, and cost-optimized manner.

Within ITIL, both the individual IT service disciplines (e.g., problem management) and interfaces to other IT service disciplines are described, such as the interaction of problem management and configuration management. Although you can immediately benefit from the practical experiences of various disciplines contained within ITIL, real success can only be achieved if you build your entire IT service gradually in accordance with ITIL.

ITIL is a combination of two core disciplines, *service support* and *service delivery*, which constitute two different levels. We won't go into detail here; interested readers should refer to the literature on ITIL. The task of the service support is to support IT services during the running of operations (at the operational level). These IT services provide direct support for IT operation. In simple terms, this can be considered 'hotline support,' and extended by the following individual disciplines or modules:

▶ Service Desk (Helpdesk)

▶ Incident Management

▶ Problem Management

▶ Configuration Management

▶ Change Management

▶ Release Management

Tasks of service support based on ITIL

Service Delivery implements planning and control processes for professional implementation of IT services at a tactical level. Therefore, the objective of service delivery is to optimally meet, plan, and monitor the requirements of customers and IT. The goal is to achieve better customer orientation, and to render and offset expenses resulting therefrom in an economically optimal manner. Service delivery consists of the following modules:

Service Delivery
tasks based on ITIL

▶ Availability Management

▶ Capacity Management

▶ Continuity Management

▶ Financial Management for IT services

▶ Service Level Management

Interested readers can refer to the special literature on this topic, see *http://www.itil.com*; and Vital Anderhub, *Service Level Management — The ITIL Process in SAP Operation*, SAP Press Essential 25, SAP PRESS, 2006.

In a nutshell, we advise IT service organizations of global enterprises to use the ITIL standards. This gains in importance as the IT solution architecture becomes more global and central.

4.6 Product

Impact of software
on the architecture

We previously learned how the modeling of global business processes and the formation of globally operating teams influence global IT solutions. To achieve a concrete system architecture that is suitable for a global IT solution, you must closely analyze the functionality and technical properties of the SAP software used. In Section 2.1, we explained that the software components used must meet the technical and functional requirements of a global solution. Often product-specific aspects restrict or even exclude the use of the originally intended architecture. Historically, global enterprises prepared a central single-instance architecture that considered the enterprise strategy and business processes. However, this central architecture failed, and the enterprises had to move to a decentralized approach, because certain software-specific prerequisites could not be met or entailed complex management.

New markets and
countries

A particularly tricky situation evolves if an enterprise wants to enter new markets and countries by using a productive SAP solution and then finds out that the existing combination of architecture and SAP software cannot be deployed — for example, when there is an expansion into China. In order to integrate the new country into a running SAP system, you must implement the country versions for both China and the Chinese language that is legally required. Say the running system is not configured for SAP Unicode; it might be necessary to establish a separate decentralized system for China. This would mean a change toward a decentralized architecture. For this reason, you must initially analyze all product-specific and software-related aspects, and align them with the enterprise plans.

In the following sections, we'll describe which functional and technical aspects, and basic structure of the used SAP software components must be taken into account to determine the appropriate architecture or adapt the existing architecture if global IT solutions have changed. We'll discuss concrete problems — for example, whether a central single-instance system is feasible for an SAP ERP system in a given SAP release, using a specific number of countries, languages, and industry solutions; or how the introduction of a new country version can affect an existing architecture. We'll also detail how an existing SAP solution must be modified to maintain the current architecture using new requirements, and when it is recommended or mandatory to change an existing architecture. In the subsequent sections, we'll analyze the following basic aspects of global IT solutions and their influence on the system architecture:

▶ Cross-application internationalization aspects:

  ▶ Technical language support and language combinations

  ▶ Time zones

▶ SAP release and availability of country versions, industry solutions, and add-ons

▶ SAP release and combination of country versions, industry solutions, and add-ons

▶ Maintenance of SAP components and SAP support packages

▶ Integration of SAP Business Suite components

Basic aspects of software for global solutions

The following descriptions will always assume a central single-instance architecture as the target architecture for a fully integrated solution. We'll also consider under which product-specific and software-related conditions the enterprise must plan and operate a central architecture global IT solution, or whether decentralized systems must be introduced. We'll only discuss software components in SAP Release 4.6C or higher, and won't detail older releases for which the SAP standard maintenance

Analysis of software for a central architecture

has expired, though there might be some exceptions for the discussion on upgrades.

4.6.1 Technical Language Support and Language Combinations

Languages and character sets

Language support is an issue that is critical for all global enterprises, and affects the entire global IT solution, and its integration into internal and external systems.[12] The global solution must be able to technically support all required languages, regardless of how the languages are used. This may include, for example, active input by the end user, installation of translations for all or specific applications, or data exchange with internal or external international business partners via various interfaces.

To process text in a local language within the global IT solution of the enterprise, the system landscape must support these languages technically correct. This means that you must be able to enter text in the local language correctly, including the entire alphabet, all characters, and their writing direction, straight into the system, as well as save, display, change, and print these documents. Because the enterprise uses its global solution in many countries, all local or official languages of these countries must be supported in the system. Even if an enterprise has established English as the global communication language and requires no translations of the user interface, the local languages are still mandatory in most countries due to legal regulations or local business practices.

Language combinations, code pages, and multilingual applications

So, if you combine multiple countries in a central architecture (or a regional or partially central architecture with multiple countries in one region, such as for Asia), you must ensure that all languages for these countries can be combined without any technical problems, independent of the SAP standard software, industry solutions, country versions, external add-ons, and customer developments. Chapter 2 gave detailed information on this topic. An SAP Unicode system is the only technically perfect language solution. You can also use a single code-page system in which all Western European languages and restrictions are accepted

---

12 See *http://service.sap.com/globalization*; *http://service.sap.com/unicode*; and Nils Bürckel, Alexander Davidenkoff, and Detlef Werner, *Unicode in SAP Systems*, SAP PRESS, 2007.

for integration with Java-based applications.[13] However, this constitutes a (perhaps very) serious problem, because in global IT solutions, you often must combine languages with different character sets. Older SAP releases, without the Unicode-supported, mixed code page solution (MDMP), are no longer supported as of ERP 6.0.[14] Table 2.6 (Chapter 2) shows an overview of the various options for technical language support. The language support is implemented across applications and systems. Consequently, it has top priority for the selection of the architecture.

Here is a short summary for language support with Unicode and non-Unicode systems:

▶ An unrestricted central architecture for global IT solutions is only possible using an SAP Unicode system.

▶ A central architecture is also possible if you only use languages of a single code page, a valid SAP language key, and accept potential limitations. Adding a new language might not be possible.

▶ The MDMP solution, which is not recommended and no longer supported as of ERP 6.0, only enables limited use of a central architecture.

▶ New languages with new character sets or language keys can only be supported in SAP Unicode. Consequently, decentralized systems are required for new languages if you don't deploy Unicode.

Unicode and non-Unicode systems

4.6.2 Time Zones

If you apply the global IT solution in countries or regions with different time zones, the software and system architecture must be able to meet time zone-specific requirements.[15]

Different time zones in a global solution

In Chapter 2, we explained how SAP software support differs over time zones. The time zone functionality mainly depends on the design of the business processes and requirements of the global IT solution expected by the end users in the various countries. For a uniform global SAP solution, the following time zones definitions are relevant:

---

13 Details can be found in SAP Note 73606 and references.
14 Details can be found in SAP Note 79991 and references.
15 See *http://service.sap.com/globalization.*

▶ **System time zone**

All technical server components of the system landscape have a system time zone. This includes the location of the data center, the server hardware (e.g., system clock), the operating system of the database and application server of the SAP system, the SAP basis modules and services, as well as other technical components. As a general rule, all technical components of an SAP system should only be operated in one time zone. This means, for example, that the SAP database must have the same time zone as the application server for the background operation of the same SAP system. But this also means that the time zones of the systems must be identical for directly integrated SAP Business Suite components — for example, SAP ERP and SAP NetWeaver BI.

▶ **End-user time zone**

You can set a time zone in the user master data of the SAP system. This time zone is static, and is usually the time zone of the office where the end user works. Dynamic adaptation without manual intervention is not possible — for example, for business trips to another country of the enterprise. In many SAP standard applications, this local time zone enables you to see the end user's local time and work in this time zone instead of in the system's time. However, this is not always possible. Particularly in technical applications, you are often displayed the system time, for example, for background processing or system log display. You can compose your own developments by means of a special ABAP function library for time zones.

▶ **Business object time zone**

Each business object that is assigned with an address in the SAP application automatically has the time zone of the geographical location.[16] For example, a business object can be a plant, a company code (location of the organizational unit of the enterprise), or the location of the customers or vendors. If transactions using business objects stretch across several time zones, this must be considered by the relevant applications. It might be necessary, for example, to correctly calculate the date.

---

16 A *business object* is an abstraction of business partners, organizations, and their locations and means, which are required to execute the business processe.

Imagine, for example, that the data center with the SAP system is located in the U.S. Pacific (UTC-8) time zone. A subsidiary in New Zealand (UTC+12) (we will ignore daylight saving time and standard time for the sake of simplification) wants to calculate the FI month-end closing for June on July 1, local time. In this case, the application must recognize that the month of June is already over in New Zealand, whereas there are still some hours left for the SAP system in the U.S. Or, if an employee in New Zealand is on vacation as of July 1, the SAP HCM application must not enter June 30 as the first day of leave, as would normally be displayed by the system. The business object time zone is particularly used for the SAP Business Suite components SAP CRM and SCM. If you want to carry out availability checks for a specific date, it must relate to the location of the plant, and not the location of the SAP system.

Whether the applications in an enterprise's global IT solution are time-zone critical or not depends on the individual situation, and on realistic and pragmatic requirements. It is neither possible nor realistic to make every date and time field in each application time-zone dependent. Most end users of a global enterprise are aware of the time zone issue, because they collaborate with colleagues on other continents.

Prerequisites for Time Zone Support

Time zone support

The influence of time zones on the system architecture can be summarized as follows:

▶ Time zones are generally supported in the SAP software; consequently they are not obstacles for a central architecture. Depending on the individual requirements of the global IT solution, you must check, however, whether the support is sufficient for the individual requirements and global processes of the enterprise. If this is not the case, and no solution can be found you must create decentralized systems with different time zones. System integration must consider the different time zones for critical applications.

▶ All technical server components of a system landscape must have the same time zone. We recommend selecting the time zone UTC for the system components, which does not require changeover between daylight saving time and standard time.

> **Prerequisites for Time Zone Support**
>
> ▸ Regarding the operation and maintenance of a central system, you must take into consideration that there is no daytime or nighttime, because global end users use the system 24/7. If you can't implement this and no other solution is possible, you must introduce decentralized systems that can be installed at a central data center location and be configured with the desired time zone. In real life, it can make sense in such a case to implement a decentralized regional architecture for the individual continents.

4.6.3   SAP Release Strategy

The SAP release strategy determines which functions and solutions are contained in the software components of a specific release.[17] It is very important for the IT department of a global enterprise to implement extensive planning that is adapted to the business strategy to ensure that the release of the software solution meets both the global solution and system architecture requirements. If the system architecture has to be changed due to new requirements (e.g., expansion into new countries, introduction of industry solutions and add-ons, upgrades, Unicode conversions, currency conversions, etc.), this must be identified as quickly as possible and implemented. In real life, however, this is not done. The results are usually some questionable 'quick and dirty' workaround solutions that are supposed to circumvent necessary upgrades.

SAP standard software and add-ons

The ideal case for an enterprise's global IT solution would be if the SAP product version used comprised all necessary functions in the standard version. (By product version, we mean a product of the SAP Business Suite in a specific SAP release — for example, ERP 6.0, including all components.). If so, (and depending on the specific product), you can assume that a global solution can be implemented with a single instance and can be maintained with moderate expenditure. The matter can become complex if you require additional software components to meet the requirements of the global IT solution. It even becomes more critical if industry solutions and country versions are required that are not contained in the SAP standard version, or cannot be activated by means of simple or moderate configuration. Then you have the problem of installing additional add-on components that may have serious effects on the existing

---

17 See *http://service.sap.com/releasestrategy.*

solution. You can obtain further information about the availability of all SAP applications at *http://service.sap.com/pam*.

> **Tip**
>
> Generally, the following rule applies:
>
> More than one (complex) add-on to the SAP standard software in a central SAP system can be problematic and should therefore be carefully analyzed or avoided!

Of course, there are some cases in which an add-on has little to no effect on the existing solution. But even for modification-free add-on country versions, you must carry out specific analyses in case of more than one add-on. This is necessary to check whether technical or functional conflicts might occur. In turn, it depends on the concrete global IT solution, and SAP can't give general information in this regard. Another problem is that you can't expect different add-on functions to match and supplement each other, even if there are not technical conflicts. There is often a misconception that the combination of industry solution and an add-on country version automatically results in a 'country version of the industry solution,' which is not the case. This can only be achieved if the industry solution has a country version, itself.

4.6.4 Industry Solutions

Chapter 2, Table 2.1 presented an overview of the SAP industry solutions. In principle, industry solutions are additional software components that are installed and activated for the existing standard software. For this purpose, the standard software is adapted to enable the execution of industry-specific functions.

Industry solutions in the SAP software

An industry solution often entails severe technical consequences: It can't be uninstalled or combined with most of other industry solutions. This seriously affects architecture considerations. If an enterprise wants to operate several SAP industry solutions, it must set up an SAP system for each solution. Consequently, only a decentralized approach is possible.

Some industry solutions were accepted for the SAP standard — for example, SAP Retail for 4.6C or SAP EH&S (Environment, Health & Safety) for

R/3 Enterprise. As a result, they can be deployed like any other standard software component and used for a central solution.

The release of SAP ERP 6.0 is includes a new innovation that transfers virtually all industry solutions to the SAP standard software by introducing the new 'switch framework architecture.'[18] However, you can only activate 1 of 12 industry solutions to keep to the technical restriction: 'one solution per system.' The advantage of this innovation is in significantly improved maintenance and future upgrades. The solutions that are technically implemented in SAP ERP 6.0 by means of SAP Enterprise extension sets enable multiple use and consequently can be combined in a central system. Table 4.1 shows an overview of the single and multiple activated industry solutions in SAP ERP 6.0.[19]

Single Use	Multiple Use (Combinations)
SAP ECC Industry Extension Healthcare 6.0	SAP ECC Enterprise Extension Consumer Products 6.0
SAP ECC Industry Extension Chemicals 6.0	SAP ECC Enterprise Extension Defense Forces & Public Security 6.0
SAP ECC Industry Extension Contract Accounting 6.0	SAP ECC Enterprise Extension Financials 6.0
SAP ECC Industry Extension Discrete Industries & Mill Products 6.0	SAP ECC Enterprise Extension FERC: Regulatory Reporting 6.0
SAP ECC Industry Extension Insurance 6.0	SAP ECC Enterprise Extension Financial Services 6.0
SAP ECC Industry Extension Media 6.0	SAP ECC Enterprise Extension Global Trade 6.0
SAP ECC Industry Extension Mining 6.0	SAP ECC Enterprise Extension Human Capital Management 6.0
SAP ECC Industry Extension Oil & Gas 6.0	SAP ECC Enterprise Extension Incentive & Commission Management 6.0
SAP ECC Industry Extension Public Services 6.0	SAP ECC Enterprise Extension Industry-Specific Sales Enhancements 6.0

Table 4.1 Single- and Multiple-Use SAP Industry Solutions in ERP 6.0

18 See *http://service.sap.com/erp*.
19 Table 4.1 refers to SAP ERP 6.0 standard solution without SAP Enhancement Packages. For more information see *http://service.sap.com/erp*.

Single Use	Multiple Use (Combinations)
SAP ECC Industry Extension Retail 6.0	SAP ECC Enterprise Extension Joint Venture Accounting 6.0
SAP ECC Industry Extension Telecommunications 6.0	SAP ECC Enterprise Extension PLM 6.0
SAP ECC Industry Extension Utilities, Waste & Recycling 6.0	SAP ECC Enterprise Extension Public Sector Management 6.0
	SAP ECC Enterprise Extension Retail 6.0
	SAP ECC Enterprise Extension SCM 6.0
	SAP ECC Enterprise Extension Travel Management 6.0

Table 4.1 Single- and Multiple-Use SAP Industry Solutions in ERP 6.0 (Cont.)

4.6.5 SAP ERP Country Versions

For country versions, the technical requirements are similar to industry solutions if you want to combine several versions in one system.[20] Regarding the global IT solution, however, there is one major difference: An enterprise usually belongs to one specific industry and consequently requires only one industry solution — in technical terms, only one add-on if the functions of the standard software are not sufficient. For country versions the situation is completely different. The global enterprise is active in many countries around the world and therefore requires many country versions in the IT solution at the same time.

Country versions for localizing SAP applications

As you already learned in Section 2.1, the SAP product strategy enables continuous extension of the number of country versions in all SAP Business Suite components and provides them in the SAP standard software. All standard countries are technically compatible and can be combined arbitrarily in the central system. These are ideal prerequisites for the single-instance architecture. You must note, however, that arbitrary language combinations are only possible in an SAP Unicode system due to the language support required for the country versions. If Unicode is not available, you might not be able to implement a single-instance architecture.

Let us take a look at the life cycle of a country version: The development and number of SAP country versions, as well as their inclusion in the

New countries; standard and add-on country versions

20 See *http://service.sap.com/globalization*.

standard software, is dynamic and follows the SAP release strategy. Initially, a new country version is only provided as an add-on that is developed, delivered, and maintained by SAP or partners. When the country version reaches market readiness, a decision is made as to whether or not the country is accepted into the SAP standard software. If so, the country version is integrated with the next SAP standard release of the Business Suite components. Consequently, the previous add-on country version requires a new installation of the current release or upgrade to the new SAP standard release in combination with a special migration, which is also referred to as a *retrofit*.[21]

SAP Standard and Add-on Release Strategy

Add-on releases

Each add-on constitutes an individual software component with different versions or releases. As a result, there is a separate release strategy for each add-on, in addition to the SAP standard. One or more add-on releases are usually closely linked to an underlying SAP release. For upgrading an SAP product to the next higher release, you normally must upgrade the add-on, as well. This is done within the SAP standard upgrade procedure by using a special add-on upgrade CD-ROM in addition the standard upgrade. Therefore, for upgrades to the SAP standard product, you must carefully plan whether a suitable add-on release and a unique upgrade path exist for the new SAP release.

Retrofit of country versions in the SAP standard and upgrade

The transfer of an add-on country version (analogous to an industry solution or an arbitrary add-on) to the SAP standard is a specific feature and is referred to as a retrofit. Here, a special retrofit migration is implemented during the SAP standard upgrade in which all objects and data of the add-on country versions are migrated to the objects and data of the standard software. For SAP ERP, the last retrofits were carried out for the countries India (R/3 Enterprise) and Russia (ERP 6.0).

Table 4.2 shows the add-on release strategy for the SAP ERP FI-CO country versions in SAP Releases 4.6C to ERP 6.0/ECC 6.0; CEE is an add-on that includes multiple, mostly European country versions. We'll explain this in the following sections in detail.

---

21 Using the new technologies — Extension Sets and Enhancement Packages (as of SAP ERP 6.0) — it is possible to introduce or transfer add-on country versions and other solutions to the SAP standard in an unchanged SAP release.

Release	4.6C (*)	R/3 Enterprise	ECC 5.0	ECC 6.0
Delivered by SAP				
Retrofit to standard		India		Russia
Integration in CEE		Kazakhstan, Russia, Ukraine, Serbia	Greece	
Add-on	CEE (*)	CEE	CEE	CEE
Add-on	Greece	Greece		
Add-on	India			
(*) Kazakhstan, Russia, Ukraine with separate SAP CCIS add-on.				
Delivered by SAP partners				
Add-on	Israel	Israel	Israel	Israel
Add-on	Iceland	Iceland	Iceland	Iceland

Table 4.2 Add-On FI-CO Country Versions and SAP ERP Releases

As you can see in the table, add-on countries are also integrated into the SAP CEE add-on package, in addition to the two retrofit countries, India (R/3 Enterprise) and Russia (ERP 6.0). We'll describe this in the following section.

SAP CEE Add-On[22]

In order to reduce the number of add-on country versions (not integrated in the SAP standard), it makes sense to provide multiple countries as a package in a technical add-on. The add-on then includes the technical conditions for combining all countries and languages. Technically, you can't install countries and languages individually, but only a combination of all countries and languages, even if you only require one country for the global solution. The advantage of this is that the issue of combining multiple technical add-on components is avoided.

SAP CEE Add-on as a "country package"

---

22 You can find more details on the SAP CEE add-on in Notes 520991 (CEE-Core or FI-CO country versions) and 524073 (HR-CEE or HCM country versions), as well as in references.

Two examples of these combination packages are the SAP CEE (Central Eastern Europe) add-on for combining multiple FI-CO country versions and SAP HR-CEE for combining multiple HCM country versions. Table 4.3 indicates the CEE add-on countries for FI-CO country versions, depending on the SAP and add-on release. This add-on includes multiple country versions for Eastern and Southeast Europe, Russia (standard as of ERP 6.0), and in some CIS countries, depending on the SAP ERP release. Because the character sets for the respective languages belong to different code pages — that is, the Eastern European or Cyrillic character set, and the Greek character set as of ERP 2004 — you should carry out the CEE add-on installation only in an SAP Unicode system for a central architecture. Otherwise, the issues for a non-Unicode system apply, and the CEE add-on will require decentralized systems.

SAP ERP Release	CEE Release	BG	SR	GR	HR	KZ	RO	RU	SI	UA
46C	010_46C				X		X		X	
46C	011_46C	X			X		X		X	
Enterprise	100_470				X	X		X	X	X
Enterprise	101_470				X	X	X	X	X	X
Enterprise	102_470	X	X		X	X	X	X	X	X
ECC 5.0	105_500		X	X	X	X	X	X	X	X
ECC 5.0	106_500	X	X	X	X	X	X	X	X	X
ECC 6.0	110_600	X	X	X	X	X	X	X	X	X

BG: Bulgaria
GR: Greece
HR: Croatia
KZ: Kazakhstan
RO: Romania
RU: Russia, as of ECC 6.0 in SAP standard
SI: Slovenia
SR: Serbia
UA: Ukraine

Table 4.3 FI-CO Country Versions in the SAP CEE Add-On

The SAP HR-CEE add-on package includes multiple HCM country versions, including those in Eastern Europe, Russia (standard as of ERP 6.0), Turkey, and Colombia (depending on the SAP and add-on release). For technical reasons, the same limitations as for the CEE add-on apply. However, the countries and languages are different.

If you want to combine the two CEE and HR-CEE add-on packages in a central system, you must note that these are two different add-ons in the technical sense, and the operation might be restricted due to add-on-specific maintenance. These restrictions must be analyzed in detail.

4.6.6 Country Versions in Industry Solutions and Other SAP Business Suite Components

In the previous sections we described the SAP industry solutions and country versions separately, and always related them to the SAP Business Suite components containing either FI-CO or HCM country versions. You can find further information on this topic in Chapter 2 and Figure 2.2. Country versions also exist for other SAP Business Suite components and SAP industry solutions. However, they are not part of the SAP ERP country strategy, but can be determined individually for an SAP product version. This also applies to the availability of translations in local languages for the various product versions.

Localized industry solutions and SAP Business Suite components

You can refer to the product documentation or contact SAP directly to determine which countries and translations are supported for which SAP Business Suite components, releases, and industry solutions, but you can't conclude that combining an SAP ERP country version and an industry solution within the same SAP system automatically means that the industry solution is functionally supported for that country. If an industry solution supports a specific country, you are either provided with industry-specific country add-ons, or the industry solution supports the country directly.

For influencing the architecture of a system landscape, the same issues apply as for the ERP country versions that were described in Section 4.6.5, "SAP ERP Country Versions."

- **Combining country versions and industry solutions in SAP ERP**

  - SAP release up to SAP ERP 2004: The combination of add-on country versions and industry solutions can result in technical conflicts and problems for continuous maintenance and future upgrades. Therefore, for a central architecture, it is only suitable to a limited extent and must be specified for special projects.

  - As of SAP Release ERP 6.0, the technical combination of an add-on country version and industry solution is generally possible due to the 'Switch Framework' functionality.

- **Country versions in SAP Business Suite components and language support**

  - An unrestricted central architecture is only possible using an SAP Unicode system.

4.6.7 Expansion into New Countries and the Effects on the Architecture

New countries and the influence on the existing architecture

An extremely critical question arises for global enterprises if they want to expand into new countries that must be implemented in an existing global solution with the given architecture.[23] Expanding into new countries could seriously affect the project effort and the architecture of an existing IT solution, depending on the country and availability of SAP components. In the following sections, we'll describe different typical scenarios, as well as their influence on the system architecture.

New languages are only unrestricted when using an SAP Unicode system

The New Country Uses a Language with a New Character Set or New Code Page

Due to the technical language support on SAP systems, you should analyze which languages and character sets are required for the new country. Whether or not a translation of the SAP software is available for this country plays a minor role, initially. Decisive factors include whether you must create company-specific documents (e.g., names, addresses, product descriptions, forms, reports, etc.) in the IT solution due to legal regulations, and/or whether you must use the local language due to the

---

23 See *http://service.sap.com/globalization*.

given business practices in order to be successful. (In Japan, for example, English is usually not accepted, and Japanese is an absolute must.) Then you must determine whether the new language is technically supported in the existing SAP system — in other words, the language key must be available and the character set or script of the language supported. Refer to Section 2.1.2, "Requirements of IT Users," Table 2.6, and the book *Unicode in SAP Systems*, for detailed explanations.

When it comes to language support, we can distinguish between the following cases:

- **The global IT solution is an SAP Unicode system**
  In an SAP Unicode system, this is always the case. In other words, the new language can be integrated into an existing SAP system without having to change the architecture.

- **The global IT solution is an SAP non-Unicode system**
  Initially, you must determine whether the new language is technically supported. If not, you can either convert the existing system to Unicode or install a new decentralized system in Unicode. If the new language is technically supported in non-Unicode, you must differentiate the following cases:

  - The new language includes the same code page as the already installed languages, and a language key is available. Consequently, you can install the language directly into the global IT solution system. You can continue to use the central architecture.

  - If the language uses a new code page, the situation is more complex. The general recommendation is to convert the SAP system to Unicode prior to introducing the new country. Or, you can install a separate decentralized system with the new language and code page to implement the new country. The result is an architecture with a decentralized orientation.

We strongly recommend not implementing the new language by means of an MDMP (mixed code page) solution into an existing system in order to keep the central architecture. Even though MDMP is supported by SAP ERP components of older SAP releases (up to and excluding SAP ERP 6.0; for SAP ERP 2004, only after upgrading; and no integration in Java-based SAP applications), there are considerable restrictions and (golden) rules, and there is a risk of data corruption (see Table 2.6).

No problems if
new country is
contained in SAP
standard

The New Country is Available as an SAP Standard Country Version of the SAP Standard Component of the Productive IT Solution

This is an almost ideal case: You can implement the new country for the existing global IT solution with moderate effort while simultaneously maintaining the existing architecture. Here, the challenge is to add the new country without influencing or impairing the current, running applications or countries. Chapter 5, "IT Implementation of Architectures," gives detailed descriptions of the required procedures and steps.

Complex, if new
country available
as an add-on

The New Country is Available as an SAP or Partner Add-on Country Version in the SAP Standard Component of the Productive IT Solution

This is a complex situation for which you must differentiate the following cases:

▶ **The existing global IT solution already contains other technical add-on components**
In this case, the general rule applies: You can't simply combine multiple add-on solutions. This is only possible when you implement an individual, customer-specific project. You must analyze, solve, and maintain any conflicts that occur, individually. Future SAP standard upgrades either require significant adaptations or are not possible. In this case, you should install a new decentralized system for the add-on country.

▶ **The global IT solution does not contain any other add-ons**
In this case, you can implement the new add-on country version in the existing system. However, you should check and manually change possible modifications of the add-on solution that are described in the respective documentation. Moreover, here you must consider that the continuous maintenance of the combination of global IT solutions and add-ons with SAP support packages, stacks, and patches is subject to certain restrictions.[24] If the add-on contains multiple country

---

24 Here, SAP Enhancement Packages must be taken into account as of SAP ERP 6.0.

versions in one package (e.g., the new country is included in the SAP CEE add-on), this information applies for the entire package. Because of the languages with multiple character sets contained in the CEE add-on, you should consider the previously mentioned issue concerning technical language support and favor an SAP Unicode system.

The New Country is Available as an SAP Standard Country Version in a Subsequent SAP Release of the Global IT Solution

Upgrade prior to introducing a new country

In this case, you should consider upgrading the existing global IT solution to the required SAP release, possibly in combination with Unicode conversion, so that you can add the new country while simultaneously maintaining the central architecture. Alternatively, you can keep the old release of the global IT solution and install a separate decentralized system in the required SAP release for the new country. This, however, will result in a transition to a decentralized architecture, and because of release differences, this might entail work-intensive integration of the new country with the old global IT solution release.

There is no SAP or Partner Country Version for the New Country

Additional effort and customer development without SAP Country Versions

This case occurs more and more often in practice and can't be solved completely. Even though new country versions are continuously developed in the SAP standard and as add-on solutions, it is not likely that all countries of the world can be included. Global enterprises, however, don't want to skip countries that could constitute new markets. But what do you have to do in this case?

For technical language support, you can introduce a new country's language in virtually all cases by means of an SAP Unicode system, because Unicode supports the character sets and scripts of all world languages. But a Unicode system features another very important function: In contrast to non-Unicode systems using 40 language keys, it provides several hundreds of language keys so that even without any character set problems, a Unicode system can become mandatory with the new language due to the language key.

To pragmatically solve the functional localization for the country version, you can apply the following frequently used practices:

▶ **Analysis of the legal regulations in the respective country and comparison with existing SAP country versions**
If you can find a suitable SAP country version, this can be used as a template for the new country and adapted (in cooperation with the IT development team) to new applications and developments.

▶ **Use in country clusters**
A country cluster is a group of countries that have similar functional and legal requirements for the localization of enterprise software — for example, financial accounting. If the new country fits into an existing country cluster with the supported country versions, it is even easier to implement the new country in the global IT solution. Figure 4.10 shows an example of country clusters for the SAP ERP FI-CO country versions. Interestingly, the country groups partly comprise geographically distant regions.

▶ **Deploying separate translations**
If you require a translation in the language of the new country, in part or in whole, which is not provided as an SAP translation, you can implement your own translation using the SAP Translation Workbench. The SAP Translation Workbench is described in Chapter 2.

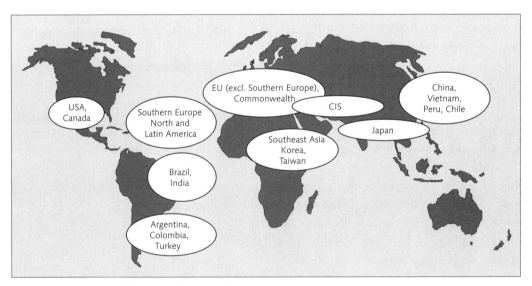

Figure 4.10 Examples of Functional Country Clusters

4.7   Summary

This chapter described in great detail all factors that can influence the selection of the appropriate system architecture. The responsibility for selecting the architecture lies not only with the IT department of an enterprise, but with the global enterprise as a whole. The design of the global IT solution is determined not only by technical IT aspects, but also by the strategy of the entire global enterprise, the business processes, and the organization structure. Combined with the properties and functions of SAP software, you can establish direct criteria for the architecture.

The three-dimensional globalization model comprises product, organizations, and process — aspects that are all relevant for determining a successful target architecture. In order to start planning the global IT project at a business process level, it is important that the business and IT teams collaborate and use suitable tools. You have learned how business process modeling using ARIS for NetWeaver, in combination with SAP Business Process Management and SAP Solution Manager, can provide valuable services.

Three dimensional model

For a successful global IT project that uses the appropriate architecture, all organizations involved in the enterprise must meet specific requirements ranging from business-related to sociocultural issues. While a well-defined, strict corporate governance is vital for the global orientation of an enterprise, the global corporate culture must be able to respect the organizations and employees in all countries, including regional specifics, and integrate them into the global project. The support organizations must be well equipped for a global project. This includes global presence, 24/7 availability, extensive expertise, and support for end users in their respective country languages. The data center responsible for planning and operating global IT solutions can either be implemented by the global enterprise or outsourced to an external global service provider. The support and data center organizations should apply the common ITIL standard for application and IT service management, and determine well-defined SLAs for the service organization and the enterprise.

SAP software used for global IT solutions directly influences the system architecture by providing clear criteria and issues that either technically

SAP software

allow a global single instance or require an architecture with decentralized orientation. Here you must consider application-independent internationalization aspects, support of country versions and industry solutions in SAP standard or as add-ons, the software release, and the integration of other SAP Business Suite components. We recommend using the current release, SAP ERP 6.0, or the current releases of other SAP Business Suite components (status 2008), because many functions and properties for the support of global solutions have improved considerably since previous releases.

Only an SAP Unicode system is suitable for unrestricted language support in a global system. Without Unicode, detailed analyses are required, or a decentralized architecture must be implemented. In SAP products, different time zones are supported to enable a worldwide, global solution. Because business processes and time-zone requirements can vary considerably, depending on the enterprise, you should carefully analyze whether the existing standard time-zone functionality is sufficient, whether you need customer developments, or whether a decentralized architecture with regional systems of different time zones is needed.

Add-ons A very crucial criterion for global solutions and their maintenance is the use of add-ons for SAP standard software. If the necessary country version or industry solution doesn't exist in the SAP standard and is available as an add-on, you must carefully check if and how installing the add-on can influence the global solution. In no case should you use multiple add-ons if the specific combination is not explicitly released. An add-on often impedes the continuous maintenance of the global solution, because it cannot always be ensured that the support package strategy of the standard software corresponds with the strategy of the add-on, which could result in dependencies and restrictions.

Future SAP release upgrades of the standard software must generally be implemented along with add-on upgrades. The new 'switch framework' technology (as of SAP ERP 6.0) comprises industry solutions in SAP standard to considerably facilitate maintenance. However, only 1 out of 12 industry solutions must be activated. SAP ERP country versions are continuously being extended, and add-on country versions are either migrated to the SAP standard (e.g., Russia for SAP ERP 6.0), or they are integrated in add-on packages, such as SAP CEE, which a combination of multiple countries (technically an add-on). Consequently, it enables the combination of these add-on countries in the global system. Country versions for other SAP Business Suite components and industry solutions follow other release and availability strategies. However, the technical factors for a global solution — in particular, language support and add-ons —still apply.

*When a global enterprise selects a specific architecture, this
architecture must be optimized for both implementation and running operations. There are many aspects that must be considered.
In this chapter, we'll describe how you can efficiently implement
the selected global architecture.*

5   IT Implementation of Architectures

For the implementation of a system architecture (in particular, a central
architecture), you must consider the following questions: How can you
enable optimal and uninterrupted operation in a global, single-instance
system? How can you manage downtimes securely to provide optimum
network operation and high performance? Project teams are concerned
about how they can manage a global project and corporate rollout that
includes a global template approach, how they can implement new countries in a global production system, and how they convert the actual
architecture of the existing system landscape into the new target architecture, among other issues.

In this chapter, we'll answer these questions, and offer valuable information and recommendations derived from numerous analyses, workshops,
concrete projects, and personal considerations. We'll focus primarily on
the central single-instance architecture, because experience has shown
that this area has the highest information requirement. However, you
can also use our suggestions for regionally oriented architectures — for
example, systems that are implemented in countries of a geographical
region, such as Asia-Pacific, which constitute a central system for this
region.

In Sections 5.1, 5.2, and 5.3, we'll discuss infrastructure aspects that
focus on the operation of a data center and hardware equipment. In Section 5.4, planning, implementation, and development will be described,
with a particular focus on the global template approach. In Section 5.5,

we'll give an overview of the functionality and use of tools for changing an existing system architecture — for example, the consolidation of two separate systems into one central system. Of course, we can't detail all aspects, because this would go far beyond the scope of this book. Therefore, we'll concentrate on the typical questions that arise for global IT solutions, and we refer interested readers to more-advanced literature on, for example, data center operation.

5.1 General Requirements for a Data Center

Discussions on the optimal architecture for a global IT solution are very complex and often controversial. The central topic here is whether and how you can implement the architecture while considering the following aspects:

▶ Profitability

▶ High performance

▶ 24/7 operation, with high availability

▶ Security

▶ Changeability

▶ Global service and support

Low TCO for the operation of of the IT solution

First, you must ensure that the total cost of ownership (TCO) is as low as possible for the implementation and operation of the IT solution. This is a natural requirement demanded by every enterprise on the IT team that is assigned with the task of implementing the global IT solution. For calculating the TCO, you must consider the costs both on the IT side and the business side, because the modeling of business processes, change tasks, restructuring processes, and so on directly influence the IT solution and architecture. Ideally, selection of an optimal architecture for the global solution doesn't just depend on IT; in practice, however, this happens only in rare cases (even if it does occasionally make sense). The criteria for selecting an architecture should be determined through collaboration between business and IT. This is particularly necessary if the enterprise has established that it is either ready for a full global solution or prefers a distributed architecture.

When it comes to IT infrastructure — that is, the performance of hardware, databases, servers, and networks — you can implement any architecture, even for high and extremely high data volumes. However, a global, central single-instance solution poses the greatest challenge in this context; there is controversy over whether IT can implement and operate a single-instance system that satisfies all requirements. But, you must be able to operate an alternate architecture cost-efficiently, quickly, and securely. This results in high demands on the IT infrastructure of the data center.

All architectures are technically feasible

In Sections 4.5.3 to 4.5.6, we explained the infrastructures, services, and processes a modern data center and operators team must provide to operate a complex global solution. An enterprise can either operate its own data center or commission a service provider. When outsourcing to a data center service provider, you must define and ensure compliance with service level agreements and processing according to ITIL standards for IT and application management (see Sections 4.5.5 and 4.5.6). Interested readers can refer to advanced literature on this topic, for example *Service Level Management — The ITIL Process in SAP Operations* by Vital Anderhub (SAP PRESS Essentials 21, 2006).

In this section, we'll detail the specific and most vital requirements of IT that are critical for implementing a global IT solution. In this context, we'll primarily focus on the central single-instance solution for a global implementation with 24/7 operation. However, the following aspects also apply for decentralized architectures, including respective adaptations.

Focus on single-instance solutions

5.1.1 Hardware Consolidation and Adaptive Computing

Today, server technology is very advanced and enables operation of multiple systems on one server, as well as the use of joint storage systems that support multiple systems. A very good example is the SAN (Storage Area Network) storage system. If you want to use a decentralized architecture for the global solution and operate a central data center at one

Server and storage consolidation

location for the entire system landscape, it is possible and efficient to operate multiple decentralized systems on shared hardware. Of course, the architecture, applications, and data remain decentralized, but the infrastructure costs are reduced due to the high-performance, shared hardware. In practice, servers and storage are often consolidated, particularly if the hardware is changed or migrated — for example, if the distributed system landscape of the decentralized IT solution is relocated from multiple data centers to one central data center.

Adaptive computing

Shared hardware has another significant advantage: With the new *adaptive computing technology,* you can dynamically assign hardware resources to the various systems, and obtain improved utilization and better response to peak situations.[1]

SAP NetWeaver has introduced adaptive computing technology especially for SAP systems. The new adaptive computing functions of SAP NetWeaver lets enterprises flexibly assign their applications and data to specific servers or storage systems, and consequently respond to changing requirements for computing power as well as changes in hardware availability. This way, you can run different software or database processes on one server in parallel. This enables data-center users and operators to better use their resources. Both aspects of hardware consolidation and adaptive computing technology are suitable for the IT infrastructure of a global IT solution, as well as for any architecture.

You can find further information about adaptive computing support in the SAP Service Marketplace *http://service.sap.com/netweaver* and the SAP Developer Network (SDN) *http://sdn.sap.com.*

5.1.2 Planning Appropriate Platforms

SAP software supports multiple operating systems and databases (platforms). Consequently, the IT team of an enterprise can select the appropriate platform. It is highly important that you only select one platform for the SAP Business Suite components, which is also designed for future plans. The *SAP Platform Availability Matrix* (PAM), which you find in

---

1 See, for example, Michael Missbach, et al., *Adaptive Hardware Infrastructures for SAP.* SAP PRESS, 2005.

the SAP Service Marketplace at *http://service.sap.com/pam,* gives detailed information on this subject.[2] The following recommendations apply:

▶ **Collaboration with SAP platform partners**
You can select the appropriate hardware — that is, the database server, the application server, the storage system, and other components — in collaboration with platform partners. They can provide detailed data, facts, and benchmarks for the available server models, and draft concrete proposals for the hardware landscape in accordance with the size requirements of the enterprise.

Platform strategy for SAP systems

▶ **64-bit strategy**
For a global system with high volume, you can only use 64-bit platforms. Today, 64-bit technology is predominant in the server market. Here you can obtain new dimensions of performance and scalability, and particularly, the 32-bit address restrictions of 4GB main memory for a process (in practice, even below this value; see also SAP Note 308375) are removed. Removing this and other limits are prerequisites for single-instance and any other decentralized architectures, including high data volumes and throughput.

▶ **Unicode support**
To enable unrestricted language support on a single-instance solution, you must use an SAP Unicode system. Many global enterprises that don't use Unicode systems yet are aware of this fact and are currently implementing or planning Unicode projects. New installations should only be implemented in Unicode; as of 2007 shipments of new SAP products will only be available in Unicode. Therefore, the platform for a global solution should be designed for a current or future Unicode platform.

When planning the database and operating system version, you must take into account when and for how long the database and hardware manufacturer must support these versions. This information must be aligned with the release strategy of the used SAP components and strictly adhered to.[3] You must analyze any exceptional rules or specifics in great

Platform release dependency

---

2 More detailed information can be found in the SAP Service Marketplace at *http://service.sap.com/platforms.*
3 See *http://service.sap.com/releasestrategy* and *http://service.sap.com/pam.*

detail. In practice, this is often considered unimportant, and consequently results in problems due to incompatibilities between the platform and SAP system.

5.2 IT Infrastructure for a Global Solution Central Architecture

The following considerations apply not only to the single-instance case, but also for any other architecture that includes large systems — for example, regional systems with many different countries and a large number of users.

Single-instance implementations

For the single-instance architecture, you must consider whether a technical implementation is possible at all. Today, IT is at a very high technological level, and consequently, even systems with tens of thousands of users and databases in the two-digit terabyte range are possible. This doesn't mean, however, that any global solution can be easily implemented as a single-instance system, because you must meet many different conditions.

When discussing the technical feasibility of a single-instance solution, first answer the question of whether a large enterprise already uses this architecture with SAP successfully. Because every enterprise (and consequently every global IT solution) has a different design, you must interpret others' experiences carefully; they only give you a general idea.

Single-instance examples

Table 5.1 gives you a general overview on whether and to what extent enterprises use global single-instance ERP systems. It shows you a small selection of known SAP production systems (as of 2007), with the following key figures:

- **Single instance:** Indicates whether it is a single-instance system.
- **Number of active users**: Average number of users that actively work on the system around the clock.
- **Database size:** Current size of the central database in terabytes.
- **ERP applications:** SAP production applications.
- **Unicode:** Indicates whether the global system runs in Unicode.

Customer	Single Instance	Number of Active Users	Database Size in TB	ERP Applications	Unicode Yes/No
1	Yes, live in EMEA and Asia; USA in 2007	30,000 planned for the end of 2009	0.7; 12 TB planned in 2009	All, excluding HCM	Yes
2	Yes	5,600	0.8	All	Yes
3	Yes	5,000	5.0	FI, CO, SD, MM, PP, WM	In 2007
4	Yes	8,000	4.8	FI, CO, SD, MM, PP	No
5	Yes, with two global systems; merger to one system planned	15,000 per system	1.8	FI, CO, MM, SD, PS, CS, AM	In 2007
6	Yes	33,000	1	SD, MM, PS, HR incl. ESS/ MSS	In 2007

Table 5.1 Real-Life Examples of Global SAP ERP Single-Instance Systems (4.7, ECC 5.0 ECC 6.0)

As you can see, the number of active users is considerably high; virtually all databases are in the terabyte range, and one example plans to consolidate two large global systems into one. We'll discuss the merger of SAP systems in Section 5.5. Note that there are live and very large single-instance systems for other SAP Business Suite components, preferably including SAP NetWeaver BI, for which implementations are known whose database sizes exceed 10TB (as of 2007).

This indicates that single-instance solutions are generally technical feasible, but it doesn't provide any information about whether this applies for the respective concrete situation. In the following sections, we'll discuss the different requirements and questions regarding the technical infrastructure of the single-instance solution, using a case-study approach.

We'll derive the facts and recommendations that you can transfer to any global IT architecture.

5.2.1 Planning for a Global, Single-Instance Architecture

Let's take a look at the following task:

Sample task

An enterprise wants to implement a global single-instance solution for all SAP ERP core applications including approximately 10,000 active users in America, EMEA, and the Asia-Pacific region. The database size is several TB, and the SAP system is operated in Unicode. The system is business-critical and consequently must be securely and efficiently available 24/7. The average response time for the end users around the world is supposed to be one second at most without considering any network latencies. The following aspects must be analyzed and clarified:
 	
▶ Server sizing and performance
▶ Network sizing and performance
▶ Infrastructure of workstation and printer
▶ Operations
  ▸ 24/7 operation
  ▸ High availability
  ▸ Planned and unplanned downtimes
  ▸ Utilization and job processing
  ▸ Maintenance work

5.2.2 Server Sizing

To determine the required hardware capacity, you must first plan the required hardware. This process is called "sizing."[4] The sizing procedure is carried out in collaboration with the enterprise's IT team, the hardware supplier or partner, and SAP, if required. SAP offers the *Quick Sizer*[5] tool, which enables you to initially estimate the required hardware

---

4 Only a short overview is given here. More details can be found in the SAP Service Marketplace at *http://service.sap.com/sizing*.

5 See details at *http://service.sap.com/quicksizer*.

performance by using technical and application-specific key data of the enterprise.

The Quick Sizer calculates the demand categories for the CPU, hard disk, and main memory, which are based on the performance key figures and the number of users for various SAP Business Suite components, and are platform-independent. The result is an estimate of the required hardware capacity, which is used as an initial approximation for hardware and infrastructure planning. In cooperation with the hardware partners, the Quick Sizer results are refined in an iterative process until the concrete plan for the hardware is available.

Quick Sizer

For appropriate hardware sizing, it makes sense to provide a platform-independent performance index that indicates hardware performance with regard to SAP applications. This enables hardware providers to measure concrete hardware models, including various equipment, and to publish their performance (similar to the horsepower of a car).

In the sizing process and the individual sizing steps, which are based on the enterprise's IT solution requirements, an index value is calculated that the hardware must deliver. On the one hand, this index is used to give a general overview of the performance of the existing installation, and on the other hand, it forms the basis for a rough estimation of the size of the infrastructure planned for the SAP operation.

The SAP Application Performance Standard (SAPS) index indicates how many SD order items (*order line items*) the SAP system can process per time unit. The SAPS value is determined by executing the SD benchmark, which is a clearly defined sequence of steps in the sales and distribution area of the SAP system. One hundred SAPS correspond to 2,000 completely processed order items per hour in the SD-application benchmark standard, or 6,000 dialog steps, or 2,400 SAP SD transactions per hour.[6]

SAP Application Performance Standard (SAPS)

The definition of SAPS is based on the business-relevant process and consequently is independent of the special configuration or the version used. Therefore, it is suitable for sizing global solutions.

---

6 See *http://service.sap.com/benchmark*.

Table 5.2 shows a benchmark excerpt of the maximum measures achieved for real production systems. This is intended to give you a general idea of the maximum possible performance of state-of-the-art hardware and show where a single-instance solution has its limits.[7]

Measurement Values	Result
Highest SD benchmark achieved in 2005	Approx. 850,000 SAPS with 16 million processed SD order items per hour
Actual number of active users	Between 3,000+ and 12,000+
Actually achieved SAPS at customers in continuous operation	>100,000
Actual database size	15 TB

Table 5.2 Selection of Maximum Benchmark References

So, if we assume 100,000 SAPS in the actual production system, this means that approximately 2,400 × 1,000 = 2.4 million SD standard transactions per hour can be achieved — a very impressive number. The technical limits of a single instance are extremely high if you combine the possible number of several thousand active users, and if you assume that Moore's law applies (see Chapter 3, Figure 3.1). Consequently, it is very likely that a single instance using SAP ERP applications for a global enterprise can be implemented on the server side; however, this is only possible if the network and the front-end infrastructure have equally high performance.

5.2.3 Network Sizing and Infrastructure

Powerful network to worldwide locations

An average response time of approximately one second is often required for the single instance and consists of multiple runtimes — essentially, the front end, the network, and the server runtime.[8] The front-end runtime is the processing time on the end user's computer. The network runtime is the transfer time from the end user to the SAP system, and vice versa. The *server runtime* is the retention period of the dialog step in the SAP system from request to response.

---

7 See *http://service.sap.com/benchmark*, **SAP Standard Application Benchmarks • Published Results**, where benchmark measures are regularly published.

8 This is a simplified model; we won't go into detail within the scope of this book.

Because the end users work at different locations around the world, high capacity requirements are placed on the remote connection network. Today, it is more likely that a global single instance fails due to a slow network than a slow server.

A rough estimate of the maximum response time of one second can be assessed to perform a server runtime of 800 msec, a network time of 100 – 200 msec and a negligible front-end runtime. Whereas runtimes for the server and front-end don't constitute problems, the network runtime is somewhat more complex.

To simplify things, let's assume that the end users work almost exclusively at the SAP GUI front end.[9] If Internet browser-based applications are used — for instance, the SAP NetWeaver portal — you must implement additional analyses.

Required network bandwidth

To calculate the bandwidth, you must evaluate how many simultaneously active users transfer data volume, respectively, per time unit bidirectionally via the network. If the end user works at the SAP GUI front end, you can assume an average of 2.5 KB to 6 KB per dialog step; for the Internet browser, it's about 15 KB. Every minute, about three dialog steps are executed by each user. If you know the number of simultaneously active users in a network segment, you can derive the minimum bandwidth for the dialog mode. For this purpose, you must add all other data flows, such as, email, printout, file transfer, Internet use, and so on.

Network *latency* generally refers to the runtime of a data package in the network. This corresponds to previously described network runtime. Example values are: 10 – 20 msec in a LAN, 50 – 250 msec in a wire-based WAN, and 200 – 600 msec via satellite. However, the data package isn't directly and immediately transferred, but travels via dial-in and via multiple intermediate stations, transmission nodes, and routers, depending on the network provider. This results in additional technical maintenance or delay times for dial-in or the transmission nodes, which can considerably extend the entire network runtime. Whereas the solution of the dial-in problem is fairly easy, the wait times in the transmission

Network latency

---

9 Details, information, and network requirements when using SAP GUI can be found in *SAP AG: Frontend Network Requirements for SAP Solutions,* vol. 5.2, March 2003; and at *http://service.sap.com/SAPGUI.*

nodes can be directly influenced. Therefore, this problem can only be solved via the network provider.

To keep the network runtime within the required time frame of approximately 100 msec, maximum, the network provider must meet the following requirements:

- High availability of the network in 24/7 operation, including an alternative, backup network
- Guaranteed minimum bandwidth, also for temporary high load
- Stable and low latency in the transmission nodes
- Minor to no data loss
- High security
- Provision of different service level agreements
- Network service and support with 24/7 availability

5.2.4 Workstation Infrastructure

To support the end users, you must establish internal IT support for all global offices to deal with the users' issues. Frequently, it is challenging to determine a company-wide global infrastructure for the end users' workstations. In particular, the local specifics in various countries are a major problem, because they require different software due to the necessary language support — for example, a Japanese Windows XP version for the subsidiary in Japan. The same problem applies for printers that require special hardware (e.g., font add-ons) to print the necessary text. This requires good planning, and the collaboration of the central IT team at the data center and the local support team at the subsidiaries. Due to local specifics in the countries, which are primarily determined by the language support, it is generally not possible to establish a globally uniform workstation infrastructure — and particularly workstation software. However, they should be central, if possible. Generally, the following recommendations apply:[10]

---

[10] See *http://service.sap.com/globalization*, *http://service.sap.com/I18N*, and the numerous SAP Notes on this subject for further details and information.

▶ If possible, use globally uniform workstation software — for example, Microsoft Windows XP.

▶ Only use different local workstation software when it's absolutely necessary, such as Japanese Microsoft Windows XP in Japan.

▶ Use uniform versions and service packs of workstation software also for special countries — for example, Microsoft Windows XP SP2 also for Japan.

▶ Establish globally uniform SAP workstations, software strategies, versions, and patch levels, in particular for SAP GUI, but also for independent software, such as Microsoft Internet Explorer for working with Web-based SAP applications.

▶ Configure local Microsoft Windows settings for the SAP GUI software, as well as for each language to enable the language support for the various countries and the optimal fonts, the character set of the language, the upload and download of files, including local text (*internationalization with the I18N flag*). This applies to SAP Unicode and non-Unicode systems, though Unicode features considerably less configuration. In order to roll out a highly global SAP GUI configuration that supports all SAP languages and enables mixed logins in SAP Unicode and non-Unicode systems on a workstation, you should use version SAP GUI 6.40 or higher and set the I18N flag independent of the SAP Business Suite components release (Menu Path in SAP GUI 6.40: **Menu • Adjust Local Layout • Options • Activate Multibyte Functionality**). Then, only minor settings for the local workstations must be implemented.

▶ Provide central and automatic update tools on the local workstations for the SAP software. To enable highly efficient maintenance and support for the workstation software, you should use appropriate tools, which will automatically import the necessary patches, updates, and so on when the computer is started.

Recommendations for uniform workstation software and configurations

Using Windows Terminal Servers

If network bottlenecks occur (probably only in specific countries), then the end users' workcenter computers are inadequately equipped, or the software maintenance of local workstations is too time-consuming. In

Citrix Terminal Server

this case, it makes sense to use Windows Terminal Servers, such as Citrix Servers.[11] The end user logs on to the terminal server via configured client software — for example, Citrix ICA — on which the complete workstation software is installed, including SAP GUI and additional software. The user's local PC then becomes a simple terminal that only manages the keyboard input and displays. The users' actual work is done on the remote server. This results in the following benefits:

▸ The workstation software is installed and maintained on a central terminal server, and the end user doesn't have to worry about anything.

▸ Today, terminal server technology is very reliable and stable.

▸ On a Citrix Server, more than 50 active users can work at the same time.

▸ Intelligent compression methods enable considerable optimization of network traffic between the user and terminal server.

▸ If mobile users must log on from outside the company network, Citrix offers an appropriate and secure solution by providing additional security hardware and software (e.g. SMART cards).

▸ To configure the workstation software, you must consider the necessary local requirements of the users, if required; for instance, you must install Japanese language support and a supported input method (IME) on the Japanese server workstation.

▸ SAP front-end printout is supported from the Windows Terminal Server.

5.2.5 Printer Infrastructure

Printer support for all languages

In general, printer infrastructure is centrally implemented by a global IT team. In other words, the printer hardware is planned and selected centrally, and then communicated to the appropriate IT support team of the respective subsidiary that purchases, installs, and connects the printers. In practice, the trend is toward the use of fast, efficient, and inexpensive network printers that enable direct printout via the company network.

---

11 For details, see *www.citrix.com*.

Often, special printer management systems are established to achieve additional functionality and a high throughput.

The ideal scenario for a globally uniform printer infrastructure is an SAP Unicode system in which you only deploy Unicode printers.[12] This enables you to print documents in any language and with any character set, without limitations and wherever you want. Today, these printers are still very expensive and slow, or they don't have the appropriate fonts. Therefore, printers are used that support only languages with a few or only one character set(s) or a code page(s) — for instance, only the Western or Eastern European languages. If you want to print other character sets or code pages (e.g., Russian or an Asian language), you must integrate special hardware add-ons with the printer, such as *font cartridges* or a *DIMM module*. You must also ensure that an appropriate SAP device type is deployed, using the correct printer configuration for this hardware add-on.

Unicode and non-Unicode printers with font add-ons

Today, there are thousands of different printer models on the market. From a technical point of view, printers are still quite standalone devices that must be provided with special configurations and programming. To some extent, you must use hexadecimal-like encoding for things like *Printer Control Language (PCL)*. In many cases, it is therefore necessary to develop separate SAP device types for these printers, including hardware extensions if they are not provided in the SAP standard. You must take this into account when planning the printer infrastructure.

Less-complex solutions without hardware add-ons use software-based procedures in which the suitable font is loaded for the required language or the printout is implemented in the SAP system via Microsoft Windows printer management, which supports thousands of printer models and all languages. For printouts via Microsoft Windows, you can create an appropriate font, including the respective character sets and the SAP device type, in the SAP Unicode system by deploying *cascading font technology*.[13] This method enables fast and easy installation of all lan-

Multilingual printouts via Microsoft Windows

---

12 SAP currently supports Unicode printers made by Hewlett Packard and Lexmark (as of 2007). Additional models are provided by SAP partners.

13 For details, see Nils Bürckel, Alexander Davidenkoff, and Detlef Werner, *Unicode in SAP Systems*. SAP PRESS, 2007.

guages. However, they are considerably slower, create higher network loads between the SAP server and the printer, and usually don't permit direct control of LAN network printers. Generally, the following recommendations apply:

▶ When planning and selecting printers, you should consider the support of all languages within the global IT solution as the core criterion, right from the very beginning.

▶ You should consider using Unicode printers.

▶ Printers with simple character sets or single code pages are supported in SAP Unicode systems and enable printing in the languages of the supported character set.

▶ It is recommendable to deploy printers with highly established printer programming languages, like PostScript or PCL.

▶ If you want to use printers with special language or font add-ons (hardware), you should gather detailed information from the manufacturers about the following issues: Which languages are supported with this add-on? Where and how can you purchase these add-ons? Does the manufacturer provide global technical support? Does an SAP device type already exist for this hardware add-on?

▶ You should implement plans for the development or adaptation of SAP device types for the selected printers and add-ons if they are not SAP-standard.

▶ When using software-based device types, take into account slower printouts and higher network loads.

▶ Printers with special hardware add-ons require collaboration between global and local IT support teams, or an expert for special solutions must be a member of the global data center team.

All of the points mentioned similarly apply to peripheral devices that are equipped with special hardware due to local requirements, such as to create and send faxes in the local language. The software adaptation and control of these devices is similar to the printers, provided that this has not yet been implemented in the standard software.

5.3   Operating an SAP Single-Instance System

In this section, we'll explain how you can ensure the secure, high-performance, and uninterrupted operation a single-instance system. If an enterprise has decided to implement a central single-instance architecture, it must consider whether it is practical to operate the system 24/7 on a global scale.

5.3.1   Downtimes and Availability

One of the greatest obstacles to the operation of a global, single-instance solution is the issue of downtime, even if the hardware and network capacity is sufficient. Due to 24/7 operation, the system must be available around the clock. There are no day shifts or night shifts for maintenance work, because the system is always in use because of the global structure of the enterprise. The question therefore arises: How do we manage downtimes?

Critical factors: downtime and availability

> **Note**
>
> We must mention one very important fact right at the beginning: 100 % technical availability of the system is not possible.

You must therefore try to come as close to 100 % availability as possible, while keeping the effort at a reasonable level. (The closer you get to the 100 % mark, availability increases exponentially.) In practice, you can achieve approximately 99.0 % to 99.9 % availability with justifiable effort. If an enterprise can't accept this limit, it should use a decentralized architecture. It is definitely worthwhile to discuss and examine all options, such as whether you must really build and operate a completely new system landscape due to a small percentage of downtime, assuming are no other reasons. Table 5.3 shows the high-availability scale for IT systems, including respective properties.[14]

---

14 More details are available at *http://service.sap.com/ha*.

Availability (%)	Downtime Per Week	Action	Downtime Per Year	Action
Hypothetical				
99.9999	0.5 sec.		26 sec.	
99.999	6 sec.	Weekly switchover (*)	5 min.	One restart per year
99.99	1 min.	Daily switchover	52 min.	One maintenance per year
Realistic				
99.9	10 min.	One restart per week	8 hr. 45 min.	One offline backup per year
99.0	1 hr. 40 min.	Offline software maintenance	87.5 hr.	Quarterly maintenance and import of support packages, upgrades, Unicode conversions
90.0	16 hr. 48 min.	One offline backup per year	36 days	Weekly offline maintenance
(*) Switchover to the standby system.				

Table 5.3 Exemplary High-Availability Scale

As you can see in the table, for a pragmatic, realistic approach, it is generally sufficient to stop the system at quarterly intervals to implement more-extensive maintenance work while the planned availability is still at 99%. These may include the import of support packages, or even an upgrade, or the implementation of Unicode conversion.

High availability   Today, every hardware manufacturer provides a suitable high-availability (HA) solution for the respective platforms. SAP technology supports and continuously extends its portfolio of HA solutions for SAP components.

You can therefore assume that suitable HA can be planned for the global, single-instance system. The following facts must be taken into account:

▶ Avoid SPOFs (*single points of failure*) — that is, technically central components whose failure affects the entire system or large parts thereof. All SPOF components must be redundantly available.

▶ Use an HA solution for the database and the application server. There are numerous solutions available on the market.

▶ Use a special and highly secure HA solution for the central SAP services message server and the enqueue server, because they constitute critical central SPOFs.

▶ Use an HA solution for shared file systems.

▶ Use HA solutions that have minimum effects on the end users.

You must generally differentiate between planned and unplanned downtimes:

Downtimes

▶ **Planned downtime**
Planned downtimes are announced well beforehand, such as to carry out specific maintenance work on the system. Reasons for planned downtimes include the import of support packages and crucial corrections, the adaptation of critical system parameters that can't be done online, upgrades to a new SAP release, migrations, Unicode conversions, and other activities that were planned far in advance.

Planned downtime is usually not very critical. You must precisely plan these downtimes for the global IT support team well in advance (about one year ahead). In practice, weekend downtimes (quarterly) are pretty useful.

▶ **Unplanned downtime**
Unplanned downtime can occur due to sudden and unexpected events, such as system failure or urgently required corrections, but also serious errors in an application that requires the recovery of the database. This may be necessary, for example, if a deletion report has incorrectly erased production data.

According to a study conducted by the Gartner Group, unplanned downtimes are caused by hardware errors (20%), operating errors

(40%), and application errors (40%).[15] Today, a modern, high-availability solution and improved operation enable you to manage any kind of system failure without data loss or long downtimes. Downtimes due to operating or application errors (80%) are more problematic, because they are the result of human error. You must also consider unexpected emergency corrections or other urgent reasons to shut down the system.

You can remedy this with improved and simplified system management, including new simple and secure tools. To reduce application problems, you can hold training, as well as improve change and problem management, and support the end users efficiently. High-quality implementation is also a very good preventive measure against the execution of unwanted deletion reports.

Figure 5.1 shows an overview of frequently required maintenance work during planned downtimes, including their intervals and durations.

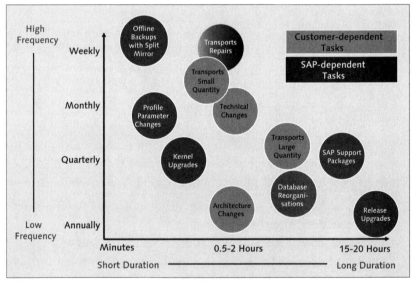

Figure 5.1 Typical Maintenance Work on Global Systems During Planned Downtimes

---

15 Gartner Group, *"Gartner Group's Networked Systems Management Research Note QA-05-2701,"* July 29, 1998, *www.gartner.com/webletter/ibmglobal/edition2/ article5/ article5.html.*

5.3.2 Specific Recommendations for Reducing Planned Downtimes

Experience with thousands of SAP production systems has shown that specific recurring activities and practices require the shutdown of the global system. In many cases, however, you can avoid shutdown by using optimal functions and measures in system administration. But these are usually not known. Moreover, SAP continuously develops improvements and new functions to reduce downtimes. In the following sections we'll present some of the most critical functions and recommendations that can reduce downtimes. Because we can't describe all methods and recommendations in this book, interested readers are referred to special documentation, such as *"Architecting a High Availability SAP NetWeaver Infrastructure,"* by Matt Kangas.[16]

▶ **Soft shutdown of application servers (as of SAP WEB AS 6.20)**   Selected recommendations
You can shutdown an application server and completely stop running activities, but you can't accept new requests that are redirected to other application servers. Therefore, the application server is shutdown in a 'soft' manner without interrupting the running operation.

▶ **Use of operation modes, and online system parameter changes**
The SAP CCMS (*Computer Center Management System*) supports the dynamic change in operation modes when changing the type of work processes. For instance, you can select the appropriate operation modes in accordance with a given time profile. For example, three additional dialog processes can be scheduled within 24 hours, each running for 60 minutes. These are required for the three continents — Asia-Pacific, EMEA, and America — when the local business hours start, and consequently system logins result in peak demands of the dialog mode. CCMS operation mode switching is also suitable for planning required background processes on a specific server for long background jobs. Using CCMS functionality, you can change many SAP system parameters in online mode without having to stop the application server. However, this doesn't apply to all parameters.

---

16 *SAP Professional Journal,* March/April 2007, *www.sappro.com.*

▶ **Rolling kernel switch**

Soon, you will be provided with a new procedure to import an SAP kernel patch, and you don't have to stop the entire system. This means that the SAP system is still available during the kernel switch. In the rolling kernel switch procedure, the application servers are provided with new kernel patches consecutively, and not simultaneously. For this purpose, you must use kernel patches that are compatible. Then you can shut down each application server individually, switch the kernel, and restart the application server. At the end of this procedure, all application servers should have the same kernel patch number. This procedure will be released in the near future. Interested readers may contact SAP to obtain further information.[17] Figure. 5.2 illustrates this procedure. Note that the SAP Message and Enqueue Service should be operated with high availability and (ideally) separately.

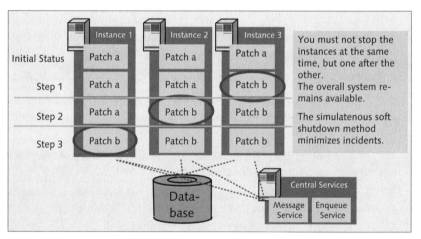

Figure 5.2 Rolling Kernel Switch Procedure

▶ **Import of support packages with minimal downtime**

In order to quickly import the SAP support packages that comprise SAP standard software components, and the add-on components of the industry solutions and add-on country versions within the planned downtime, you should use the following procedures and techniques:

---

17 See *http://service.sap.com/patches*.

Using the *shadow import method*, you import support packages into shadow objects without interrupting online operation. Then, you must stop the system to transfer the shadow objects to the active objects and activate them. The advantage of this is that the long import time for the objects is omitted during downtime. Figure 5.3 shows an overview of this procedure.

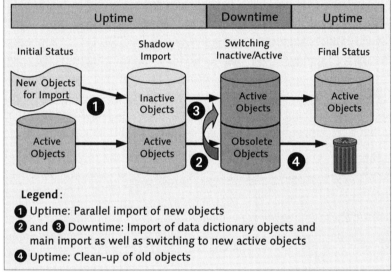

Figure 5.3 Support Package Shadow Import Procedure

Many activities and checks occur once per support package queue — for example, the creation of objects. If not defined otherwise, you should import queues including as many support packages as possible so that these checks are carried out only once. You can combine this with the quarterly planned downtime, because several support packages accrue during this time period. This information about the support packages also applies to other packages that are installed using the same or a similar technique — for example, the SAP Enhancement Packages available as of SAP ERP 6.0.[18]

---

18 See *http://service.sap.com/erp*.

Daylight saving
time and standard
time

▸ **Changeover from daylight savings time to standard time, and vice versa**

If the time zone of the global system includes daylight savings time, the system times are adjusted by one hour twice per year. For the end users, this can constitute a deviation of up to two hours when the clocks are adjusted to daylight savings time in the northern hemisphere and to standard time in the southern hemisphere (or vice versa). The changeover from standard to daylight savings time usually does not constitute any problems and requires no downtime, while for the changeover from daylight to standard time, it is recommended to stop the system for two hours. We recommend using the UTC (Universal Time Coordinate) system time zone, which doesn't have any standard or daylight savings time, to avoid the problems that occur during the changeover from standard to daylight savings time. For more information, please refer to Section 4.5.2, "Time Zones."

If this is not an option, and if this planned downtime cannot be used for maintenance activities, you can consider using a new special feature as of SAP WEB AS 6.40:

During the changeover from daylight savings time to standard time, the 'double hour' (usually between 2:00 a.m. and 3:00 a.m.) runs twice within a period of two hours, whereas the clock of the SAP system runs at half the speed and consequently progresses by only one hour. Therefore, the backward leap in time is avoided. The deviation of the SAP system time and the official time increases to –30 minutes during the first hour, then leaps to +30 minutes, and finally goes back to zero minutes in the second hour. The values of the SAP ABAP system time and date (SY-UZEIT/SY-DATUM fields), for example, do not correspond with the official time during changeover. Please refer to SAP Note 7417 for further details and prerequisites.

5.3.3 Utilization and Job Processing

High continuous
load around the
clock

Another very critical issue for the global single-instance solution is how the high loads of job processing (background processing) match with the dialog processing of the end user. Due to the 24/7 operation around the globe, there is no night during which you can carry out resource-intensive background jobs and similar administrative activities. Consequently, you must take specific measures to manage the continuous load of dialog work and background jobs.

Practical experience has shown that successful global single-instance customers always use strict plans with predefined time windows that must be met for job processing. First, you must determine the load distribution for dialog and background operation within 24 hours. This forms the basis for the measures to be taken. Figure 5.4 shows an example of a typical load distribution for an accepted global single-instance system with end users in America, EMEA, and Asia.

Strict time windows for job processing

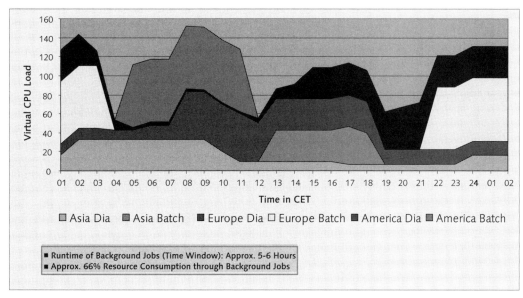

Figure 5.4 Example of CPU Load Distribution for Dialog and Background Operation (Batch) Within 24 Hours

You can see that approximately three time windows of up to six hours must be provided for the background jobs (batch) for each continent/region. This means that the background jobs run for two-thirds of the day and consequently require 66% of the CPU. The following general recommendations for managing this situation have proven themselves in real global single-instance systems:

Job processing recommendations

▶ Strictly organize and schedule background jobs in the given time windows (it may be helpful to use an external job-management system).

▶ Use time-dependent SAP CCMS operation modes to configure more or less background work processes for specific times.

▶ Use one or more separate application servers only for background operation.

▶ Use adaptive-computing technology to dynamically connect additional hardware resources for peak loads.

▶ Analyze and tune programs for the background operation. Frequently, background jobs are unnecessarily long because the design or the selection parameters arc unfavorable. Or, they are customer developments whose programming has low performance and high-tuning potential.

5.3.4 SAP Solution Manager

Universal tool for support

You can use SAP Solution Manager to efficiently support the running operation.[19] It includes numerous functions (e.g., system monitoring and service desk for user support) that enable optimal support of global solutions and help reduce downtimes. Further critical functions are the change management and test management that are used to reduce the effort for recurring maintenance work — for example, support package imports. Here, a central test management is implemented along with automated test tools, such as SAP eCATT, *extended Computer Aided Test Tool*, or *Mercury Loadrunner*.[20] SAP Solution Manager complies with ITIL standards for IT service and application management, and can easily be integrated with the service and support processes of a data center. Figure 5.5 shows an overview of SAP Solution Manager functions.

Of course, there are more aspects that play decisive roles for the planning and operation of a global single-instance solution. To describe them in great detail, however, would go far beyond the scope of this book. Interested readers may refer to the numerous special literature that is available at the SAP Service Marketplace *(http://service.sap.com)* and the SAP Developer Network *(http://sdn.sap.com)*.

---

19 See Matthias Melich and Marc O. Schäfer, *SAP Solution Manager*. SAP PRESS, 2006; and *http://service.sap.com/solutionmanager*.

20 See *www.mercury.com* for more details.

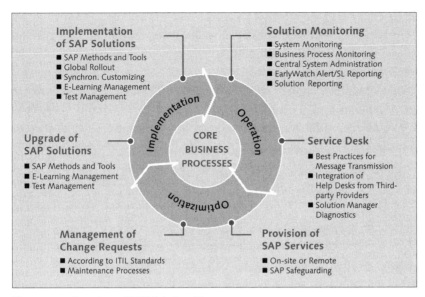

Figure 5.5 Overview of SAP Solution Manager

5.4 Implementing Global SAP Projects in the Selected Architecture

In addition to the critical question of the operation of a single-instance solution, planning and implementation of global projects also places high demands on the IT team. In this section, we'll describe how to set up an appropriate customizing and development environment for a global project, appropriate procedures for internal release and project planning, as well as the proven global template procedure for the corporate rollout.

5.4.1 Global System Development and Configuration

A very critical factor for selecting the appropriate architecture is the question: How can the global solution be implemented and maintained with regard to development and customizing? In Chapter 4, we described the different architectures and explained the most critical aspects. We established that you can centrally set up development and customizing, even for a decentralized architecture.

Complex and extensive development in global projects

223

In practice, large global enterprises often complain that the entire global IT solution has become unclear over the years, and that they have neither complete documentation or personnel with an overview of all live, used developments. As a result, thousands of customer developments are created and must be maintained. Most of them are independent of each other and have function redundancies. Therefore, the question arises as to whether a central development is possible in addition to decentralized development in an architecture with a decentralized orientation.

Three-system transport landscape and client concept

For the development and configuration of an SAP ERP system, you must consider how many SAP clients are required and for what purposes. Concerning this matter, there is no perfect solution, because the client characteristics depend very much on the individual requirements, the organization of the development and configuration project team, and the defined processes. The following recommendation applies to the often exceptional case that the development and configuration work is coordinated centrally, and that it follows the general SAP recommendations for a three-system transport landscape, including a DEV system for development and customizing, a QAS system for consolidation and testing, a PRD system for live operations, as well as (potentially) additional systems for training, sandboxing, and so on.

You can take corrective measures directly in the PRD or QAS system in case of emergency. However, they must always be integrated with the DEV system to ensure the source principle. In other words, you must maintain the latest version of each development object centrally to avoid inconsistencies due to different versions. This sounds reasonable and simple, but in practice, implementation is rather difficult and requires careful planning in a large global project with thousands of development objects.

The following recommendations for client configuration primarily apply to a central architecture, but can also be used for other architectures. We would like to point out that the client concept is only suitable for ABAP developments and applications, and other procedures apply to Java-based development and configuration. We won't detail these; rather, interested readers are referred to the documentation and relevant literature, for instance: Karl Kessler, Peter Tillert, and Panayot Dobrikov, *Java Programming with the SAP Web Application Server* (SAP PRESS, 2005).

Figure 5.6 shows a typical client concept for a global solution, central architecture.

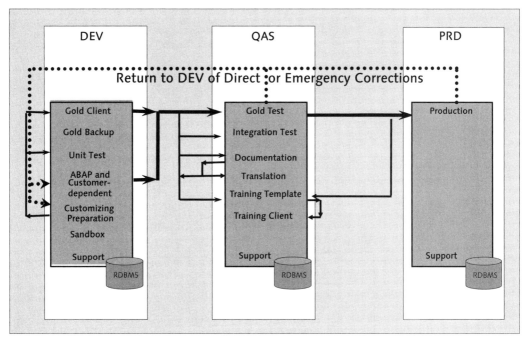

Figure 5.6 Client Concept in a Global System Landscape

Table 5.4 explains the individual client functions.

Client	Function
DEV System	
Gold client	Final customizing and configuration for QAS and PRD
Gold backup	Backup of the gold client
Unit test	Simple modular test for validating customer developments and simple applications
ABAP and client-independent objects	ABAP development
Customizing preparation	Customizing and configuration of the project

Table 5.4 ABAP Client Concept in a Global System

Client	Function
Sandbox	Playground
Support	Special client for SAP support
QAS system	
Gold test	Gold client for test
Integration test	Central test client including all master and transaction data, as well as interfaces for integration tests
Documentation	Documentation (if required)
Translation	Translation of customizing if not possible in DEV
Training template	Training for end user original
Training client	Hands-on training for end users, arbitrarily rebuilt, based on template
PRD system	
Production	Production client

Table 5.4 ABAP Client Concept in a Global System (Cont.)

You might be wondering why our global system client concept differs only slightly from the standard lifecycle recommendations for development and customizing in a simple system. Due to the (very) high volumes of development and customizing, this proven procedure is also a critical instrument for extensive global projects and an efficient lifecycle of the global IT solution, not only during the implementation phase, but also for maintenance in the production phase.

Client variants

Of course, there are many different variants of the clients and their functions, and every enterprise can set up additional clients. But, you should strictly ensure that the source principle is observed — in other words, that the developments and configurations, as well as their changes, are implemented at a central point. The settings for a client's changeability must be made accordingly. But you must also consider that you might not be able to manage the client administration via transports or RFC due to high volume if too many clients exist. Note that a client represents a logical system and consequently defines the architecture. So if you carry out development, final customizing activities, or the live operations in multiple clients, this is called a decentralized architecture.

5.4.2 Development and Configuration in Different Architectures

In a purely decentralized architecture, a three-system transport landscape is normally built for each production system. You therefore implement a separate development and configuration for each decentralized system. Generally, only a few or no joint objects exist that can be used for all systems. We have already explained in previous chapters that the distribution and independence is usually disadvantageous for a globally efficient IT solution, because all decentralized systems still belong to the same enterprise. Nevertheless, this architecture makes sense and is the only solution in specific cases, if, for example, SAP components with different releases are used due to their different scope of functions, or if an SAP Unicode system is mandatory for the introduction of new countries and languages, and the existing system landscape can't be converted into Unicode (yet).

The other architectures that use shared services (described in Chapter 3), and the centralized decentralized architecture and its variants enable a central development and configuration design by establishing the development and customizing system as a shared service system. You can also set up another central variant, which is referred to as a "template" system, in which you develop and configure the global template of the corporate headquarters. In both variants, central development and the template system play essential roles for the entire system landscape.

Template system

Ultimately, there is another variant that enables an even higher focus on the central architecture (although not central single instance). Using this variant enables you to centrally develop and consolidate in the global systems by means of global processes and the template method; the live operations, however, are always distributed to multiple systems. Therefore, this is also referred to as a *quasi-global architecture*. The reasons for distribution to multiple production systems may technical in nature — for example, performance or security reasons, or you are required to establish one production system per code page of a language group because no Unicode system exists.

To illustrate this situation, Figures 5.7 and 5.8 show four different global solution transport landscapes, from a decentralized architecture with regional alignment toward a central architecture — in this example, including Europe and Asia-Pacific. The figures show the following transport landscapes:

▸ **Three-system transport landscape per region**
This is the classical case of a fully decentralized architecture. A separate development system, DEV1 and DEV2, exists for each decentralized system, in which you can develop and configure locally. Transports are carried out for testing in the local QAS1 and QAS2 systems, and then in the local production systems PRD1 and PRD2. Overall, these are two independent, three-system transport landscapes that have only little or nothing in common.

▸ **Regionally coupled transport landscape**
This is a partially centralized development and configuration. A global development system, DEV, exists that is especially useful for creating corporate-wide global templates, which means that it performs a dedicated global partial function. The global template is then transferred to the decentralized development systems DEV1 and DEV2, in which you can implement local developments, depending on the requirements and the globally defined development processes and guidelines. Then, the global template is transported to the follow-up systems QAS1 and QAS2 for testing purposes. Subsequently, it is transferred to PRD1 and PRD2 for production. For this variant, it is vital to clearly define whether and which parts of the global template may be changed in DEV1 and DEV2. Generally, this should be limited, and changes should only be made if absolutely necessary, such as for urgent legal changes. The corporate-wide global development process is only harmonized to a limited extent.

A similar variant of this scenario has already been presented in Figure 3.10 (Chapter 3, "Overview of Architectures"). This variant has only one global development system instead of multiple regional development systems, so its combination with the global template system results in a higher degree of harmonization.

▸ **Regionally centralized transport landscape**
This is another centralization of the development. The decentralized development systems from the regionally coupled landscape are omit-

ted so that you can carry out the development and configuration of the global IT solution fully centrally. You determine a central development and configuration system in which all developments and configurations of all dependent decentralized systems are implemented. The decentralized systems only comprise QAS and PRD systems, and you may make only minor changes, if any at all. This is a shared services architecture, and its global IT solution development process is almost identical to the central single-instance architecture.

▶ **Centralized landscape using multiple production systems**
Here, central development is carried out in the central DEV system, and the consolidation and tests are also implemented with a central global approach in the QAS system. Only the live operation is distributed to multiple systems PRD1 and PRD2. All developments, configurations, and processes have a highly global alignment and support the global template approach. The production systems are often subdivided for technical reasons.

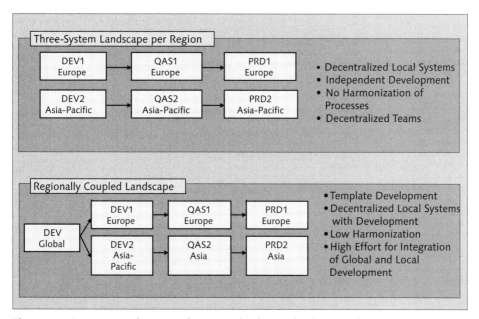

Figure 5.7 Transport Landscapes with Decentralized Centralized Oriented Architectures (1)

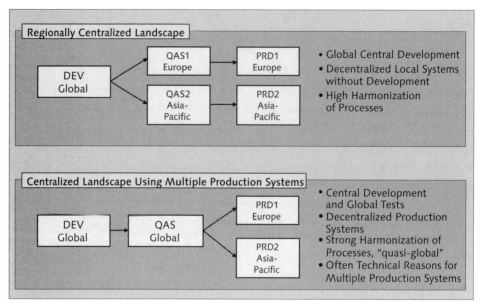

Figure 5.8 Transport Landscapes with Decentralized Centralized Oriented Architectures (2)

5.4.3 Release Management of Global IT Solutions

Customer release strategy for global solutions

In general, global solutions are highly dynamic. They are continuously developed to implement new countries or to install new applications and processes. The production system must also be maintained regularly. You must remedy errors and bugs, implement changes to the production solution (e.g., due to legal regulations), optimize critical functions, or modify configuration and customizing settings. For this purpose, you can use a more or less standardized development and transport process in the transport landscapes for the various architectures described in Section 5.4.2. This means that you can plan and implement new projects in addition to running the maintenance activities supported by different project, maintenance, or support teams.

New projects within the global IT solution are generally implemented in the underlying SAP release of the used components if no upgrade of the IT solution (or parts thereof) to a new SAP release is required due to other reasons — for example, if the project requires new functions that are not contained in the existing SAP release. For a central architecture approach that includes a central global system landscape, or for a combined architecture comprising a central development system, you must consider how to manage the combination of running maintenance and new project work with regard to the developments and configurations. Simply put, you must consider how to clearly separate developments, corrections, and configurations into maintenance and new projects within an existing global system landscape.

In practice, these are often underestimated. Consequently, development and customizing activities are implemented in a central development system without a clear definition of how you can separate them, customized to the concrete company-specific IT solution. The tools of the SAP development and transport environment provide suitable functions — for example, the SAP Transport Organizer, which supports the developments of project teams, the version management of the ABAP Workbench, or the namespace concept. Nevertheless, in large global systems, these are often not sufficient to ensure smooth live operation or introduce new complex projects and rollouts. A new project or rollout of the global enterprise may perform like a new SAP release of the underlying software components or add-ons of an industry solution. This means, however, that a new and particularly large project represents a new IT-specific, internal release of the existing solution.

Parallel maintenance and project work

But how can you implement the parallel operation of maintenance and new projects in the system landscape architecture efficiently? Here, it is reasonable to introduce a release management customized to the global IT solution, which is common practice in general IT. The release management has the following general tasks:

Recommendations for custom release management

▸ Determine the functional scope of the solution or project.

▸ Determine the exact schedule of the release rollout in coordination with project or product management.

▸ Monitor compliance with the criteria determined in the project or product management for release creation.

▸ Document the scope and changes, in particular, description of properties relevant for backward compatibility.

▸ Manage the version history (versioning) and consequently ensure reproducibility.

Therefore, the IT department of a global enterprise determines a custom internal release, and complies with the established standards and processes of the software lifecycle for each release. The release management considerably influences the system landscape architecture of the global IT solution. In other words, it significantly changes the system landscape, such as during an SAP upgrade or Unicode conversion. During an upgrade or a Unicode conversion, you must create new systems on which you can implement the necessary adaptations prior to the upgrade or Unicode conversion of the production system. This means that the entire system landscape comprises these additional systems for the duration of this activity. Therefore, we can subdivide the entire landscape of the IT solution — that is, all systems used for the running operation and new projects — into a maintenance landscape and project landscape.

For determining the system landscape for the internal release management, the conditions are similar to an SAP upgrade. However, there is one major difference: In contrast to a single SAP upgrade or a single Unicode conversion, at least two (or even more) internal releases must be supported for the entire system landscape. This is also called a "release" or "phase" system landscape. You require one release for the maintenance landscape of the running, live operation and one or more releases for the project landscape, including the development and consolidation system. In the following sections, we'll describe two general approaches of how you can implement a phase-dependent system landscape that results from the release management.[21]

In addition to the maintenance of the production components, you must also have an infrastructure that supports the implementation of new projects during live operation. The global IT solution therefore comprises multiple phases. For example, let us say the release status of the running production system is Release x, and the new project uses Release $x+1$. These release names are used only internally and only refer to the custom global solution. Generally, they are independent of the release status of the SAP production components. You can use them to better structure and manage your large global solutions. If you must upgrade the SAP components, this also comprises a new internal release status.

---

21 This description is highly simplified. The specific case must be considered carefully.

There are two basic options for implementing the phase-dependent system landscape:

▶ **Two transport landscapes for maintenance and project work**
For the running operation of the production component in Release x, the existing three-system transport landscape is used, which is also referred to as the maintenance landscape.

For the new project with Release x+1, another transport landscape (project landscape, release landscape) is used with a custom development and consolidation system. All corrections made to the maintenance landscape in Release x must be transferred to the project landscape of Release x+1 and synchronized with the new development.

This transfer and synchronization can be rather complex, and must be elaborated in great detail. It is decisive that the maintenance and project landscape system coexist in the entire system landscape architecture. If the new project goes live with Release x+1, all new developments and configurations are transported to the production system during the transfer (switch-over), and the production system is upgraded to Release x+1. The previous development and consolidation system becomes part of the maintenance landscape for production Release x+1, and the previous development and consolidation system with Release x+1 becomes part of the project landscape for another new project with status Release x+2. For an SAP upgrade or other migration activity (e.g., Unicode conversions, operating system and database migrations, system consolidations, etc.), you generally must use this procedure.

Coexistence of the maintenance and project landscape

Figure 5.9 shows the solution landscape, including the maintenance and project landscape. The maintenance landscape comprises the systems DEV1, QAS1, and PRD; and the project landscape consists of DEV2 and QAS2. You can implement all developments and corrections intended for Release x centrally in DEV1. If the developments in the maintenance area are transported to the test system QAS1, and subsequently to the production system PRD, they must also be transported or replicated to the system DEV2, because each change in Release x must also be implemented or synchronized in Release x+1.

If you work on the same object in DEV2 that was changed in Release x, such as new functionality, the problem arises of how to synchronize the changes of Release x with the developments of Release x+1. So, if you transport the object from DEV1 to DEV2, you overwrite possible changes in Release x+1. In this case, you must use specific procedures, such as version management and solutions from the SAP software logistics (e.g., transport workflow), which we won't detail here. At this point, we would like to mention that the functions in the change management of SAP Solution Manager 4.0 provide good support in this matter.

When Release x+1 goes live, the production system is changed, and all new developments and configurations from Release x+1 are transported to PRD. Here again, you must ensure synchronization with Release x. Figure 5.9 shows this approach with two transport landscapes, including a (simplified) maintenance and project landscape.

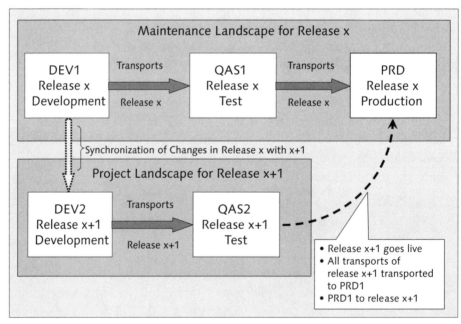

Figure 5.9 Maintenance and Project System Landscape

▶ **One transport landscape for maintenance and project work**
You implement the new project on the existing transport landscape. That is, there is no separation between the running maintenance of the production component in Release x and the implementation of the new project in Release x+1.

To ensure a clear separation of maintenance and project work — which can be very complex in a large global solution — you must define a very clear process for separating the development and configuration of maintenance in Release x and project work in Release x+1. For this purpose, you can deploy a sound versioning concept. To support these processes, special tools are developed and used. This concept is only possible if the underlying SAP components change only slightly (or not at all) from Release x to Release x+1. It can be used for Unicode conversions (due to the support of mixed Unicode/ non-Unicode transports, which is not recommended), but not for SAP upgrades or migrations.[22]

Versioning Concept

5.4.4 Corporate Rollout that Includes a Global Template Approach

Globally active enterprises often want to implement projects that concern the entire corporate structure and consequently have a pronounced global character. Most of these enterprises, however, are not able to use the central global single-instance architecture for their global IT solution. There are many reasons for this.

Global rollouts

A major problem exists if the system landscape has a historically decentralized development so that consolidation in a central system is too complex, and the processes and data are implemented and operated individually and locally at the global locations without a common basis for the corporate headquarters.

Subsequently, most of these enterprises have discovered that it can be beneficial and cost-efficient for IT to centralize specific components in the system landscape, and harmonize and standardize certain processes

---

22 This is possible if the SAP release supports the live Unicode components. See *http:// service.sap.com/unicode* and SAP Note 79991 for details.

and data that are uniform for all countries and enterprise departments that must be compatible with the local solutions. The degree of freedom for the individual solutions will be reduced at the local locations.

Therefore, you must find a common denominator for the SAP concept that is based on global requirements. Building on this, you can develop a basic solution that is rolled out to the various subsidiaries and then individually extended.

Global template approach

A sound approach for a global project that uses these determining factors is the corporate rollout, including a global template approach (introduced in Section 3.2), which we considered for our architecture discussions. A global template defines the common elements, processes, data, and objects across all enterprise areas and departments, and includes regional and local specifics if the components are mandatory for the business model. The template often contains all master data, standards, and definitions of the business 'best practices' that are implemented across the entire group. This enables you to centrally control the global business processes and data, and make the necessary changes and adaptations at the local locations. This approach particularly enables you to efficiently use either a partially or fully central system architecture, as displayed in Figure 5.8.

We want to illustrate this in a concrete example. A customer uses a shared services or centralized decentralized architecture and wants to replace his locally operated SAP ERP system (which has evolved over several years) with a global SAP ERP template. This template was created by corporate headquarters and has been operated in some countries. Multiple country organizations have already been merged into a local SAP system whose classification has been ensured by means of different company codes. Other countries will introduce the new template at the same time as the customer. In this project, an extensive testing period is granted. In addition to the new 'custom' SAP world, it must also be ensured that all peripheral applications affected by the changes and the 'going-live' scenarios are subject to intensive tests. Multiple test cycles should be carried out: unit tests, integration tests, and dry runs. In this context, numerous activities must be closely coordinated with the areas of responsibility within corporate headquarters and the participating country organizations. Another critical task in this project is the organizational preparation of the business areas for the software conversion and subsequent modification of the daily processes. How can this project be achieved?

A well-established change concept for the global template is the three-level approach:

Three-level change concept

1. The first level comprises global elements that are planned, implemented, and maintained exclusively by a central team at the corporate headquarters, and which must not change in decentralized systems or organizations. Examples are corporate-wide reports that are identical in all national organizations, or the central assignment of numbers to the various business objects — for instance, orders that must be clearly determined across all organizations and systems. From the technical point of view, this concept corresponds to a GUID (*Globally Unique Identifier*).[23]

2. The second level consists of harmonized elements. The central team plans and creates these elements, as well. Unlike unchangeable global elements, however, these can be changed to a certain extent by the local organizations and systems; for example, master data of business partners must contain additional fields due to legal regulations in the various countries (for instance, for tax purposes), and this must be reflected on the respective systems. These special fields can be added and processed locally (changeability) without changing the company-wide master data (enabling only specific changes).

3. The third level contains local elements that can be changed completely and processed by the local team in coordination with the central team. Of course, the local changes must be in line with the global

---

23 A *Globally Unique Identifier* is a unique number that is used in distributed computer systems. A GUID is an implementation of the *Universally Unique Identifier standard*. For example, a group of eight subsidiaries has multiple customer files with customer numbers. The customer number is supposed to be unique within the group. The members of the group agree that the numbers added at Location One always end with the number one. Accordingly, the numbers of Location Two would end with two, and so on, see also *http://en.wikipedia.org/wiki/GUID*).

solution and must not exceed certain limitations. Local elements are particularly required due to legal regulations of the respective countries, or if a given application, business process, or part thereof is definitely inappropriate for a global or harmonized element.

Figure 5.10 illustrates the three-level concept of a global template.

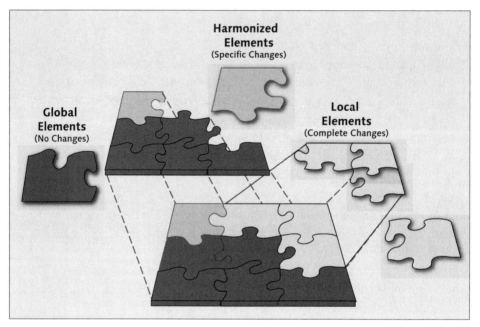

Figure 5.10 Three-Level Global Template Concept

Gradual/Phased rollouts in new countries

Gradual, or phased, rollouts enable you to implement partially central developments and configurations for a global IT solution controlled by local systems. This usually entails a significant improvement of the entire global IT solution. This approach is well suited, for example, for introducing a group of new countries (e.g., Asia). The used architecture still allows enough room to locally implement the legislations and business practices that may vary considerably in the various countries, while simultaneously keeping the global processes and data of the enterprise. You can use multiple tools, methodologies, and procedures to implement a global template project. SAP Solution Manager provides dedicated functionality for global template projects and corporate rollouts, which we'll summarize in the following sections.

Global Template Implementation Using the SAP Solution Manager

SAP Solution Manager provides a global template approach and corporate rollout functionality with which you can define business processes and customization centrally in a template. Within a corporate rollout scenario, one or more templates are defined at corporate headquarters that can be included in scenarios, blueprint documents, and configurations. The global team can decide which parts of the template are relevant for the subsidiaries — that is, for their decentralized systems — and whether, or to which degree the subsidiaries may change the template in the rollout projects.

The centrally defined template is transported to the subsidiaries' systems via transport tools. There, the template is used in the implementation project to implement local solutions in compliance with global specifications.

The corporate rollout project is supported by the Global ASAP (*Accelerated SAP*) procedure and methodology via a *Global Template Roadmap* that is provided in SAP Solution Manager (a screenshot of the roadmap is shown in Figure 5.11).[24] During individual project phases, you carry out project-specific activities — from planning to global rollout and commissioning of the decentralized production systems at the subsidiaries, to continuous maintenance. All developments and customizing activities in a central reference system are implemented as a development and configuration system, and distributed to the decentralized systems via transport mechanisms. It is defined which changes can be done centrally or decentralized.

Global ASAP

Figure 5.12 shows how you can develop the topology for the global development system within the system landscape during phase two: the global business blueprint of the Global Template Roadmap.

---

24 Additional information, references, and details can be found at the SAP Service Marketplace: *http://service.spa.com/asap* and *http://service.sap.lcom/solutionmanager.*

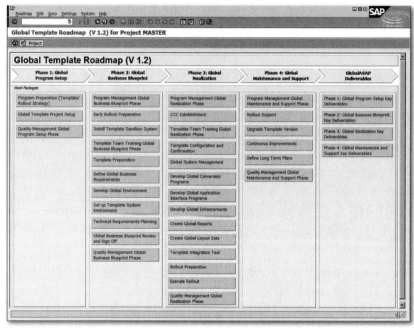

Figure 5.11 Global Template Roadmap in SAP Solution Manager

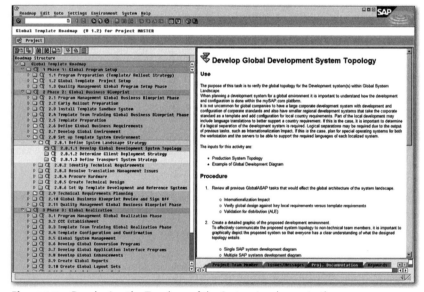

Figure 5.12 Developing the Topology of the System Landscape in the Global Template Roadmap

<table>
<tr>
<td>

Example of a Corporate Rollout in Asia, Using the Global Template

In a concrete project of an international enterprise, SAP ERP was supposed to be introduced in six Asian countries after the implementation in Europe.[25] Here, the global template approach would be applied and the business processes standardized as much as possible. The architecture of the system landscape corresponded to the regional, centralized landscape, including multi-client systems (comparable to Figure 5.8).

In addition to the installation of five SAP application modules (FI, SD, MM, CO, PP, and the SAP BW (Business Warehouse) components, including seven FI-based Infocubes and multiple external third-party systems), data was migrated that mainly originated from SAP systems and other legacy systems. Initially, the prevailing opinion was that the Asian countries all had to be lumped together, and that global processes and data needed to be highly standardized.

However, it was quickly determined that this approach could not easily be implemented for the Asian countries. Working out the details was tricky. Each country had its own specifics. In China, for example, data was still maintained in Microsoft Excel sheets. In Thailand, however, frequent job rotations prevented the effectiveness of training. The newly acquired knowledge was not needed for the new job, and thus was completely useless. They came to the conclusion that generalization had to be handled carefully regarding the globalization of IT in Asia. There was no uniform model for Asia. Each country was unique and must be considered as such. This fact could be taken into account in IT using the global template approach.

</td>
<td>

Considerable differences in Asian Countries

</td>
</tr>
</table>

5.4.5 Implementation of New Countries in a Central System[25]

A frequently recurring case is the extension and rollout of the existing global solution into new countries. This is done if an enterprise wants to develop new markets in new countries, or if an enterprise has decided to integrate existing countries with the global system. In the latter case, countries with decentralized SAP systems are either relocated to global SAP systems — for example, due to a centralization of the architecture (not necessarily a global single-instance architecture) — or countries that are operated on non-SAP systems using third-party software are sup-

Expansion in new countries

---

25 The project was presented in Rob Woof, "Implementing an SAP Global Template in Asia," SAP Globalization Symposium, 2006; see *www.sap.com/community/pub/events/2006%5F10%5F30%5Fglobal%5Fsymposium/*.

posed to be migrated to the SAP system. In either case, you must extend an existing global SAP solution by one or more countries. This should be done as smooth as possible and without interrupting the running operation. Often, a group of countries will be integrated, such as when an enterprise explores new regions (e.g., Asia) so that the new implementation can include a complete country group.

Recommendations for implementing new countries into a global system

First you must determine if SAP supports the new countries and their languages. Note that the global system should use Unicode for language support so that technical problems do not occur *a priori* as a result of the new languages. Ideally, these are standard SAP countries, which will help you keep the implementation effort at a low level, and the existing architecture can be used for an SAP Unicode system. New countries must be implemented decentralized if Unicode is not used.

If the new countries are available as add-ons, you must determine whether the add-on might seriously influence the existing architecture, as was described in Section 4.6.5. If modification-free add-ons exist for the new countries, and if no additional add-ons have been installed, you can generally implement the new countries with the existing architecture. Otherwise, you must carry out the implementation on a separate system. If SAP or SAP partners do not support the new countries, you can proceed as described in Section 4.6.7. In this case, you develop a minimum solution within the implementation. An SAP Unicode system should be available to implement the countries and languages with the existing architecture.

Harmonizing the templates

When the basic conditions have been determined, you can start the project for the new countries. We recommend applying the global template methodology described in Section 5.4.4. The main task is to harmonize the company-specific global template with the templates of the new countries. Generally, the following rule applies: You must provide experts for the project teams of each new country that know the legal regulations, the common business practices, and functionality of the SAP country versions, and (ideally) are fluent in the local language, both spoken and written.

Because the task of introducing new countries into a global SAP solution is of utmost importance, we'll describe the necessary steps in the following section. First, we'll summarize how a new country is usually installed in the SAP ERP FI-CO components.

Country Installation Program

The best way to explain the installation and activation of a new country is to describe a new installation of SAP. The pre-configured customizing settings for each country are absolutely essential. These settings are summarized in a country template and comprise multiple, country-specific configurations that SAP only delivers in client 000 for a new installation or an upgrade. In Section 2.1.1, typical examples were presented of a country template — for instance, country-specific taxes, or formats for payment programs or depreciation plans.

The country installation program adapts the country template to the given country's sample organizational units, primarily the company code.[26] The standard company code is always set to 0001 — in other words, upon execution of the country installation program, all elements of the country template are allocated to the company code 0001 and its dependent organizational units, such as sales organization 0001 and plant 0001.

Country installation during a new SAP installation

You must perform the following steps to install a new country:

1. Select the country template in client 000, depending on the new installation or the add-on installation.
2. Copy client 000 to a new work client.
3. Execute the country installation program: **SAP Transaction SPRO (SAP IMG) • SAP Reference IMG • Company structure • Localize sample organizational units • Country Versions • Two-digit Country Code • Execute (Test Run possible)**. After the execution has been completed, all country template values are allocated to the company code 0001 and additional dependent organizational units.

---

26 You can find more details at *http://service.sap.com/globalization,* and in the documentation for the country installation program at *http://help.sap.com/erp2005_ehp_02/helpdata/en/5a/d34a9f544811d1895e0000e8323c4f/frameset.htm,* and *http://help-sap.com.*

4. If you want to select a company code other than 0001 for the country template, you can copy the company code after the country installation program under **SAP IMG · Company Structure · Financial accounting · Copy Company Code**.

5. Subsequently, you must perform any additional actions described in the documentation. The country can be installed for the implementation. Moreover, you probably must import the language using Transaction SMLT if a translation is available and necessary for the country.

Figure 5.13 shows an overview of the individual country installation steps.

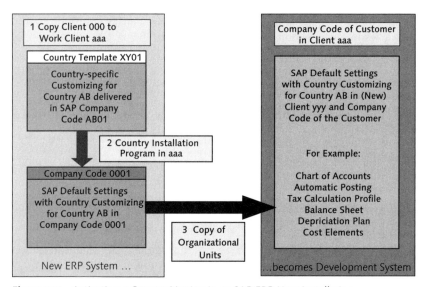

Figure 5.13 Activating a Country Version in an SAP ERP New Installation

Special country installation for a global SAP production system

If you want to install one or more countries in an existing SAP system in which multiple countries have already been implemented, which is generally the case, you can't use the country installation program at all, or only to a limited extent, as was previously described. The problem is that you already have a configured production client, and this could result in conflicts between the country template of the new country in client 000 and the customization in the production client. You have two solution approaches:

▶ You can configure the new country manually in the new client. In other words, you create the country template of client 000 manually in the customized preparatory client of the development system to manually solve possible conflicts.

▶ You install the new country in the customized client using a modified country-installation program procedure.

In the following example of a rollout in Asia, we'll explain the manual installation procedure.[27]

Example: Installation of New Countries for a Rollout in Asia	Manual installation

Let's assume that you have a global production system with multiple countries in America and EMEA, and you use an SAP ERP 6.0 Unicode system. Your enterprise wants to expand to Asia and implement the countries China, Korea, Japan, and Thailand within the Asia rollout project. All these countries are part of SAP standard and technical language support for a global system, available due to Unicode. But how can you add these countries to your existing system?

The SAP country installation program is not suitable here, because you want to implement multiple new countries, and because the system has already gone live.[27] Therefore, we'll explain the manual installation method. In this context, it is vital that the implementation team include experts for country versions. This is a new project, and consequently it is a new, internal company release. You should start the project work in a new development system, as was described in the previous sections. You must implement the following basic steps to integrate the country templates in the work client. Then you can start the actual project work:

1. **Copy the client 000 into the new sandbox client for reference and testing purposes.**
   This is provides a reference client for the new countries and for implementing tests, and, if required, training for the new countries.

---

27 This restricted procedure can be found in the SAP documentation at *http://help.sap. com*.

Example: Installation of New Countries for a Rollout in Asia

2. **Analyze the country template — that is, the country-specific customizing.**
   For initial assessment, you can use the control tables TCUSC and TCUSF; for additional customizing settings, refer to the country version's documentation or contact your consultant. This also applies for add-on country versions. You can find an appropriate document that describes the customizing objects typically required for the new country at SAP AG, Solution Management Globalization Services, "Including New Countries in the Delivery System — Setting up a New Country," *http://service.sap.com/globalization*, Media Library, 2003.

   Work in the customizing client of the development system.
   Analyze potential conflicts between the country template and the customizations already set in the running SAP system. For this purpose, you can create and use SAP BC Sets (Business Configuration Sets) for the country template, because they are suitable tools for a template-based project and lay the foundation for integration into other clients. A BC Set is a collection of customized settings that are recorded and stored as snapshots. The BC Set can be used as a static template for implementation projects, which you can't overwrite. You can compare the BC Set including the country template with the customization settings in the work client by using the SAP Customizing Cross-System Viewer (Transaction SCU0). Possible conflicts are displayed as single table entries, enabling you to solve them quickly. During project work, it is useful to create separate BC Sets per country for company-specific country settings.[28]

3. **Use sound documentation and a common language.**
   Configuration, customizing, and additional settings relevant for the new countries should be documented uniformly, comprehensibly, and in one common project language — for example, English. This is required to provide all information during implementation and maintenance to all teams involved.

   Moreover, we recommend determining a uniform translation strategy for the country-specific settings, because it is a global project. You should always translate all local text objects, particularly customizing and reporting texts, and appropriate forms of the countries into the common project language to ensure that all multinational members of the global team can collaborate efficiently.

4. **Start project work.**
   Subsequently, you can start the project work implemented (preferably) using the global template approach to include new countries.

---

28 For more details on BC Sets, refer to the SAP online documentation at *http://help.sap.com*.

5.5   Tools for Changing Existing Architectures

Now that we have thoroughly explained the implementation of global projects in a given system architecture, in this section, we'll detail how you can change the architectures of existing system landscapes — for example, how you can merge two decentralized systems into one central system, or how you can divide a central system.

5.5.1   System Landscape Optimization

Large global enterprises are often required, or companies want to change their system landscapes, which are frequently very complex. Organizational changes, such as a company merger, have a direct influence on the existing system landscape, because the IT systems of two companies must be combined. But restructuring is often not necessarily required for a global enterprise to recognize that the existing system landscape needs improving, either from a technical, application, or process-specific point of view. Here is a classic, real-life example.

Several years ago, a global enterprise started to introduce SAP and other ERP software on a global scale. Over the years, a separate IT system, including a separate data center and an operators' team, was introduced for each country. The applications and processes were planned, developed, and implemented locally. Analyses of company-wide cost-cutting measures revealed that IT costs were unexpectedly high. It was established that system consolidations would result in considerable cost reductions, particularly for the running operation. Moreover, after an in-depth analysis involving business consultants and application experts, selected applications and processes were planned to be optimized. For this purpose, the existing implementations would be changed, and the enterprise's master data that used to be processed across the enterprise would be harmonized. This is a very complex optimization task for which the system landscape must be restructured, and the implemented applications and processes changed.

The System Landscape Optimization (SLO) provides methods, tools, consulting and project support for such a complex restructuring and optimization measure in SAP, and enables larger change tasks in the SAP pro-

Tools and services for changing the architecture

duction solution.[29] SLO facilitates the comprehensive implementation of business-related changes in the customer systems and enables an effective optimization of the system landscape. They ensure and support the adaptability of SAP solutions over the entire lifecycle of the product.

After analyzing the customer requirements and the relevant areas of the SAP systems concerned, SLO selects the appropriate approach from their range of services to optimally meet customer requirements and proposes a solution. SLO plans and implements the selected solution — also in close collaboration with the customer's project team — and if required, offers support by means of specialized development teams. Customers often ask about typical scenarios for software adaptations. These include:

Reasons for
changing an
architecture

- ▶ Consolidation of complex IT landscapes
- ▶ Spin-off of company divisions
- ▶ Integration of enterprises
- ▶ Reorganization and restructuring within the enterprise
- ▶ Optimization of business processes

Furthermore, there are numerous, often business-related or legally required changes, such as changes to the charts of accounts or currency changeovers (e.g., the introduction of the euro some years ago) that necessitate significant changes and migration of the IT systems. SLO offers the following typical services:

Application-
specific changes

- ▶ Chart of accounts changes
- ▶ Fiscal year change
- ▶ Customer conversion
- ▶ Vendor change
- ▶ Material change
- ▶ Material group changes
- ▶ Changes to the cost centers or other objects of the CO component

---

29 You can find more details at *http://service.sap.com/slo;* and SNP AG, *"SNP SLO System Landscape Optimization,"* Product flyer, at *http://snp.de/media/0000000141.pdf,* and references.

- Company code renaming

- Controlling area renaming

- Plant renaming

- Renaming of logical systems

- Asset class changes

- Controlling area change to 'all currencies'

- Currency key renaming

In the following sections, we describe typical scenarios for architecture adaptations involving some of these services.

Consolidation of Decentralized SAP System Landscapes

Let's assume that in a large, international group, a wide range of SAP systems was installed at various locations over the years. During an analysis for reducing the total cost of ownership (TCO) of the system landscape, the persons responsible establish that work is redundantly performed in many places, the implementation of individual systems is only controlled to a limited extent, and some systems are not fully utilized. The TCO can be reduced by consolidating these redundant systems.

Different solutions are possible, depending on the specific requirements of the project. The easiest way is to copy multiple clients from the distributed systems into one common system to create a central, multiclient system without any additional standardization.

Approaches for system consolidation

Alternatively, you can migrate data from one client to another client by means of a data migration method — for example, the *SAP Legacy System Migration Workbench* (LSMW), the new *SAP Accelerated Data Migration* (ADM), or the *SAP Migration Workbench* (MWB).[30] Large enterprises using a decentralized system landscape may want to consider whether it is cost-effective to carry out a new implementation that includes selective data migration from decentralized legacy systems, such as customiz-

---

30 For more details, see *http://service.sap.com/lsmw,* SAP AG: "*MIGRATION SOLUTIONS FROM SAP*"; SAP Decision Support Brief, "Accelerated Data Migration (ADM) and Legacy System Migration Workbench (LSMW)"; and *http://service.sap.com/slo.*

ing data, master data, and open items of transaction data. This procedure is also referred to as a "green field" approach.

The best integration can be achieved by merging clients, using a special conversion technique. We will detail this in the following sections.

Spin-off of Company Divisions

If a group sells a specific company division to another enterprise, the data and configurations of the sold company divisions must be deleted in the existing IT systems without affecting other applications and data. From the technical point of view, you can consider this as a client separation in the SAP system. In other words, a new client, including the data of the sold company division, is created based on the common client, while the common client still contains all data of the remaining company divisions. The data of the new SAP client can be migrated to the new owner via several technical methods.

SAP SLO offers two different solutions for separating clients: The data intended for the spun-off enterprise is migrated to a new client via data migration (Legacy System Migration Workbench or Migration Workbench); or a client copy is created for the spun-off enterprise, from which the data that is no longer relevant is removed by using the *Delete company code* SLO service.

Integration and Restructuring Within an Enterprise

When an enterprise acquires or takes over another enterprise, the IT data of the acquired enterprise must be adapted to the data of the existing implementation. This often requires special data conversions, such as the material numbers of the acquired enterprise that have different formats and different naming conventions than the acquiring enterprise. All material numbers must have the same format after the integration has been completed. For this purpose, you must convert the material numbers of the acquired enterprise.

A similar scenario applies to the restructuring and reorganization of enterprises. For example, your enterprise used to be organized according to regions, and your SAP system is structured accordingly — typically with a region-decentralized or a shared services architecture. A detailed analysis of the business processes reveals, for example, that a central organization would enable more-efficient control. For this purpose, you must adapt the controlling areas in which the structure of the enterprise is mapped in the SAP system. You could also be required to merge some or all decentralized systems into one central system.

The material number change SAP SLO service is used to update the material numbers of the acquired enterprise and adapt them to the naming convention of the acquiring enterprise. This is done via the *SLO Conversion Workbench*, which we'll describe in Section 5.5.2. The *controlling area consolidation* SLO service is based on the same tool, and enables you to consolidate the previously regional controlling areas to central units required for the restructuring. For consolidating decentralized systems, you can use client merging, which we'll describe in the following section. There are many more SLO services for similar scenarios, which you can find at *http://service.sap.com/slo*.

Material number change and other SLO services

In the following section we'll discuss system consolidation, which is vital for system architecture adaptation. For this purpose, you must merge clients.

Example: Merging Clients for Consolidating of Separated Systems

Globally active enterprises that use a decentralized architecture (with or without shared services) often have a high number of individual, distributed systems, frequently one for each country or organizational unit. These have accumulated over the years because few to no global processes and teams have existed in the enterprise's IT. The first strategy to reduce costs is to consolidate the systems. We'll explain this process by describing client merging. The merging of physically distributed systems into one central, multiclient system is the first step toward consolidation. However, this doesn't enable a real central architecture in the sense of a single-instance solution. So, you have to merge at the client level to obtain a single-instance solution. Figure 5.14 shows the initial situation of a typical example.

Migrating decentralized systems to a central system

You can implement a simplified client merge by using data migration from the source client(s) to the target client — for example, using the SAP Legacy System Migration Workbench, which is included in standard SAP functionality. In this process, only specific enterprise data (usually

Merging of clients using SLO or standard SAP tools

master data, open items, activities, or orders) is migrated from the source clients on a specific key date. This approach is particularly useful if the target client (more generally, the consolidated system) doesn't have to access historical data or all transaction data, and if the clients involved have different structures that will be rebuilt.

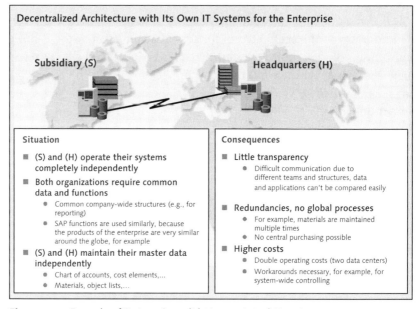

Figure 5.14 Example of System Consolidation — Actual Situation

In general, the migration of historical data is not possible at the detail level. You can only migrate key date or total values, or transactions not completed. Because you can't migrate transactions and their previous processes and data, you must temporarily implement additional technical or organizational solutions for daily business. For this reason, the LSMW approach is only suitable for simple cases. For complete client mergers that include all data and customizations, you must use additional SLO-specific tools.

SLO Migration and Conversion Workbench

A comprehensive solution for complex cases that can't be handled by LSMW can be achieved by combining special technical functions — in particular, *SAP SLO Migration Workbench* (MWB), *Conversion Workbench*

(CWB), and conversion rules. The rules are already preset for numerous SAP objects. You can identify and integrate additional objects and customer developments. These objects are consistently implemented in all SAP applications, independent of the key date and at a high speed.

Ultimately, the target client appears as if it had existed in this form from the very beginning of the system's operation, because the historical data, open items, and processes were all adapted according to the new specifications. This approach enables users to use all data and functions in the new consolidated client immediately after the conversion, and to the customary extent. Figure 5.15 shows the result of this example.[31]

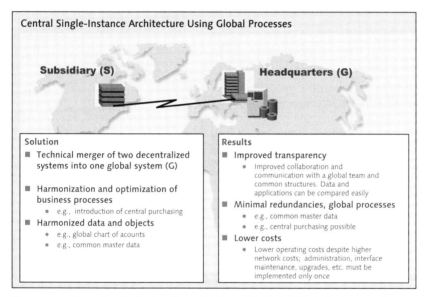

Figure 5.15 Example of a System Consolidation with Global Single Instance as the Target

In the following sections, we'll describe the general functions of the *Migration Workbench* and *Conversion Workbench tools,* which are vital for this procedure.

---

31 Please note that these assumptions and results originate from many concrete projects. However, you must analyze each system consolidation case individually to assess the degree of optimization.

253

5.5.2 Special Technologies: Migration and Conversion Workbench

To give you a more detailed overview of the functionality of the tools that are used for adapting the system architectures, in this section we'll describe the *Migration Workbench* (MWB) and *Conversion Workbench*. These are two essential tools on which most adaptations are based. The SAP SLO team developed them particularly for this purpose. They are used in combination with the previously described SLO services.

Migration Workbench

The MWB (see Figure 5.16) is used to migrate data — ranging from table contents to complete business objects — from the sender system to the receiving system. During migration, you must explicitly determine which data will be moved and where. Both the Migration Workbench (which we'll describe in the following) and the Conversion Workbench work at database level to achieve high throughput.

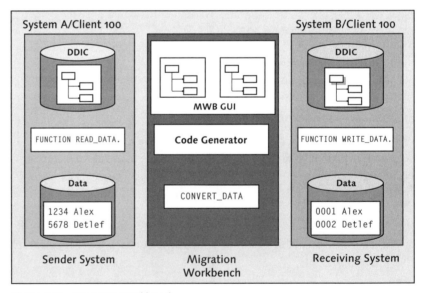

Figure 5.16 Migration Workbench

Defining the sender and receiver structure
First, you must define the sender and receiving structure. For this purpose, enter the tables and their hierarchical dependencies. In the Migra-

tion Workbench, store these structures in separate containers for the sender and the receiver.

Subsequently, the Migration Workbench reads the field information of all tables stored in the container from the respective SAP Data Dictionary (DDIC) and stores it. Then you define the relationships between the sender and receiving structures, and establish rules according to which the data is supposed to be migrated from the sender system to the receiving system. Based on these rules, the Migration Workbench code generator creates SAP ABAP function groups and modules, as well as methods that carry out the migration. They read and convert data from the sender system and implement it in the receiving system. The data is then implemented in these steps.

Depending on the quantity, data is implemented in one step or gradually in several steps. The entire migration process is stored in a log. All SAP systems involved must be locked for this purpose.

Conversion Workbench

The CWB (see Figure 5.17) is used to make necessary data changes — for example, coming from business applications, such as in number ranges for charts of accounts or material numbers — directly at the database level. Depending on the where-used list of the *SAP Data Dictionary*, an SAP ABAP conversion program and (if necessary) a conversion view is generated for each table to be implemented.

The data to be implemented is stored in a *conversion cluster* and read for conversion. The database table is then updated with the implemented data. The cluster technique enables you to reset an implementation, because the original data still exists in the cluster. Or, you can implement multiple tables at the same time. The generated implementation programs then implement the values in the database. After conversion, only the new values will be found in the system.

Cluster technique

With this type of conversion, all involved SAP system components are considered. The conversion comprises master data, transaction data, and customizing data. Tables that are part of the standard are converted automatically, but tables that the enterprise has created itself, as well as modifications of standard tables, are generally converted automatically, also.

255

The Conversion Workbench forms a base that is also used in conversion solutions for other tasks, such as for merging company codes or deleting control areas. Similar to MWB, the system must be locked for CWB during the conversion to ensure the integrity of the data.

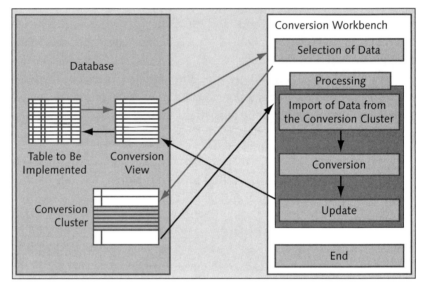

Figure 5.17 Conversion Workbench

5.6 Summary

This chapter gave you a comprehensive overview of how a global solution can be implemented in a given architecture — from planning the infrastructure to live operation, to migration of architectures due to external or internal factors.

When an enterprise has decided on a central single-instance architecture, setting up the appropriate IT infrastructure and ensuring the smooth operation of the central system is a big challenge. Because today's technology generally provides sufficient computer and network capacity to operate even extremely large global systems that involve tens of thousands of active users, the question arises as to how the downtimes and high load of a 24/7 operation can be securely managed.

Despite state-of-the-art, high-availability solutions and additional techni- No 100%
cal facilities for security (e.g., disaster recovery centers), you can't plan plannable
for 100% availability, because specific maintenance tasks can only be availability
carried out when the system is shut down. We explained how you can
achieve an availability of nearly 100% by implementing good global
planning, and by using specific tools and practices for maintenance
optimization.

In order to plan, implement, and gradually roll out a global project, it Maintenance and
makes sense to subdivide the system landscape into a maintenance land- project landscape
scape for global live production and a project landscape for the selected
architecture's new projects. You can continuously extend your global IT
solution via custom release management (e.g., by rolling out a group of
new countries at a specific time).

You can use the global template approach to plan and implement a global Global template
project. The global template includes global processes, data structures, approach
and configurations that can be adapted to local requirements, for example, due to the legal regulations of specific countries. The global template
approach also enables you to achieve central development in a decentralized, production system architecture.

This chapter gave you important information on the general procedure
for introducing and integrating individual new countries or country systems into an existing system. Due to language support, this is only technically feasible in an SAP Unicode system. Local expert advice for the
countries (from advisors who are members of the project team) is indis-
pensable for the implementation.

If you want to change the architecture of the existing system landscape System Landscape
to either optimize IT or because of external influences (e.g., the restruc- Optimization
turing of the enterprise), you are provided with SAP System Landscape
Optimization services and tools to manage these complex tasks. Using
these, you can implement the consolidation of complex IT landscapes,
spin-off of company divisions, integration of enterprises, reorganizations and restructurings within the enterprise, or optimization of business processes in the existing system landscape to achieve the target
architecture.

Now that you have read the previous chapters, you are probably wondering: "So which system topology is best for my enterprise?" This chapter provides the answer to that question. It also contains a decision matrix — newly introduced at this point in the book — which helps you to select a topology.

6   Customer Scenarios and Decision-Making Processes

So far, this book has provided a lot of information on system topologies and their conditions. Now, analyses from the customer's point of view follow. From an SAP perspective, customer examples illustrate how technical, geographical, or even political aspects may affect the system architecture. Due to the variety of enterprises, there is not just one preferred system topology; rather, a recommendation for an architecture approach will emerge when reading this chapter. A new decision matrix, which is introduced for the first time in this book, enables you to determine the best system topology for your specific company situation.

6.1   Experiences of SAP Customers with Different System Topologies

Due to their positions as solution managers for internationalization issues in the area of SAP Globalization Services, this book's authors know hundreds of customer implementations and their details. Discussions with decision-makers, IT teams, project managers, and customer service representatives provided valuable information on these aspects. On the one hand, typical implementation procedures become obvious, while on the other hand, the very different reasons for the selection of individual architectures are revealed.

A historical trend for global systems in one installation, sometimes with satellites for shared services or specific functions, can be recognized. It replaced the single-box approach of the mainframe era (SAP R/2) and the tendency to use largely distributed architectures (beginning with SAP R/3 client/server installations), as shown in Figure 6.1.

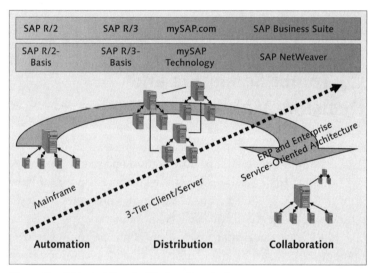

Figure 6.1   Historical Trend of System Topologies

The following sections describe the four basic and most frequently used system architectures in more detail, list the arguments of SAP customers for or against the individual architectures, and highlight factors that are critical for implementation. A real-life example of a typical customer project illustrates the path from a distributed architecture to a central system.

6.1.1   Central System

The approach that is most frequently used for a global installation is the implementation of a central system (single box).[1] Here, there is a global SAP ERP system based, for example, on powerful hardware. All processes are implemented in the SAP ERP system, and all users directly access the system. Processes and data can be easily standardized and harmonized due

---

1 In this chapter, we use "single box" and "single instance" synonymously.

to the high degree of integration. Reporting processes can be directly carried out without difficulty. Another advantage of the single-box approach is the easy-maintenance concept with central system control.

> **Recommendation**
>
> The various advantages of a central system mentioned earlier are very impressive and not the only reason SAP recommends the single-box approach whenever this system architecture can be implemented.

SAP recommends the single box

The challenge of this topology is to manage the global complexity on one system (combine country versions) and differentiate between business processes with different business area requirements. In addition, you must technically reduce the high failure risk and provide appropriate hardware, considering the size of the installation to ensure sufficient performance. Translations for different languages are another important subject to create acceptance among users, business partners, or government agencies. Figure 6.2 provides an overview of these aspects.

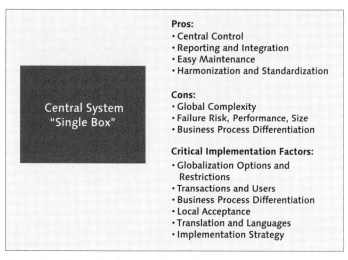

Central System "Single Box"

Pros:
- Central Control
- Reporting and Integration
- Easy Maintenance
- Harmonization and Standardization

Cons:
- Global Complexity
- Failure Risk, Performance, Size
- Business Process Differentiation

Critical Implementation Factors:
- Globalization Options and Restrictions
- Transactions and Users
- Business Process Differentiation
- Local Acceptance
- Translation and Languages
- Implementation Strategy

Figure 6.2 Single-Box Customer Scenario

Discussions have been held with several company representatives in order to obtain information on the reasons that enterprises have for implementing central systems (single box). Table 6.1 lists the reasons most frequently mentioned and offers comments.

Reasons customers implement a central system (single box)

Reasons for a Single Box	Comments
Improved control and transparency of business processes	All processes are implemented in only one system and can therefore be optimally used or changed uniformly, if required.
Global view of datasets	No consolidation of datasets in distributed individual systems required, because all applications can directly access the same dataset without having to synchronize the distributed systems.
Reduction of organizational obstacles regarding procurement	Implementing the procurement chain is a clear and consistent process without interruptions between the individual components.
No data distribution problems	There is only one system; therefore, no distribution is required.
Easy system administration	There is only one system on which one team can focus, and the definitions are globally uniform.
More transparency for employees	All employees work in the same system, global access via the Internet is no problem from the technical point of view, and you can use a Unicode-based installation to combine any user languages without problems.
Improved information flow	The information flows in the enterprise are processed according to standards as well as directly forwarded to communication partners. Specific interfaces or conversion tools are not required.
Highest possible use of the functional integration of SAP software	All functions that an enterprise uses are implemented and customized in the same system. Therefore, 'distribution' is not relevant.
Reduction of current maintenance costs	Only one system requires maintenance; costs can be saved within the IT team and due to uniform hardware.
Use of corporate-wide reporting standards	Uniform reporting standards in the enterprise are globally defined, and processes and evaluations work with uniform datasets.
Centralized user support and resource management	This refers to internal support: Users are supported by one global team. However, appropriate measures must be taken to ensure support 24/7. For example, this can be achieved by operating three support centers (one for each region), which then work in overlapping shifts according to the 'follow-the-sun' concept.

Table 6.1 Reasons Customers Implement a Central System

Reasons for a Single Box	Comments
Simplified distribution scenarios	This refers to the connection of third-party systems — for example, data exchange with suppliers or wholesalers.
Easier maintenance of (fewer) interfaces	Since there is only one internal system, you must only implement and maintain the interfaces to external systems. Experience has shown that this is an essential cost advantage.
Consistent and harmonized master data	After the master data structure has been planned or harmonized once, you can maintain datasets centrally. In this way, you can avoid redundant products that are identical but have different names.
Standard business processes	All business processes are centrally implemented and run on one system. They provide the same functions for all users.
Reduced (total) costs	Here, the total of all cost savings mentioned earlier is generally offset against costs for the more-complex hardware of the single-box approach.
Central purchase of administration and IT products	The products are almost always globally purchased. This standardization can reduce the costs (e.g., fewer suppliers, higher quantities).
Corporate identity	Experience has shown that customers can also use their single box to harmonize all processes and activities included in the corporate identity.
Global definition of data and processes	After the master data structure has been planned or harmonized once, and the business processes have been defined, you can use and maintain datasets and processes centrally.
Shared use of best practices at a global level	Best practices that have been proven and must be implemented only once are usually available for all users on a global basis.
Improved services for global customers	Let's take a look at an example: If availability is requested, it must be searched only in one system/database.
Easier implementation of global businesses	You can uniformly implement all components required for the implementation of a global business (e.g., business processes, software components, data, etc.) and then directly use them globally.
Real-time access to all information	Ideally, the system runs 24/7 and is always globally available so that required information can be accessed uniformly. Errors due to missing data synchronizations are not possible in single-box topologies.

Table 6.1 Reasons Customers Implement a Central System (Cont.)

Reasons for a Single Box	Comments
Integration of all business transactions in one database	Not only do the software components run on one system, they also uniformly access one database. Therefore, no synchronization is required.
Faster internal and external communication, improved integration of information transfer	The data throughput is optimized, because internal interfaces are avoided where possible, and external systems are connected uniformly. The efficiency also increases, because potential errors are reduced, such as through conversions.
Optimal use of IT for corporate-wide processes	Additional hardware (or software) requirements are reduced by using a single system. In contrast to distributed systems, redundant implementations of processes, or redundant installations of software can therefore be avoided.
Faster global response times and reactions	The system runs 24/7 and is always available.
Specific and standardized integration of partners and suppliers	You define processes and technical interfaces in the same system.
Increased IT efficiency due to shared resources	There is usually only one central IT team that works either at the system location or in the regions as a virtual team.
Simplified development of global templates	Because you have to design a template to plan the system rollout, local and global aspects can be planned in the best possible way, right from the start. Hence, a uniform approach is created.
Easy transformation of the enterprise's future visions	Global templates completely cover the enterprise's visions and can be easily modified with global effects when future changes occur.
Globally adapted processes and data definitions, which have been jointly specified	After the master data structure has been globally adapted and planned or harmonized once, and the business processes have been defined, you can use and maintain datasets and processes centrally.
Continuous increase and homogeneous coverage of the required processes toward the enterprise's vision	The system is optimized over time, and you can harmonize all processes.
A 'dedicated team'	This holds true for IT groups as well as for sales departments. Collaboration takes place in a uniform system, which is used as a base.

Table 6.1 Reasons Customers Implement a Central System (Cont.)

Reasons for a Single Box	Comments
The SAP system is the leading system	If it is required to connect other systems, the 'master' is set by default.
Minimum changes to standard software	Software components run on a single box with optimal data exchange. Since you usually combine only standard country versions, even for country-specific functions, you can avoid using modifications or add-ons.
Option to implement global e-business	Uniform access to exactly one backbone system is provided.
Easy connectivity to other business partners' systems	You can easily define the interfaces if the system runs under Unicode.
Global supply chain and customer relationship management	In addition to cost savings due to global purchases (see above), additional programs, such as CRM, can also be integrated — including easy data migration on the single box.
Faster use of best practices by all users: ▸ At all locations ▸ In new countries ▸ For new or modified business processes	For example, if a process is modified, it is immediately available for all users and doesn't have to be distributed first.

Table 6.1 Reasons Customers Implement a Central System (Cont.)

6.1.2 Decentralized Approach with Individual Systems

Enterprises that want to enable the highest possible degree of freedom for local locations or functional units (e.g., regional sales departments) select a decentralized approach — sometimes with a very high number of individual systems.

The main advantage of this topology is that the local system administrator is responsible for all processes required for the implementation. The administrator can therefore decide in which time frame and with which release the relevant business processes are supposed to be implemented.

The local team is also responsible for selecting the supported languages, the scope of required translations, as well as planning the upgrade strategy and maintenance window. Theoretically, it is not absolutely necessary to adapt the satellite systems exactly and regularly in the individual countries (apart from consolidating data that is required for profit-and-loss or financial statements).

High costs for redundant or incompatible systems
Despite the high degree of freedom for local teams, this solution has various disadvantages, which usually eliminate the advantages if you compare them in detail. The high number of (perhaps) redundant or incompatible systems is associated with considerable operation costs, and the SAP support required increases.

Furthermore, there are almost countless interfaces. These usually lead to a nearly exponential increase in the operating costs and are also potential sources of errors.

The implementation of global processes or maintenance strategies cannot be easily managed when the decentralized approach is used. It may also lead to a lot of redundancy, and you cannot take advantage of synergy effects.

For this system topology, it is generally important to realistically assess the costs. This applies particularly to the global costs for incompatibility, complex implementations, and maintenance. Figure 6.3 summarizes these issues.

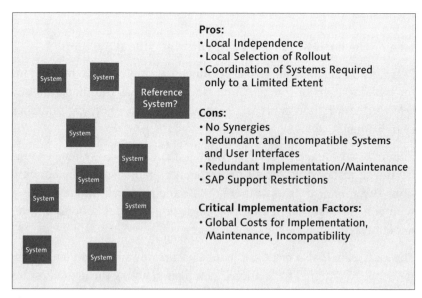

Figure 6.3 Customer Scenario with a Decentralized Approach, with Individual Systems

Table 6.2 lists the most frequent reasons that SAP customers implement a decentralized system, including comments.

Reasons customers implement decentralized systems

Reasons for Decentralized Systems	Comments
Flexibility for organizational changes	You can quickly assign other tasks to each system. The systems, which are partly assigned to individual organizations, can be configured independently and run automatically. Local teams are independent in how they use their systems.
Virtual organizations or joint ventures can be easily mapped	For example, abstract business units or external systems are treated as local installations and integrated into the distributed architecture via interfaces. This is easier than configuring them independently in a single system.
Sufficient communication infrastructure	This is often a political approach — for example, when local organizations want be independent of corporate headquarters and consequently communicate only infrequently.
Use of different SAP versions	This is a weak argument, because you generally should consolidate different SAP versions as quickly as possible.
Applications run on different platforms/hardware	If the applications use different platforms, they have to be distributed across the respective hardware. This situation can often be found in legacy systems that are combined with SAP installations, or when companies are acquired (the entire IT must be integrated into new system landscape).
Many large non-SAP systems available	In this case, you must change to SAP systems before you can consolidate the systems.
Implementation in subsequent phases	For a start, you implemented separate ERP units in the individual countries correspondingly — for example, in accordance to the temporal growth of the enterprise or acquisition.

Table 6.2 Reasons Customers Implement Decentralized Systems

Reasons for Decentralized Systems	Comments
Individual locations with different historical developments	This is similar to the previous comment. However, in this case, local installations could develop independently at the same time. Consequently, different software components or release statuses were implemented.
Flexibility for upgrades	Of course, the individual systems can execute upgrades, install new software components, or change platforms (almost) completely independently of each other.
Local systems are owned by subsidiaries and/or only partly involve the parent company.	This refers to local systems in the system group that can only be connected via interfaces, because the systems aren't owned by the parent company and therefore cannot be modified.
Product of "mergers and acquisitions"	This can often be found today: When companies are acquired, new systems with different SAP releases or non-SAP software are added. They should be integrated as quickly as possible.
High failure safety	Today, this does no longer count as a good argument, because the hardware can also be set up in a fail-safe manner for other topologies.
Incompatible country versions	In individual cases, this argument may also count against the single-box approach; consequently, an additional system may be required.

Table 6.2 Reasons Customers Implement Decentralized Systems (cont.)

6.1.3 Distributed Systems with Integrated and Consolidated Business Processes

In global SAP installations, you can often find topologies with (a few) distributed systems on which integrated and consolidated business processes are implemented. In addition to a central system, they frequently also include satellites that are customized and optimized for specific functions, business areas, or regional locations.

In this case, a distribution model is usually used that ensures data and process harmonization, and that can also be automated. Basically, successfully installed systems provide well-planned communication and definitions of uniform standards (whenever possible). Furthermore, individual systems can be maintained independently, and release strategies can be planned for each location, separately.

However, this topology has also disadvantages. It is often difficult to control systems globally, and a complex network of installations that execute the business processes is created. From the point of view of the local systems, this situation is often not considered the best solution. Although it allows freedom at the local level, functional scope is limited. When distributed systems are implemented, including integration and consolidation, it is very important to find an appropriate distribution model and implement all related scenarios.

Distribution model for implementing distributed systems

How the systems are supposed to cooperate must also be analyzed, as well as if the satellites are sufficiently locally accepted. Figure 6.4 summarizes these assessments.

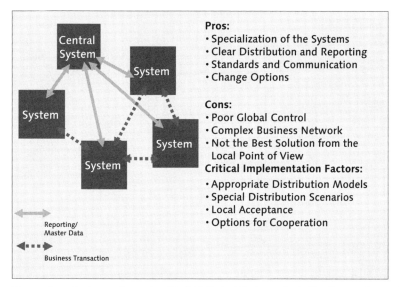

Figure 6.4 Customer Scenario with Distributed Systems, Including Integration and Consolidation

SAP customers most frequently mention the reasons listed in Table 6.3 for their decisions to implement distributed systems that include integration and consolidation. Like in the previous tables, comments are included.

Reasons customers implement distributed systems including integration and consolidation

Reasons for Distributed Systems, Including Integration and Consolidation	Comments
Different time zones, parallel implementation	Although implementations of software have been largely standardized, the systems are operated in various time zones — that is, maintenance work or rollouts are performed at different times. Highly specialized systems, which distribute load-intensive processes (e.g., monthly payrolls) in accordance with the time zones, may also be considered.
Globally shared master data and reporting are sufficient	Master data is distributed across the individual systems according to a defined schema, and shared reporting processes are carried out. All other functions can be implemented and operated independently on individual systems.
Flexible/larger maintenance window	You can operate the individual systems separately to a large extent. After the systems have been maintained, the data is synchronized again.
Best flexibility for regional configurations	The individual systems are assigned to regions, which are then configured independently of each other. This can also include the installation of different software or other hardware platforms if it meets the business requirements in a better way.
Diversification easily possible	This applies to different areas — from hardware and software to characteristics of local requirements, to customer-specific developments.
Reduction in technical dependencies	This argument applies, for example, to the installation of different software, non-uniform platforms, non-standard SAP country versions, or SAP industry solutions.

Table 6.3 Reasons Customers Implement Distributed Systems, Including Integration and Consolidation

Reasons for Distributed Systems, Including Integration and Consolidation	Comments
Higher transparency of organizations	This is a rather political consideration.
No generalization of business processes possible	This can often be found in large global enterprises that are active in several industries and have very diversified rollout concepts or diverse, incompatible business processes.
Good coverage of country-specific requirements	This is relevant, for example, for incompatible country versions.
Regional requirements for Customizing, modifications, or developments	Regional units want to respond comprehensively to the local requirements and be determined by global standards only to a limited extent. This often applies when non-standard SAP country versions are used.
No single point-of-failure risk (as is the case with single-box scenarios)	This aspect is no longer relevant, because hardware can be set up in a fail-safe manner.
Corporate culture	This is a rather political issue. Enterprises have traditional, historically grown, autonomous and separate units with specific systems and their own ITs.
Different mentalities	This is also rather politically inspired. It often applies to sales organizations that work on different regional bases and want to map this situation in their sales system.

Table 6.3 Reasons Customers Implement Distributed Systems, Including Integration and Consolidation (Cont.)

6.1.4   Decentralized Approach with Shared Services

When an enterprise wants to enable different business processes on a local, regional basis — for example, in places as large as America, Asia, or Europe, or even in individual countries where stores are based — the decentralized approach with shared services is frequently selected.

Redundant functions inevitably occur, such as for HR processes. By using a global and dedicated shared services system, you can avoid this problem, as well as save maintenance costs.

Disadvantage:
interfaces

Interfaces between the systems must be implemented, maintained, and face incomplete integration of business processes, which are disadvantages of this topology. You must pay attention to good data harmonization and standardization when rolling out and planning a decentralized approach with shared services. In addition, the costs for a global implementation and the maintenance of different systems should be accurately calculated, as shown in Figure 6.5.

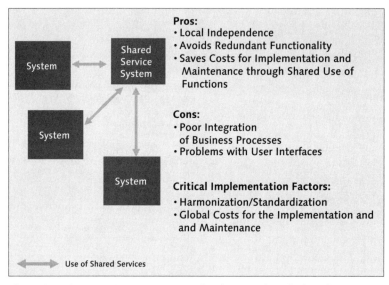

Figure 6.5 Customer Scenario: Decentralized Approach with Shared Services

Table 6.4 lists and comments on the reasons SAP customers implement a decentralized approach with shared services.

Reasons customers
implement
decentralized
systems with
shared services

Reasons for Decentralized Systems with Shared Services	Comments
Shared data and processes	A shared services system manages important enterprise data and (global) business processes. Consequently, uniform datasets and processes are provided. This is often used in personnel administration, including payroll processes or invoice management.

Table 6.4 Reasons Customers Implement Decentralized Systems with Shared Services

Reasons for Decentralized Systems with Shared Services	Comments
Dedicated systems	Dedicated systems are combinations of shared services systems that are specialized for specific functions — possibly with other systems assigned to specific functions or geographically separated installations.
Autonomous business areas	In addition to using globally shared, uniform processes, and their data, the individual business areas can act independently on a local basis and consequently optimize implementations.
Performance	This argument is no longer of particular importance, because hardware has sufficient performance, even for single-box installations.
Synergies	This refers to the fact that enterprises outsource identical or similar processes that must sometimes exist on all shared services systems redundantly in order to work more efficiently.
Independence regarding upgrades and the selection of processes	All corporate group systems (including the shared services system) can be changed almost completely independently of each other, even when there are release changes or implementations of new functions.
Higher flexibility within the organization	In addition to using globally shared, uniform processes and their data, the individual organizations can locally act independently and consequently respond quickly, such as to changes in the local markets (by changing business processes or implementing new legal regulations in individual regions, which is very important for some countries).
Different time zones	This argument greatly depends on the individual business processes and involved functions. In some cases, or when enterprise-specific requirements must be met, distributed systems may be more flexible to adjust.

Table 6.4 Reasons Customers Implement Decentralized Systems with Shared Services (Cont.)

Reasons for Decentralized Systems with Shared Services	Comments
Enterprise units with different requirements (e.g., local)	If individual enterprise areas have specific requirements — for example, if they are active in an industry other than the parent company's — you can selectively configure the settings of a dedicated system.
Different central and regional standards	If it is only required to define basic standards globally (e.g., consolidation or personnel administration), you can customize local or regional systems individually.
Users can be connected to the central or regional system	All users use the central system/shared services system for things like travel expenses, submitting invoices, or ordering office equipment; as well as use the local system for things like sales processes or customer support.
Different industry solutions	This refers to enterprises that are active in more than one industry and therefore want to use several SAP industry solutions.

Table 6.4 Reasons Customers Implement Decentralized Systems with Shared Services (Cont.)

6.1.5 Sample Project: From Distributed Systems to Single Box

The previous sections provided information on the topologies that SAP customers prefer, and listed reasons that led to their decisions. Now, a specific sample project is explained to illustrate a way to migrate from a distributed architecture to a single box. This example represents many nearly identical, real-life projects of large installations, and therefore provides a good overview of the processes involved.

Sample enterprise   The sales level of the enterprise in this example typically amounts to tens of billions of dollars, its number of employees exceeds 50,000, and it is globally active in more than 50 countries. The global installation consists of three individual live systems in different regions, which communicate via a comprehensive distribution model and are provided with changes via several development channels.

This complexity involves numerous problems: In addition to the generally high costs for operation and maintenance, the interfaces cause problems, basically due to different code pages. By definition, data that is exchanged between systems is only supposed to be provided in English (7-bit ASCII) in order to avoid incompatibilities that may occur due to special characters that the various code pages define or contain in different ways. Experience has shown that this procedure (called the "Golden Rule" by SAP) often hasn't been observed (usually by insufficiently trained users). In some cases, the characters were even deleted. You could completely solve this problem by using a Unicode-based single box in the planned target system.

Usability and transparency were insufficient, and functional restrictions were detected — at least partially due to interruptions in the execution of processes when changing from one system to another. As the introduction of other SAP solutions (e.g., SAP CRM, SAP SRM, or SAP SCM) were planned, it was obvious that the complexity would again increase.

To solve these problems, a project was started that was supposed to transfer all existing systems into a single, Unicode-based global installation. This installation can then be supplied from a single development pipeline at a later stage. For the system consolidation, it was also decided to integrate two of the existing systems into the third system. This is the planned single box, which represents the new system topology. Figure 6.6 illustrates this approach.

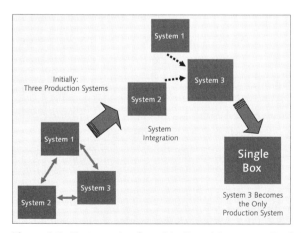

Figure 6.6 Restructuring from Distributed Systems to Single Box

At the beginning of the project, many questions arose referring to the consequences of this procedure. The following aspects were considered as particularly critical:

▸ Will the single-box hardware work with sufficient performance?

▸ How much downtime must be expected, and how will it affect the daily business?

▸ Can data that had been archived before the system was converted be read correctly afterward, and after a later Unicode conversion has been completed?

▸ In particular, is financial data correctly transferred? In times of challenging SOX (Sarbanes-Oxley Act) specifications, this is a decisive aspect.[2]

▸ What will be the business benefits of this project (in addition to IT savings)?

The project team has already answered these questions in advance:

▸ All of the three systems had a database size of approximately two terabytes, and the resulting single box was considered to have a final size of four terabytes due to data consolidation and previous archiving processes. Consequently, the hardware could be set up respectively in collaboration with the manufacturer.

▸ Experiences from other projects and test runs led to the assumption that the systems could be converted with a maximum downtime of 96 hours. This downtime was barely acceptable to the enterprise.

▸ The test runs should particularly be mentioned: For all projects that required downtime, SAP customer experience has shown that the hardware considerably influences the time in which the system is not available. For example, Unicode conversion for a system with a one-terabyte database may last 20 hours or several days, although the same procedure is used. SAP therefore recommends copying the live system first, and then 'testing' the desired process several times. Only

---

2 The Sarbanes-Oxley Act of 2002, a U.S. federal law, is a binding regulation for company reporting.

after these tests will you know how long the downtime for an implementation of the live system will take.

▶ Archiving is always a sound recommendation.

▶ Upon consultation with SAP, it could be determined that data archived before a system is converted into Unicode can be read in Unicode systems without problems (automatic conversion). It is therefore generally recommended to convert as much data as possible prior to each system conversion.

▶ Once again, to ensure data consistency (which SAP guarantees anyway), it was decided to verify data consistency (particularly financial data) by using external auditors. Therefore, any doubts regarding SOX compatibility can be eliminated.

▶ The analysis of the business advantages provided by the new single-box system showed that many of the advantages of this topology mentioned in Section 6.1.1 could also be applied to this enterprise. Have you already recognized the improvements that have been described in this customer's experience? The essential aspects are once again summarized:

  ▶ No data distribution problems

  ▶ More transparency for employees

  ▶ Improved information flow

  ▶ Highest possible use of the functional integration of SAP software

  ▶ Reduction of current maintenance costs

  ▶ Easier maintenance of (fewer) interfaces

  ▶ Standard business processes

  ▶ Corporate identity

  ▶ All business transactions in one database

  ▶ Faster internal and external communication, and improved integration of information transfer

SAP SLO (*System Landscape Optimization*), which was described in detail in Section 5.5, was extensively used in processes in which systems were consolidated and modifications were carried out — for example, when adjusting internal organizational structures, data was harmonized, or

Consolidating systems using SAP SLO

277

the existing landscape was restructured. According to organizational and business definitions, SAP SLO analyzed existing datasets, selected appropriate conversion tools, and adapted the tools to project-specific requirements.

6.2 Guideline for Decision-Making Processes

Decision matrix for selecting the appropriate system architecture

Previous chapters provided much information on the different criteria that influence your choice of the system topology. Now you know that the single box is usually recommended. This section introduces a tool that can be very useful for selecting the appropriate system architecture: the decision matrix.[3] It particularly considers the individual business processes. To explain this tool, we use the example of a virtual enterprise that has typical parameters and problems, which is frequently found in our work with SAP customers.

You must 'only' transfer this decision-making process, which this section will roughly outline, to your specific questions and enterprise characteristics to determine the optimal topology for your enterprise. Interestingly, this example shows that it sometimes can be useful to not adhere to the SAP recommendation (single box), not only because of functional reasons, but also for business aspects.

Let's first take a detailed look at the virtual enterprise, which we'll refer to as *SAPdemo*, to outline its current problems and management expectations.

> **Sample Enterprise**
>
> SAPdemo produces pharmaceutical products: generics. Generics are drugs that can also be sold by other companies at considerably lower prices after a period of several years has expired. In this defined period, only the original producer may sell these drugs.
>
> SAPdemo's headquarters are located in Boston (U.S.), and it has production plants in the U.S. and Europe. Sales are executed globally with three centers in the U.S., Europe, and Asia. In total, SAPdemo has 2,000 employees and a global sales level of US$2 billion.

---

3 The decision matrix was developed by SAP's Sven Scharfenberg and Dr. Detlef Werner.

From a business point of view, the pharmaceuticals industry has some specific characteristics. Therefore, SAP provides a customized solution for this industry (*SAP Pharmaceuticals*), which SAPdemo uses to a large extent. The following aspects are critical success factors of this industry:

▶ **Sales management**
The pharmaceutical industry is probably the only industry that does not know its end customers: the patients that take the drugs. Therefore, third parties execute the sales processes. These parties are usually physicians in practices or hospitals that prescribe the products and, at the same time, are the contacts for sales representatives of the pharmaceutical enterprise.

▶ **Cost issue**
The cost issue is one of the most important aspects for generics producers, because drugs by different producers, which have the same active ingredient, are differentiated mainly by the sales price.

▶ **Optimizing the supply chain**
It is also critical to optimize the supply chain, because smooth production, as well as the ability to respond quickly to changes (e.g., to select new, cheaper suppliers), must be ensured.

The pharmaceutical industry is subject to strict conditions and specific legal regulations, which can differ depending on the country. Examples are the FDA (*Food and Drug Administration*) in the U.S. and the *Federal Institute for Drugs and Medical Devices* in Germany, which are responsible for the authorization of medicinal products for human use.

SAPdemo purchases raw chemicals from different manufacturers for use in producing active agents for their generics in a first production step. This agent is the actual active ingredient of a drug. Active agents may also be purchased from third-party producers. These substances are used to produce the final drugs (e.g., pills or coated tablets), which are then packed before they are delivered to distribution centers.

Wholesalers in the individual countries buy the drugs and deliver them to drugstores or directly to hospitals. Usually the end customers (patients) buy the products drugstores after the physicians have prescribed them. Figure 6.7 illustrates the procurement chain of SAPdemo, considering regional structures.

Success Factors in the Pharmaceutical Industry

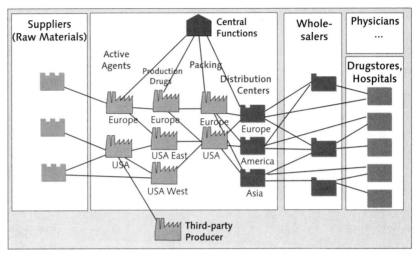

Figure 6.7 Pharmaceutical Procurement Chain of SAPdemo

Covering all
business processes
of SAPdemo by
using a single box

Currently, SAPdemo covers business processes globally with a central
SAP system that still runs with SAP R/3 Enterprise and is configured with
MDMP, because SAPdemo is active in various regions where different
languages are spoken (see Section 2.1.2, "Requirements of IT Users").
The single box provides central functions, such as personnel accounting, controlling, or reporting. It also controls procurement, sales, and
production processes.

Suppliers, customers, and a warehouse management system are connected via various interfaces. Figure 6.8 illustrates the actual situation.

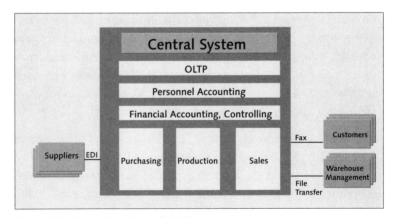

Figure 6.8 System Topology of SAPdemo

SAPdemo's management analyzed the actual situation described in coordination with the stores, which are distributed across different countries, and prepared the following list of requirements and aspects to be optimized:

▶ In general, costs must be reduced in order to maintain competitiveness. Particularly, increased stocks of active agents and unpacked drugs caught their eyes.

▶ Performance was insufficient when computationally intensive processes were required, such as for month-end closings.

▶ External systems were insufficiently integrated; there were too many semi-automatic interfaces (e.g., fax, file transfer).

▶ Information flow was insufficient. External market data was not considered in sales planning, or the sales department was not provided with information as quickly as required.

▶ An important political argument: The sales organizations want to work independently of each other.

▶ Logistics need improving: Wholesalers are supposed to be better integrated, which would also lead to improved inventory management.

▶ The system is supposed to respond quicker to market changes.

Considering these aspects (and of course many other detailed requirements), SAPdemo prepares a clearly defined roadmap in the first step. This roadmap describes how the enterprise wants to achieve the target status, using specified business strategies based on the actual status. Figure 6.9 illustrates this approach as an example.

Defining the strategy

At this point, SAPdemo defines the basic principles for the decision matrix by precisely analyzing different areas of the enterprises and roughly categorizing them. For example, the core business, with the following parameters, comes first:

▶ Legal requirements, regionally characterized
▶ Reporting
▶ Homogeneous procurement chain
▶ Production
▶ Sales

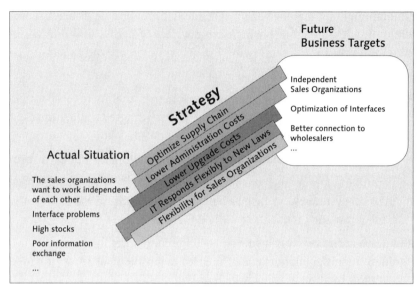

Figure 6.9 Strategy Definition for SAPdemo

The next step is to determine the focus areas for the organizational units, such as:

▶ Defining reporting for each organizational unit,

▶ Developing a 'high-level plan' for purchase and production,

▶ Harmonization of master data, and

▶ Identification of the essential business processes.

Decision matrix template — These parameters can then be used to generate the template for the decision matrix in which the enterprise's point of view is compared with business process aspects. For SAPdemo, the matrix is generated from the following business-critical processes:

▶ Production of active agents

▶ Production of drugs

▶ Packing

▶ Delivery

▶ Sales analysis

▶ Financial accounting

These processes are then compared with regard to the different organizational units. In addition to the headquarters, organizational units are located in North America, Europe, and Asia. Therefore, a matrix is generated as shown in Figure 6.10.

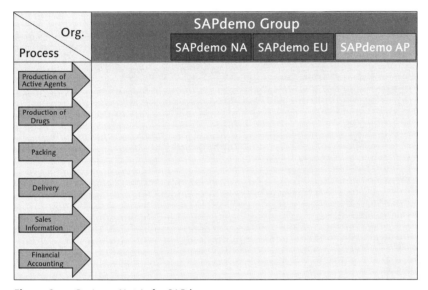

Figure 6.10 Business Matrix for SAPdemo

Based on this matrix, the following questions arise about the core business processes and their interdependencies with different business units:

Core business processes and their interdependencies with business units

► Who is responsible for the processes?

► What are the exact process steps?

► How can and must processes be standardized?

► What kind of information flow is given?

► Which processes run between the separate business units?

► What kinds of relationships exist between the individual processes?

► How are reporting processes carried out?

If you transfer the answers to these core questions into the matrix, the results will be as shown in Figure 6.11.

While the entire production process is carried out in North America and Europe, the drugs are sold in Asia. Consequently, all three regions are included in the global business. Reporting sales revenues and all other business transactions that are important for financial accounting processes are directly forwarded to headquarters.

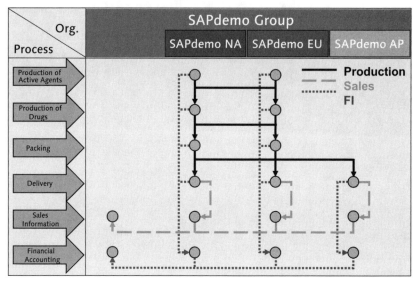

Figure 6.11 Core Business Processes and Their Interdependencies with SAPdemo Business Units

Business cluster – combining business processes

After the preceding considerations have been made, the decisive step now follows: introducing a cluster of business processes, which provides a high integration level. Due to this integration level, you can also technically implement the business processes in a single system. The following applies to the analysis of possible system topologies:

One business cluster = one system

If all of the enterprise's business processes considered here were distributed across more than one business cluster (the single-box approach), it would be a distributed scenario. Therefore, determining the information flow between the systems in a distribution model is required.

According to the requirements for optimizing SAPdemo business processes (described at the beginning of this section), different business cluster alternatives are now set up to analyze their best possible uses for adjusting new or modified business processes. Here, the following five core strategies should always be considered:

▶ Uninterrupted integration of the procurement chain

▶ IT administration costs

▶ Flexibility for upgrades

▶ Flexibility regarding regional regulations

▶ Flexibility for sales organizations

Core SAPdemo strategies to be analyzed

Variant I: One Central Business Cluster (Single Box)

The first variant corresponds to the actual SAPdemo situation — that is, all business processes are mapped and integrated into one central business cluster (single box), as shown in Figure 6.12.

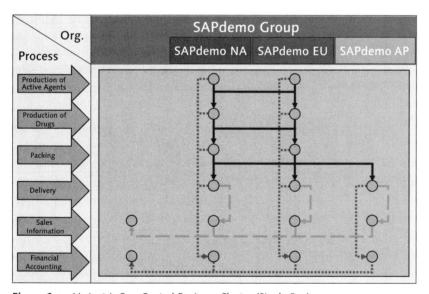

Figure 6.12 Variant I: One Central Business Cluster (Single Box)

When analyzing the implementation of the five core strategies mentioned, the result of topology Variant I is as follows (+ means positive, – means negative, 0 means neutral):

▶ **Uninterruptible integration of the procurement chain**
(+) Very good integration, because all processes are implemented in one system.

▶ **IT administration costs**
(+) Manageable IT administration costs, because only one SAP ERP system is operated.

▶ **Flexibility for upgrades**
(–) Very inflexible, because the entire system is always affected.

▶ **Flexibility regarding regional regulations**
(0) One system must cover all local (legal) requirements, which can be achieved when using SAP standard country versions.

▶ **Flexibility for sales organizations**
(0) Not particularly flexible, because the three sales organizations can only be differentiated by using different customizations.

Variant II: Distribution of Business Clusters by Organizational Unit

The second topology variant for SAPdemo considers four business clusters: one system for each of the three sales organizations and another for all other business processes, as illustrated in Figure 6.13.

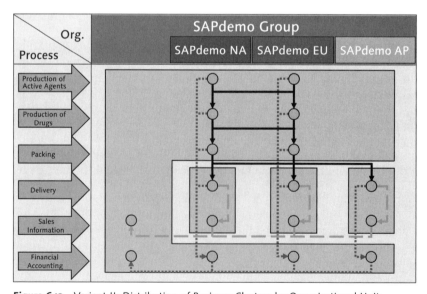

Figure 6.13 Variant II: Distribution of Business Clusters by Organizational Unit

You can immediately see that there are numerous interfaces between the systems. These interfaces must be configured to ensure smooth data flow.

This approach again analyzes the implementation of the five core strategies mentioned, resulting in the following for topology Variant II:

▶ **Uninterruptible integration of the procurement chain**
   (–) Poor integration, because production and sales processes are separated.

▶ **IT administration costs**
   (–) Very high IT administration costs, because four SAP ERP systems must be operated. You can also expect high interface costs.

▶ **Flexibility for upgrades**
   (+) Very flexible, because each of the four systems can be updated separately.

▶ **Flexibility regarding regional regulations**
   (+) All local (legal) requirements can be covered separately in the individual systems.

▶ **Flexibility for sales organizations**
   (+) Very flexible, because each of the three sales organizations has a specific system.

Variant III: Distribution of Business Clusters by Function

Alternative III distributes SAPdemo business processes across two business clusters. Therefore, global sales has one dedicated system, and procurement chain processes and production are implemented on a second business cluster. Figure 6.14 illustrates this approach.

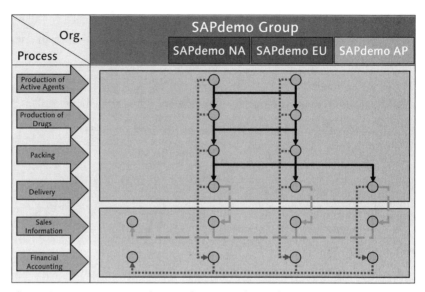

Figure 6.14 Variant III: Distribution of Business Clusters by Function

Using topology Variant III with two systems, SAPdemo came up with the following result after having analyzed the implementation of the five core strategies in two business clusters:

► **Uninterruptible integration of the procurement chain**
(+) Very good integration, because all processes are implemented in one system.

► **IT administration costs**
(+) Manageable IT administration costs, because only two SAP ERP systems must be operated, and the number of interfaces implemented and maintained is not that high.

► **Flexibility for upgrades**
(0) Relatively flexible, because two systems can be upgraded independently of each other.

► **Flexibility regarding regional regulations**
(0) Particularly the sales system must cover all local (legal) requirements. This can be achieved when using SAP standard country versions.

▶ **Flexibility for sales organizations**
(0) Not particularly flexible, because the three sales organizations can only be differentiated through customizations.

Variant IV: Distribution of Business Clusters by Region

The fourth system topology proposed for SAPdemo distributes all business processes according to regional aspects. There is one system for each region: America, Europe, and Asia. This system assumes all tasks, from purchase to production to sales. In addition, a business cluster is used for internal processes, such as accounting. Figure 6.15 illustrates this approach.

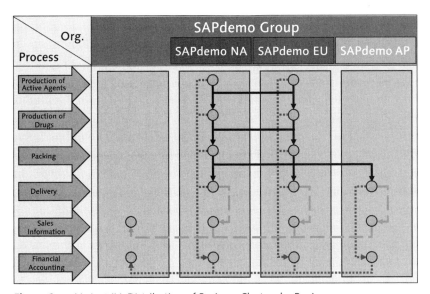

Figure 6.15   Variant IV: Distribution of Business Clusters by Region

When analyzing the implementation of the five core strategies, the result of topology Variant IV is as follows:

▶ **Uninterruptible integration of the procurement chain**
(–) Very poor integration, because cross-region processes disintegrate in multiple instances.

▶ **IT administration costs**
(–) Very high IT administration costs, because four SAP ERP systems must be operated. You can also expect high interface costs.

▶ **Flexibility for upgrades**
(+) Very flexible, because the regional systems can be upgraded separately.

▶ **Flexibility regarding regional regulations**
(+) All local (legal) requirements can be covered separately in the individual systems.

▶ **Flexibility for sales organizations**
(+) Very flexible, because each of the three sales organizations has a specific system.

Decision matrix for determining the best possible topology

Evaluation of Variants I–IV and Determination of the Best Possible Alternative

After having set up and evaluated four possible business cluster variants for SAPdemo, the results are now prioritized in a decision matrix to determine the best possible variant.

This two-dimensional matrix contains the five core strategies. It weights the strategies according to management's plans and the enterprise's vision. This weighting categorizes them as "high" or "medium" priority. The core strategies are then compared with the list of four system topologies.

In the first step, for each topology, enter the degree of coverage and feasibility of implementation for the strategies that were discussed, respectively, in the context of the individual alternatives. In this example, you can enter values from one to five, where one refers to the "best possible" strategy, and five is a strategy that is "less or insufficiently" useful. That is, for better analyses, the entries are more differentiated than those that were categorized with +/0/– (positive/neutral/negative).

In the second, decisive step, multiply the individual values by the weighting of the core strategies. The coverage values are multiplied by two if they are "positive" and remain unchanged if they are "neutral." If you add all final values (that is, after their multiplication) for each system topology, you receive the final ranking:

The smallest value represents the optimal topology (in this case, for SAP-demo). In our example, if you take a look at the entries for Variant III, you receive a ranking value of 18:

((1 + 2 + 3) × 2) = 12, for the strategies categorized as "high,"
plus (3 + 3) = 6, for the two strategies categorized as "medium,"
for a total of 12 + 6 = 18

If you perform this calculation for all other alternatives, you will determine that Variant III (the distribution of business clusters by functions) shows the best value — namely, a ranking of 18. Consequently, it can be considered the ideal system topology for SAPdemo. Figure 6.16 shows the previously described decision matrix.

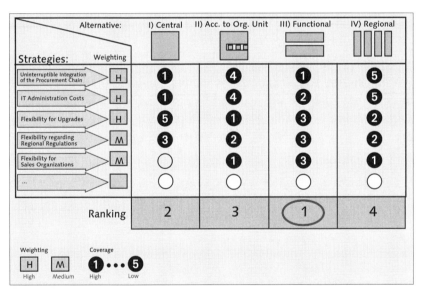

Figure 6.16 Decision Matrix for Evaluating the Best Possible Topology Alternative

How can this result be interpreted? In contrast to the general single-box recommendation by SAP, a distributed topology was considered for this example.

Comments on the result

According to strategic considerations of SAPdemo, the following strategies had the highest priority:

► Reduce costs,

► Enable you to respond to market changes in a flexible way, and

► Ensure smooth procurement chain operation.

These were covered in the best possible way by Variant II with two business clusters.

Because the flexibility regarding regional legal regulations can be implemented in SAPdemo countries via standard country versions, this aspect is not critical, and therefore was categorized as less important for the strategy.

Furthermore, the issue of sales organizations wanting to be more independent, which is a rather political one, was also considered less important. The three sales organizations will be sufficiently differentiated by using different Customizing.

Work to be done after the system topology has been determined After the best possible system topology has been determined, SAPdemo will expand the considerations (which previously were limited to core business processes) to all business processes and integrate them into or assign them to the defined business clusters. Depending on the enterprise size, this may involve a great deal of effort, but is nevertheless necessary.

It will also be required to distribute individual processes across both systems, or even integrate non-SAP systems, such as those of suppliers or wholesalers. This process requires a precise analysis of the interfaces to ensure problem-free data exchange.

After completing these detailed tasks, you must prepare the actual project plan with regard to technical and practical, as well as temporal aspects. The project plan could include the following essential aspects for SAPdemo:

► **Splitting the single box:**

▸ Setting up two systems with new/modified hardware

▸ Release upgrades

- ▶ Implementation of country-specific functions (country versions)
- ▶ Unicode conversion
- ▶ Tests
- ▶ **Implementing new and modified processes:**
  - ▶ Distribution model, interface definition
  - ▶ Implementation of processes
  - ▶ Master data definition and harmonization
  - ▶ Tests
- ▶ **Maintenance aspects and internal services:**
  - ▶ Preparing the maintenance plan for the systems (time schedule)
  - ▶ Emergency plans
  - ▶ Planning user support (e.g., hotline, etc.)
- ▶ **Rollout:**
  - ▶ Informing and training all users and departments
  - ▶ Informing partner companies, suppliers, and others about the improvements

Well, now SAPdemo has successfully completed the system topology conversion. The project issues listed are standard project work that you are already familiar with because of your own experiences with specific SAP installations, which the literature describes in detail.

6.3   Summary

The last part of this chapter focuses on an analysis from the customer's point of view.

Among other tools, these reports show how technical, geographical, or political aspects might affect system architectures. Due to the variety of enterprises, there is not one preferred system topology, but nevertheless, a recommendation by SAP emerged: SAP absolutely recommends the single box whenever possible!

SAP recommends the single box

A real-life sample project illustrated the way from a distributed to single-box architecture. Finally, a tool was provided that can be very useful for selecting the appropriate system architecture: the decision matrix. In particular, it considers the individual business processes.

Interestingly, the evaluation of the decision matrix for the sample enterprise, SAPdemo, showed that it can sometimes be useful to disregard the SAP recommendation (single box), not only due to functional reasons, but also business aspects.

You can now transfer the decision-making process, which this chapter roughly outlined, to your specific enterprise characteristics to determine the optimal topology for your enterprise.

7   System Topology Summary for the Global Solution

Which system topology should be used to integrate the software solution? In this book, we answered this core question about the planning and operation of a global SAP ERP installation.

Initially, you learned that the ERP software is the essential prerequisite for a long-term and successful positioning in the international market for a globally active enterprise. Subsequently, we discussed the requirements the business world poses on software, as well as on the implementation of the appropriate hardware.

You also became familiar with the different topology options for global systems — ranging from single-box to distributed systems. We described the planning and implementation of IT infrastructures and introduced the utilities that are available for implementing, maintaining, and operating them.

SAP customers with different architectures shared their experiences and provided information on the benefits of individual solutions. Specific guidelines supplemented the suggestions and tips provided in this book. Enterprises can use these guidelines to select the appropriate system topology, based of their own business processes as well as other aspects.

In conclusion, we want to mention two essential aspects:

▶ Ideally, integrate all functions in one single installation (single box) that can be accessed by all international users (the reason why SAP recommends this option).

SAP recommends the single box

▶ Still, there isn't a system topology that should be preferred for all cases, because your decision on an installation variant depends on several enterprise-specific factors.

Finally, we want to provide you with a rule of thumb for planning your global implementation:

Always plan as globally as possible and as locally as necessary!

A   Glossary

ALE: Application Linking and Embedding (also, *Application Link Enabling*); SAP interface technology for asynchronous connection of systems.

ANSI: *American National Standards Institute;* also Microsoft's name for Windows code pages.

API: *Application Programming Interface.*

Application server: Computer that executes programs.

Asynchronous transmission: Data transmission between systems that are not continuously connected.

Backup: A duplicate copy of saved data for restoration in case of computer failure.

Bandwidth: Transmission speed.

Batch: Messages or records that are bundled and processed together.

BDC: *Batch Data Communication*, a synonym for batch input.

BTF: *Behind the firewall.*

Bi-directional: Writing system that can run either right to left or left to right.

Big Endian: Computer architecture that puts the most significant byte (MSB) first for numbers consisting of multiple bytes.

Binary files: Files with data that are not in text format (e.g., hexadecimal).

Blended code page: SAP code page that allows the combination of languages from different code pages (e.g. Latin-1 and Japanese) in a single code page (with some limitations). Since the advent of Unicode, this is considered an obsolete technology.

BOM: *Byte order mark.*

Byte: Smallest storage unit addressable, eight bits.

Byte-swapped: Swapped order of a byte sequence.

Case: Some alphabets contain letters in different forms (e.g. different sizes). In Germany, for instance, upper case and lower case are possible.

CBL: *Common Business Library*, an open XML specification for the exchange of business documents (industry-independent).

CGI: *Common Gateway Interface*, a data transmission interface.

Character: The smallest unit of a written language.

Character encoding form: Mapping of characters to numerical expressions.

Character encoding scheme: Character encoding with serialization. There are seven different ones under Unicode: UTF-8, UTF-16, UTF-16BE, UTF-16LE, UTF-32, UTF-32BE, and UTF-32LE.

Character set: Set of characters and letters that make up a language.

CJK: Abbreviation for Chinese, Japanese, and Korean.

CJKV: Abbreviation for Chinese, Japanese, Korean, and Vietnamese.

Code page: Encoding of a character set — for example, Latin-1 for Western European characters.

CPU: *Central processing unit*, the processor.

Data transformation: To change data between different storage formats.

DBCS: Double Byte Character Set.

DMZ: *De-Militarized Zone*, the neutral zone between the intranet and extranet.

Double-byte character set: Sets in which characters are encoded by two bytes for each character, such as for Chinese or Japanese.

EBCDIC: *Extended Binary Coded Decimal Interchange Code*, character sets (for mainframe computers) that encode characters with eight bits. The first reserved positions (x00 through x3F) are control characters, and the range from x41 to xFE are graphical characters. The English characters are divided into upper- and lowercase ranges, with capital letters from xC1 to xC9, xD1 to xD9, and xE2 to xE9; and lowercase letters from x81 to x89, x91 to x99, and xA2 to xA9.

eCATT: Extension of the *Computer-Aided Test Tool,* can create test procedures from business processes.

EDIFACT: *Electronic Data Interchange For Administration, Commerce, and Transport,* the standard format for transmission of structured data in business data exchange.

Encoding form: Short for "character encoding form."

Encoding scheme: Short for "character encoding scheme."

EUC: *Extended (enhanced) Unix Code,* method for the parallel use of single- and multibyte character tables.

External vocabulary on table: UMGPMDIT-based vocabulary for the transfer of assigned vocabulary entries to other SAP systems.

Failover: Process for fail-safe systems.

Flag text language: In English, "text lang" indicator to determine the relevance of language key for the code page dependency of the table entry.

Font: Style of displayed characters.

FTP: *File Transfer Protocol*, for data transmission.

German ASCII: Variant of the *American Standard Code for Information Interchange* with German special characters added.

Global template: One or more centrally created templates made available to relevant projects in the subsidiaries and other organizations participating in the global project for introducing, implementing, and maintaining a global rollout. The templates comprise global scenarios, blueprint documents, configurations, and developments. The degree to which subsidiaries may change the central templates is centrally defined.

Glyph: Graphical representation of a character.

GUI: *Graphical User Interface.*

Hangul: Korean language script.

Hint: Help for assignment words to language codes in the system vocabulary, based on arbitrary attributes. Used during the preparation of MDMP-systems for a Unicode – conversion: The code page used for the creation of texts has to be determined properly.

HTML: *Hypertext Markup Language,* text description language that combines un-

formatted text with formatting information. HTML is the language most used for Websites.

I18N: Acronym for internationalization, between the "I" and the "N" there are 18 letters.

IDoc: Standard SAP format for electronic data exchange between systems with special message formats (*IDoc types*).

INDX-type Table: Tables that have a transparent and binary area, which must be handled specially in Transaction SPUMG.

Interface: The connection between two or more systems exchanging data.

ISCII: *Indian Script Code for Information Interchange.*

ISO: *International Organization for Standardization.*

ITS: *Internet Transaction Server*, interface between the Internet and SAP applications.

J2EE: *Java-2-Platform Enterprise Edition,* development platform for (Web) applications in Java.

JDBC: *Java Database Connectivity*, programming interface for Java applications and databases.

JTA: *Java Transaction Application programming interface*, programming interface for Java and transaction programs/monitors.

Kanji: Japanese name for Han characters, one of two Japanese syllabaries.

Katakana: One of two Japanese syllabaries, often used for the display of 'difficult' kanji characters.

Cryptography: Encryption technology.

Latency: Time required for transmitting a message from the sender to the recipient. Latency comprises three components: migration delay, transmission delay, and wait time.

Latin-1: Character set for Western European languages.

Latin-2: Character set for Eastern European languages.

Latin-3: Character set for Southern European languages.

Latin-4: Character set for Nordic/Baltic languages.

Little Endian: Computer architecture that puts the least significant byte first for numbers consisting of multiple bytes.

Load balancing: Process for distributing processing load over multiple computers and servers.

LSB: *Least Significant Byte.*

Markup: Command for structuring and/or formatting a document in a page description language.

MBCS: *Multi Byte Character Set.*

MDMP: *Multi-Display Multi-Processing,* process for using different code pages in one system. The logon language determines the code page used. Since the advent of Unicode, this technology is considered obsolete.

Message broker: Server for the distribution of messages between different applications.

Message queuing: Method for time-offset data transmission between applications.

Middleware: Programs for data exchange between different applications. Conversion rules may also be applied.

MSB: *Most Significant Byte.*

Multibyte character set: Character set with a different number of bytes for the encoding of characters.

Network latency: See "Latency."

NNTP: *Network News Transfer Protocol,* protocol for the exchange of news articles on Usenet.

Octet: Eight bits, or one byte.

ODBC: *Open Database Connectivity,* database (Web) interface.

OS: *Operating System.*

Patch: Program change for the correction of errors or extension of functionality.

PCL: *Printer Communication Language,* printer protocol from Hewlett-Packard.

PDF: *Portable Document Format,* Adobe format for text and graphics, with a precisely defined layout.

Plain text: Text that consists entirely of encoded characters without any formatting information.

Portal: Website used to access the Internet, intranet, or a network. Consists of a group of links, content, and services adapted to the needs of a user or group of users.

R3load: Kernel-level tool for import and export during system installation, upgrade, and migration, as well as for the conversion of a system to Unicode.

RAID: *Redundant Array of Independent Disks,* a cluster of multiple hard disks.

RAM: *Random Access Memory,* working memory of the computer (processor).

RFC: *Remote Function Call,* SAP interface protocol that simplifies the programming of communication between systems.

Rich text: Text that contains both encoded characters and formatting information (e.g., information about fonts and colors).

RMI: *Remote Method Invocation,* calls methods or objects on different computers.

Routing: The direction of data packages in the network.

SAPS: *SAP Application Performance Standard,* 100 SAPS are defined as 2,000 completely processed order items per hour in the SD-application benchmark standard. This throughput is achieved by implementing 6,000 dialog steps and 2,000 updates per hour, or 2,400 SAP transactions per hour.

SBCS: *Single-Byte Character Set,* character set using only one byte for the encoding of one character.

Script: A defined set of letters and/or characters for the representation of a language. Example: Russian is written with a subset of the Cyrillic script.

SGML: *Standard Generalized Markup Language,* the standard for markup languages for digital documents, standardized by the *International Standardization Organization* as ISO 8879.

Sizing: Definition of the hardware requirements for an SAP system, such as the memory requirements, network bandwidth, or CPU power.

Shift-JIS: Encoding for Japanese characters, often used in PCs.

SJIS: Short for "Shift-JIS."

SOA: *Service-Oriented Architecture,* software architecture enabling the design, development, identification, and use of standardized services for the entire enterprise, whereby service reusability is a core benefit.

SPUMG: Code page scanner, transaction for the preparation of an MDMP system for Unicode conversion. Texts in tables without a language key can be assigned to the code pages used during creation.

SQL: *Structured Query Language,* language for database queries.

Synchronous transmission: Transmission of data between directly connected devices with immediate (not time-offset) response.

SLO: *System Landscape Optimization,* portfolio of services for process optimization, from individual applications to the harmonization of complete SAP environments.

SUMG Transaction: Tool for the post-processing step after conversion of an MDMP system into Unicode.

System vocabulary: List of words that must be assigned a language code within SPUMG Transaction.

Template: One or more centrally create data files that comprise preconfigured solutions. They are provided via transports or similar procedures. The templates are transferred and adapted for a project's final solution.

TCP/IP: *Transmission Control Protocol/ Internet Protocol.*

UCG: *Unicode Conversion Guide,* top-ranking guideline for conversion of an SAP system to Unicode.

UCS: *Universal Character Set,* character set according to international standard ISO/IEC 10646.

Unicode: International standard in which every character in a script is assigned a uniform code.

Unicode encoding format: Format for representing Unicode characters. These include UTF-8, UTF-16, and UTF-32.

Unicode encoding scheme: Unicode character set.

Unicode transformation format: Another term for *Unicode encoding scheme.*

US-7-ASCII range: Corresponds to seven-bit ASCII. English characters, symbols, and numbers are included in every code page.

UTF: *Unicode Transformation Format.*

UUEncode: *Unix to Unix Encoding,* 'packed' encoding of binary data as ASCII text.

VoIP: *Voice over IP,* transmission of voice in digital form via the Internet Protocol.

W3C: *World Wide Web Consortium,* *www.w3c.org.*

WML: *Wireless Markup Language,* page description language for Websites that can be displayed on mobile terminals, like cell phones.

WSDL: *Web Service Description Language,* XML language for the description of Web services.

XBRL: *Extensible Business Reporting Language,* XML-based protocol for the transmission of financial documents over the Internet.

XHTML: *Extensible Hypertext Markup Language,* XML-compatible HTML.

XML: *Extensible Markup Language,* used for the transmission of structured data, using the Unicode character set as standard.

B   Literature

B.1   Books and Articles

▶ Anderhub, V., *"Service Level Management — der ITIL-Prozess im SAP-Betrieb."* SAP Essentials, No. 25, SAP PRESS, 2006.

▶ Bengel, G., *"Verteilte Systeme."* Vieweg, 2nd Ed., 2002.

▶ Blumenthal, A. and H. Keller, *ABAP — Fortgeschrittene Techniken und Tools.* SAP PRESS, 2005.

▶ Bürckel, N., A. Davidenkoff, and D. Werner, D., *Unicode in SAP-Systemen.* SAP PRESS, 2007.

▶ Comer, D. E., *Computernetzwerke und Internets.* Addison-Wesley, 3rd Ed., 2001.

▶ Fox, J., "Consider These 3 Questions When Deciding to Upgrade to mySAP ERP." *www.sapinsider.com*, October - December 2005.

▶ Fritz, F.-J., "Take Note! Custom Applications and Standard SAP Solutions: What's the Difference When It Comes to Lifecycle Management?" www.sapinsider.com, January - March 2005.

▶ Fritz, F.-J., "Take Note! Unicode: Overhead or Necessity?" www.sapinsider.com, April - June 2006.

▶ Gammel, R., "SAP in der Pflicht: Global denken, lokal puzzeln." Manager Magazin, January 2007.

▶ Gartner Group, Gartner Group's Networked Systems Management Research Note QA-05-2701, July 29, 1998, *http://www.gartner.com/webletter/ibmglobal/edition2/article5/article5.html*.

▶ Harold, E. R., *Java Network Programming.* O'Reilly, 2nd Ed., 2000.

▶ Heuvelmans, W., et al., *Enhancing the Quality of ABAP Development.* SAP PRESS, 2004.

▶ IDS Scheer Expert Paper, "Geschäftsprozessdesign als Grundlage von Compliance Management, Enterprise Architecture und Business Rules," May 2005, *http://www.aris.de*.

▸ IDS Scheer white paper, "ARIS for SAP NetWeaver — The Business Process Design Solution for SAP NetWeaver," October 2006, *http://www.aris.de.*

▸ Janssen, S., "Targeted Methods and Tools for Right-Sizing Your Hardware Landscape," Performance & Data Management Corner, January – March 2006, *www.sapinsider.com.*

▸ Kangas, M., "Architecting a High Availability SAP NetWeaver Infrastructure." SAP Professional Journal, March/April 2007, *www.sappro.com.*

▸ Keller, H. and J. Jacobitz, *ABAP Objects.* SAP PRESS, 2003.

▸ Keller, H., ABAP-Referenz. Updated and extended in 2004, 2nd Ed., SAP PRESS, 2005.

▸ Kessler, K., et al., Java-Programmierung mit dem SAP Web Application Server. SAP PRESS, 2005.

▸ Korpela, J., *Unicode Explained.* O'Reilly, 2006.

▸ Kurchina, P., *"Gegenwart und Zukunft der IT gestalten."* SAP INFO deutsch Home ePaper, No. 144.

▸ Missbach, M., et al., *Adaptive Hardware-Infrastrukturen für SAP.* SAP PRESS, 2005.

▸ Oswald, G., *SAP Service und Support.* SAP PRESS, 2006.

▸ Ranum, A., "Open Integration — Tips & Tricks: SAP Infrastructure 3.0 — Enterprise Ready!" April - June 2004, *www.sapinsider.com.*

▸ SAP AG, "Frontend Network Requirements for SAP Solutions, Version 5.2," March 2003.

▸ SAP AG, *"Migration Solutions from SAP,* SAP Decision Support Brief: Accelerated Data Migration (ADM) and Legacy System Migration Workbench (LSMW). 2004"

▸ SAP AG, *"SAP NetWeaver and Globalization: Meeting Local and Global Requirements."* SAP AG white paper, Material No. 50057742, Version 2.0, 2005.

▸ SAP AG, "Solution Management Globalization Services: Including New Countries in the Delivery System — Setting up a new country." Media Library, 2003, *http://service.sap.com/globalization.*

▸ Schäfer, M. and M. Melich, *SAP Solution Manager.* SAP PRESS, 2006.

▶ Schneider-Neureither, A., *Optimierung von SAP-Systemlandschaften.* SAP PRESS, 2004.

▶ SNP AG, "SNP SLO System Landscape Optimization," *http://snp.de/media/0000000141.pdf.*

▶ SNP AG, "SNP SLO System Landscape Optimization," *http://snp.de/media/0000000141.pdf.*

▶ Vanstechelman, B. and M. Mergaerts, M., *The OS/DB Migration Project Guide.* SAP PRESS, 2005.

▶ Wong, C., *HTTP kurz & gut.* O'Reilly/VVA, 2000.

▶ Woof, R., *"Implementing an SAP Global Template in Asia,"* SAP Globalization Symposium, 2006.

B.2 Links

B.2.1 General Links

▶ *ftp://ftp.denic.de/pub/rfc/rfc2616.txt*

▶ *http://de.wikipedia.org/wiki/Corporate_Governance*

▶ *http://de.wikipedia.org/wiki/GUID*

▶ *http://de.wikipedia.org/wiki/Service-Level-Agreement*

▶ *http://en.wikipedia.org/wiki/Latency_(engineering)*

▶ *www.aris.de*

▶ *www.citrix.com*

▶ *www.itil.com*

▶ *www.mercury.com*

▶ *www.unicode.org*

B.2.2 SAP Links

▶ *http://service.sap.com/benchmark*

▶ *http://service.sap.com/bpm*

▶ *http://service.sap.com/consulting*

▶ *http://service.sap.com/erp*

▶ *http://service.sap.com/globalization*

- *http://service.sap.com/globalization*
- Service offerings: *http://service.sap.com/goinglivecheck*
- *http://service.sap.com/goinglive-fu*
- *http://service.sap.com/ha*
- *http://service.sap.com/I18N*
- *http://service.sap.com/instguides*
- *http://service.sap.com/localization*
- *http://service.sap.com/lsmw*
- *http://service.sap.com/message*
- *http://service.sap.com/migrationkey*
- *http://service.sap.com/notes*
- *http://service.sap.com/pam*
- *http://service.sap.com/partners*
- *http://service.sap.com/patches*
- *http://service.sap.com/performnace*
- *http://service.sap.com/platforms*
- *http://service.sap.com/quicksizer*
- *http://service.sap.com/releasenotes*
- *http://service.sap.com/releasestrategy*
- *http://service.sap.com/sizing*
- *http://service.sap.com/slo*
- *http://service.sap.com/solutionmanager*
- *http://service.sap.com/support*
- *http://service.sap.com/systemcopy*
- *http://service.sap.com/unicode*
- Unicode Library: *http://service.sap.com/unicode@sap*
- *http://service.sap.com/upgradeservices*
- *http://service.sap.com/xi*
- *http://www.sap.com./solutions/business-suite/erp/pdf/BWP_SB_Global_Solutions_Without_Boundaries.pdf*
- *http://www.sap.com/community/pub/events/2006%5F10%5F30%5Fglobal%5Fsymposium/*

C   Authors

After his studies in electrical engineering and completing an engineering doctorate at the University of Karlsruhe (Germany), **Alexander Davidenkoff** joined SAP AG at the end of 1992. He started in R/3 basis support and technical consulting, and was soon concentrating on international topics, such as language and code page technologies in SAP products. He began collaboration with national organizations in Eastern Europe and Russia, supported colleagues, customers, and partners in numerous activities and projects, and contributed significantly to the improvement of language support in SAP R/3. Since the late 1990s, Davidenkoff has been working closely with countries in the Asia-Pacific region.

In 1996, Davidenkoff moved to international Development/Globalization Services at SAP, where he became responsible for country versions project management, as well as globalization, localization, and translation issues. He now works for SAP Globalization Services as a solution manager for the Unicode rollout, global solutions, time zones, global integrated solutions using SAP NetWeaver, the architecture of complex system environments, and related topics. He also supports, advises, and trains numerous colleagues, clients, and partners in many countries.

Detlef Werner earned his doctorate in 1989 from the University of Hamburg (Germany) as a chemist, where his work included computer-supported analytics. After an international career at medium-size companies, Werner joined SAP AG in 1998, working first on construction and conversion of the Internet Business Framework. Other work areas at SAP have included global partner management, the design of marketplaces for customers on issues involving international implementation of business processes, and related IT structures.

Werner is currently working as a solution manager for SAP Globalization Services, where system topologies, country versions, and languages (introduction of Unicode in SAP) have been core topics for many years. Since 2003, he is teaching at the International University of Bruchsal, Germany, as a visiting professor for international management and e-business.

Index

D

Your complete guide to individual service-oriented architectures

Industry-specific solutions for implementing enterprise SOA

Volumes of lessons learned and best practices for re-designing your system architecture

417 pp., 2008, 69,95 Euro / US$ 69.95
ISBN 978-1-59229-162-5

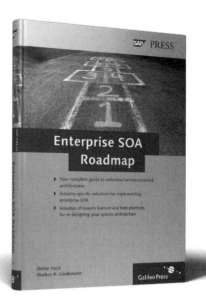

Enterprise SOA Roadmap

Stefan Hack, Markus A. Lindemann

Enterprise SOA Roadmap

This book, intended for business leaders, IT managers and consultants, guides you step-by-step along the path to enterprise service-oriented architecture. Using a detailed analysis of more than 500 SAP Consulting projects in different industries as a basis, the authors deliver concrete recommendations on how best to roll out enterprise SOA in your own organization. You'll learn how SAP supports enterprises along their individual adoption paths, and benefit from the many lessons learned that are described in the book. In addition, you'll discover how to apply specific implementation options, arguments and best practices in your enterprise and how to sidestep potential implementation risks.

Understand the principles of
administration and
development

Gain insights on KM,
collaboration, unification,
application management, and
the transport system

462 pp., 2008, 69,95 Euro / US$ 69.95
ISBN 978-1-59229-145-8

SAP NetWeaver Portal

www.sap-press.com

Valentin Nicolescu, Katharina Klappert,
Helmut Krcmar

SAP NetWeaver Portal

This book introduces IT managers, portal administrators and consultants to the structure and application
areas of SAP NetWeaver Portal (Release 7.0). A main
focus is to describe key portal functions and the
underlying architecture — all from the technical
viewpoint. Topics covered include role management,
authentication mechanisms, knowledge and content
management, developing and administrating applications, application and system integration, as well as
many more. Readers gain a solid technical grounding
in all the relevant aspects of the SAP NetWeaver
Portal, and the skills needed to effectively implement
them in practice.

**Improve your Design Process
with "Contextual Design"**

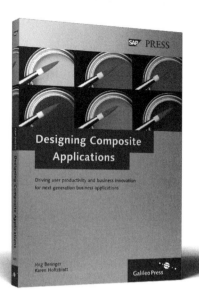

182 pp., 2006, 49,95 Euro / US$ 49,95
ISBN 978-1-59229-065-9

Designing
Composite Applications

www.sap-press.com

Jörg Beringer, Karen Holtzblatt

Designing Composite Applications

Driving user productivity and business innovation for
next generation business applications

This book helps any serious developer hit the ground
running by providing a highly detailed and
comprehensive introduction to modern application
design, using the SAP Enterprise Services
Architecture (ESA) toolset and the methodology of
"Contextual Design". Readers will benefit
immediately from exclusive insights on design
processes based on SAPs Business Process Platform
and learn valuable tricks and techniques that can
drastically improve user productivity. Anybody
involved in the process of enterprise application
design and usability/quality management stands to
benefit from this book.

The benchmark work for release 4.0

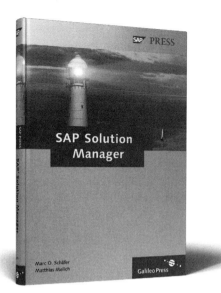

500 pp.,2006, 69,95 Euro / US$ 69,95
ISBN 978-1-59229-091-8

SAP Solution Manager

www.sap-press.com

M.O. Schäfer, M. Melich

SAP Solution Manager

This unique book helps administrators and IT managers to quickly understand the full functionality of SAP Solution Manager, release 4.0. Readers get a thorough introduction in the areas of Implementation and Operations, especially in the scenarios Project Management, Service Desk, Change Request Management, and the brand new function Diagnostics (root cause analysis).
The integration capabilities with third-party tools from the areas of Help Desk and Modelling, as well as the relation between the functionality and ITIL Application Management are also dealt with in detail.

Implementing ITIL Processes in Your SAP Department

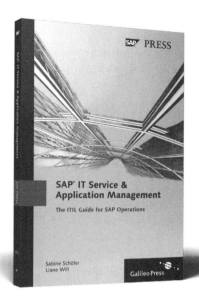

96 pp., 2006, 19,95 Euro / US$ 29.95
ISBN 978-1-59229-094-9

SAP IT Service & Application Management

www.sap-press.com

S. Schöler, L. Will

SAP IT Service & Application Management

The ITIL Guide for SAP Operations

With this one-of-a-kind pocket guide you learn how to fill the ITIL processes of IT Service Management and Application Management with real "SAP life" and you get recommendations on which SAP tools and services are available to best support you in this effort. The integration processes between both areas are also covered in detail. This is a must-have reference for IT managers responsible for optimizing SAP operations and cost structures.

Learn the most efficient ways to implement SAP-related change in your organization

Understand the unique challenges of change in an SAP environment and avoid problems before they occur

Learn strategies for successfully conquering each phase of your implementation

364 pp., 2007, 69,95 Euro / US$ 69,95
ISBN 978-1-59229-104-5

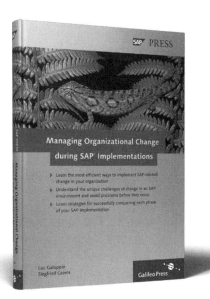

Managing Organizational Change During SAP Implementations

www.sap-press.com

Luc Galoppin, Siegfried Caems

Managing Organizational Change During SAP Implementations

Many SAP implementations are not successful because proper change management procedures are ignored. This book helps you prepare for change in an organized manner. This practical guide takes a holistic look at an organization, the impact of an SAP implementation on it and how negative impacts can be lessened or, in most cases, negated early on. Taking a real-world, practical approach this book focuses on actual challenges and details how they can be overcome with relative ease.

Enterprise Data Management
with SAP NetWeaver MDM

www.sap-press.com

Andrew LeBlanc

Enterprise Data Management with
SAP NetWeaver MDM

Build Foundations for Continual Improvements
with SAP MDM

Master data is your company's DNA, and effective
master data management demands extensive preparation. This book is the key to developing and
implementing your own comprehensive SAP MDM
strategy. Readers get all the essential prerequisites
for building a successful and sustainable MDM
strategy. Fully up-to-date for SAP MDM 5.5 SP04,
this comprehensive book contains all the resources
needed to set your own MDM strategy.

**Revised new edition,
completely up-to-date
for SAP ERP 6.0**

**New functions and
technologies: Archive Routing,
Transaction TAANA, XML-based
archiving, and many more**

405 pp., 2. edition 2007, 69,95 Euro / US$ 69,95
ISBN 978-1-59229-116-8

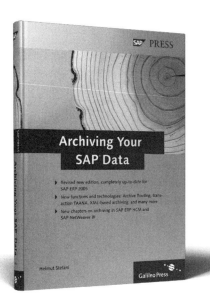

Archiving Your SAP Data

www.sap-press.com

Helmut Stefani

Archiving Your SAP Data

This much anticipated, completely revised edition of our
bestseller is up-to-date for SAP ERP 6.0, and provides you
with valuable knowledge to master data archiving with SAP.
Fully updated, this new edition includes two all-new
chapters on XML-based data archiving and archiving in SAP
ERP HCM and contains detailed descriptions of all the new
functions and technologies such as Archive Routing and the
TAANA transaction. Readers uncover all the underlying
technologies and quickly familiarize themselves with all
activities of data archiving—archivability checks, the
archiving process, storage of archive files, and display of
archived data. The book focuses on the requirements of
system and database administrators as well as project
collaborators who are responsible for implementing data
archiving in an SAP customer project.

Fundamental knowledge and in-depth administration advice

Expert advice on key areas like planning, administration, and development

Includes extra chapters on backup, recovery, restoration, SAP NetWeaver BI, and more

818 pp., 2008, 89,95 Euro / US$ 89.95
ISBN 978-1-59229-120-5

Michael Höding, André Faustmann, Gunnar Klein, Ronny Zimmermann

SAP Database Administration with Oracle

Oracle is one of the most significant, but also one of the most complex, DB platforms available for SAP systems — so why hasn't someone written a book on how to configure the interaction? Well, here it is: With this in-depth reference book, administrators get much needed background knowledge, as well as complete details on architectural and software/logistics issues, in addition to step-by-step instructions for all of the most important administration tasks. Every aspect of system landscape planning and maintenance is covered, helping administrators hone their problem solving skills. Bonus chapters deal with Java, SAP NetWeaver BI, and the highly complex issues of Backup, Recovery, and Restoration.

SOX and CobiT Overview

All relevant Cobit Controls
and their relevance for
SAP Operations

All tools necessary for
implementation

196 pp., 2007, 34,95 Euro / US$ 34,95
ISBN 978-1-59229-128-1

CobiT and the Sarbanes-Oxley Act

www.sap-press.com

Sabine Schöler, Liane Will, Marc O. Schäfer

CobiT and the Sarbanes-Oxley Act

The SOX Guide for SAP Operations

This pocket-sized guide is your roadmap to implementing the relevant CobiT Controls using SAP tools. Starting with the business/IT requirements dictated by the Sarbanes-Oxley Act, the authors explain the relevant controls of the CobiT framework and show you exactly which tools and services SAP provides for the smooth implementation of these controls within your IT operations.

>> www.sap-press.de/1438

ABAP Objects

www.sap-press.com

H. Keller, S. Krüger

ABAP Objects

ABAP Programming in SAP NetWeaver

This completely new third edition of our best-selling ABAP book provides detailed coverage of ABAP programming with SAP NetWeaver. This outstanding compendium treats all concepts of modern ABAP up to release 7.0. New topics include ABAP and Unicode, Shared Objects, exception handling, Web Dynpro for ABAP, Object Services, and of course ABAP and XML. Bonus: All readers will receive the SAP NetWeaver 2004s ABAP Trial Version ("Mini-SAP") on DVD.